SEEKING TRUTH

HOW TO MOVE FROM PARTISAN BICKERING TO BUILDING CONSENSUS

ELGIN L HUSHBECK JR.

Energion Publications
Gonzalez, Florida
2022

Copyright © 2022, Elgin L. Hushbeck, Jr.

Scripture taken from the Holy Bible: International Standard Version® Release 2.0. Copyright © 1996-2013 by the ISV Foundation. Used by permission of Davidson Press, LLC. ALL RIGHTS RESERVED INTERNATIONALLY.

ISBN: 978-1-63199-810-2
eISBN: 978-1-63199-811-0

Energion Publications
P. O. Box 841
Gonzalez, FL 32533

energion.com
pubs@energion.com

For
Eleanor and Michael

Acknowledgments

While I formally started work on this book in 2009, following the publication of *Preserving Democracy*, in many respects, this is a book I have been researching and thinking about for most of my adult life. As I wrote in *Faith and Reason*, which is in some respects a more religiously oriented companion volume, even as a teen, I wondered how people could hold such different opinions and, more importantly, who was correct. Soon this became an interest in the questions, how you know what you know; why do you believe what you believe?

Over the years, many people have influenced and shaped my views, which eventually became this book. I saw many people in discussions, some doing it well, some doing it poorly. There were many people I talked to, either directly or online. There were the teachers I had, and then the students in my classrooms later. A lot of people help shape the book.

When it comes to individuals, the most important has been my wife, Hanna, as she is in virtually all aspects of my life. She has always been there for me, supported me, and encouraged me. None of my books could have been written without her love and support.

I also want to thank Niles Bindel and Jonathan Williams, as they, in many ways, epitomize the good things in this book. We all three disagree on many things and, in fact, on some of the things in this book. We have also had many wonderful conversations about the subjects in his book and many other wide-ranging areas. We do not always agree. In fact, we normally disagree but we do challenge each other to move closer to the truth. At least on one occasion, following an evening of drinks, dinner, and discussion, we had a waiter at the restaurant we were at come over and say how much he enjoyed listening to our discussion.

In addition, I want to single out Niles. Niles read early versions of the manuscript and gave me extremely valuable feedback concerning the areas where we disagree. His feedback was incorporated, and it made the book better.

Finally, I want to thank Helen Wisniewski for her detailed editing on several early drafts. Also, my friends at Energion, my editor Chris Eyre, someone else I frequently disagree with, but whose critical but helpful eye helps me think better. Then, of course, my publisher Henry Neufeld for his kind support and encouragement over the years.

Table of Contents

Introduction ix

Part I: Truth and Knowledge   1

1   Down the Rabbit Hole 3
2   I Think; Therefore I Am, I Think 29
3   I Exist, You Exist, Maybe 49
4   Can We Know Anything? 61
5   What is Truth? 79

Part II: Disagreement and Error   99

6   Agreeing to Disagree 101
7   Disagreeing Agreeably 127
8   The Importance of Error 145

Part III: Seeking Truth   163

9   Know Thyself 165
10   Open to Open-Mindedness 183
11   Avoiding Errors 201
12   Evaluating Claims, Reaching Decisions 239

INTRODUCTION

We live in a world that is not governed by truth. Many people make decisions and judgments, not because they are true, correct, or even supported by reason and evidence, but for a whole host of other reasons. It fits their agenda; it makes them feel better about themselves; it is what they want. The people advocating it are on their side of the political spectrum or part of their religious group. Perhaps the person opposing it is someone they do not like. You can find people who will support a position when advocated by someone they like but oppose the same position when argued for by someone they don't.

In one instance, a minor crisis that politicians face from time to time, a person tweeted about how uncaring a newly elected official was for ignoring the problem leaving people to suffer. This showed that people had voted for the wrong candidate. When someone pointed out that the official in question had not yet been sworn in, and that their preferred candidate was still running things, they did not miss a beat, switching to how wonderful their guy was at handling the problem. The facts of the situation had not changed, the only thing that changed was who they thought was in charge. Whatever the reason, whether something is true or false is often secondary.

C. S. Lewis, noted Oxford professor and author of *The Chronicles of Narnia*, was concerned with the intellectual changes he saw taking place around him. He wrote about them in several of his books, such as *The Abolition of Man*. Using a fictional setting, he did so in *The Screwtape Letters*, a book Lewis dedicated to his friend J.R.R. Tolkien, author of *The Hobbit* and *The Lord of the Rings*.

Written and published during the early part of World War II, Lewis saw *The Screwtape Letters* as "kind of a joke," but one that would attract the reader to a serious topic they normally would not consider. Originally published in an Anglican periodical called the Guardian (not to be confused with the newspaper of that name), at least one reader did not appreciate the humor. A clergyman canceled his subscriptions calling the letters "diabolical."

The Screwtape Letters contains 31 letters written by Screwtape, an older demon, to his young nephew, Wormwood. His nephew was new to the art of temptation, and Screwtape was helping him to guide his "patient" on to the wrong path. This literary device allowed Lewis to comment on some serious and harmful trends he saw in the broader culture, yet do so in an entertaining way. He opens the first letter with the changing attitudes towards concepts like true and false.

My dear Wormwood,

I note what you say about guiding your patient's reading and taking care that he sees a good deal of his materialist friend. But are you not being a trifle naif? It sounds as if you supposed that argument was the way to keep him out of the Enemy's clutches. That might have been so if he had lived a few centuries earlier. At that time the humans still knew pretty well when a thing was proved and when it was not; and if it was proved they really believed it. They still connected thinking with doing and were prepared to alter their way of life as the result of a chain of reasoning. But what with the weekly press and other such weapons we have largely altered that. Your man has been accustomed, ever since he was a boy, to have a dozen incompatible philosophies dancing about together inside his head. He doesn't think of doctrines as primarily "true" or "false," but as "academic" or "practical," "outworn" or "contemporary," "conventional" or "ruthless." Jargon, not argument, is your best ally in keeping him from the Church. Don't waste time trying to make him think that materialism is true! Make him think it is strong, or stark, or courageous—that it is the philosophy of the future. That's the sort of thing he cares about.[1]

The change Lewis was pointing out in the 1940s continues to the present day. This change has been very fundamental and, as we will see, has been going on for hundreds of years. Still, it shows up in subtle ways. The columnist George Will noticed one such change in the early 1990s. Following a presidential debate, Will was struck by the change in poll questions. After the Kennedy-Nixon debate in 1960, people were effectively asked, "What did you think about the debate?" Will pointed out that this question had changed to, "How do you feel about the debate?"

These are not the same questions. The first calls for thinking. An intellectual analysis of what the candidates said and, your judgments about it. The latter asks for an emotional response which might include some intellectual analysis, but it need not. More importantly, an intellectual analysis could be wrong; the truth was still important. An emotion cannot be wrong; it is what you feel; the truth is not as important.

This change has significantly impacted various issues, such as choosing leaders like presidents. Just consider the memorable moments from presidential debates over the last several decades. These have tended to be soundbites and trivial things that can be exploited, such as candidates looking at their watch. Now candidates don't wear watches less they be portrayed as bored and disinterested.

Perhaps the most memorable moment from the 1976 Carter-Ford debates was Ford's misstatement of the USSR's domination over Eastern Europe. During the Dukakis-Bush Debate in 1988, the takeaway was a lack of emotion by Dukakis when answering a death penalty question. Gore's sighs were the big issue in the 2000 Gore-Bush debate. In the 1970s, it was a key policy issue. By the 1980s, it was a lack of emotion. By 2000 it was sighing. As annoy-

---

[1] Lewis, C. S. (1942). The Screwtape Letters: Annotated Edition Kindle Edition. New York: HaperOne.

ing as Gore's sighs may or may not have been, is this really an issue that should determine a presidential election?

Nor have things gotten better since 2000. More recent debates have turned on a whole range of things. These have been simple mistakes or one-liners that may or may not be humorous, depending on whether it helps or hurts your candidate. Now, some of the most memorable lines do not even come from the debates themselves but rather from comedians portraying the candidates on shows like *Saturday Night Live*. In an era that does not value truth, that matters little. What is really important is the line is memorable, whether said by the candidate or a comedian.

Today we live in a world that not only depreciates truth but rejects it as a guiding principle. Truth is relative. You have your truth; I have mine. For some, truth is just a power structure, a tool for oppressors to use on the oppressed. That the things a person believes are internally inconsistent or even contradictory is not only irrelevant but to be celebrated. Truth is found not in objective reality but subjective experience with all its emotions and conflicts.

Following the terrorist attacks on September 11, Americans virtually unanimously condemned them as evil in no uncertain terms. The concept of evil would normally imply something that clearly violates an absolute standard of right and wrong. Yet, in a survey conducted shortly after the attack, most Americans said "truth is always relative to the person and their situation."[2]

How can these views be reconciled? To ask the question misses the point. As Screwtape would have said, most people are now accustomed, from their youth, "to have a dozen incompatible philosophies dancing about together inside" their heads. It does not matter that these views are incompatible; that both cannot be true.

Beliefs are not just individual pieces of information. They comprise a network of interrelations and justifications. In a coher-

---

2 Barna. (2002, Februrary 12). *Americans Are Most Likely to Base Truth on Feelings*. Retrieved from Barna.com: https://www.barna.com/research/americans-are-most-likely-to-base-truth-on-feelings/

ent, well-thought-out system, all the various pieces of information would fit together like puzzle pieces; the picture they form would be reality. What Lewis was pointing out was for many, this was no longer even the goal. Rather than being coherent, many people's beliefs were a jumbled mess, conflicting and even contradictory at times.

Beliefs exist in a hierarchy, with more fundamental beliefs supporting others. For example, working backward, the recent developments in cosmology are grounded in earlier findings, which are grounded in the basics of physics and chemistry, which are based on a general view of science, which is grounded in the importance of empirical evidence and a belief the world around us is structured and well ordered enough for us to learn about it. Nor do the foundational beliefs stop there.

Yet today, many people not only accept, but argue vigorously for beliefs without understanding where they came from or the foundation upon which they are based. At times, they even reject the foundations of their own beliefs, completely unaware they are effectively refuting themselves. It would be like someone arguing for the latest discovery in cosmology while rejecting the importance of evidence.

Some people do reject the notion of absolute objective truth. They argue all truth is relative and subjective. Yet this does not prevent them from arguing for their views and condemning those who disagree with them. As for conflicting beliefs, people will use one or the other as best fits the needs of the moment. To ask for logical consistency is to be an oppressor.

I reject such views and argue in this book that there is such a thing as absolute objective truth, and perhaps, more importantly, we can know it to at least some extent. For many, that statement will be extremely uncontroversial. Some might even ask how it could even be controversial? Even with the depreciation of truth that has taken place in so much of society, truth, as a concept, has not gone away. Truth is just made subservient to other things. It becomes a tool in one's intellectual toolbox to be pulled out and used when convenient and left in the toolbox when it is not. The goal, however, is not truth but something else; something else is dominant.

The ultimate goal will change from person to person and even for individuals from one time to the next. The ultimate goal might be to defend a political idea or a religious belief. It could be to achieve something desired or to avoid something undesirable. Whatever it is, the truth is made to serve another master. This can, at times, lead to a short-term advantage. A well-placed lie can cause your candidate to win an election. A well-placed lie can get you out of a bad situation. At an individual level, this can work on occasion. You just need to have a goal other than the truth. Though as the lies accumulate, they can make things more difficult in the long run.

At a societal level, falsehoods rarely make a solid foundation for good public policy. This is particularly true in a democracy depending on voters, who in turn depend on good information upon which to base their votes. Democracies have a problem focusing on too many issues at once. Bad information can result in leaders focusing on problems that are exaggerated or even non-existent. When this happens, it will be at the expense of real problems, problems that will be ignored, or wasted resources that could have been better spent elsewhere.

Even worse, when truth is relative, with each person having their own version of the truth, there are no rational means to reach a consensus; the consensus needed in a democracy. There must be some unity to keep it together if a nation or group is not to tear itself apart. When unity cannot be achieved by consensus, it will come by force as a last resort. Political decisions and the country's direction will no longer be based on working out a compromise among the various groups but on which side is stronger. Polarization is sure to follow. If history is any guide, in the absence of persuasion, violence usually comes at some point. In the United

States, we already have polarization and are beginning to see violence.

In some respects, this book is radical. Some might even consider it dangerous. It is a call for truth. While many call for truth, few like being shown they are wrong. As such, we tend to erect intellectual barriers to protect our beliefs, to keep them from being challenged. Apply the things suggested in this book, and it is almost certain some of what you believe will be shown to be false and need to be modified or even rejected.

Some will not like this book for that reason. But this book is a call to see truth as preeminent. Truth first, then everything else. It is a call to seek truth and to speak it. While many will claim the banner of truth, far fewer are willing to commit to it. Committing to truth requires placing it above your beliefs. It is a willingness to admit errors and correct them. It means placing truth ahead of an agenda. It often requires courage to speak in the face of those who are invested in a lie. It can also take courage to hear the truth when we are wrong.

History is full of examples, some of which we will discuss in this book, of those who suffered for speaking the truth. Those with a vested interest in a lie may simply ignore you or attempt to silence you. They may protest against you. They can cost you your job and your livelihood. In some places, they will imprison or even kill you. The truth may set you free, but often speaking the truth is not without consequences. Currently, the trend in the broader society, a society split with polarization where even simple discussions can be risky, is not positive.

This is not inevitable. It can be reversed. What is needed is a general reaffirmation of the importance of a truth that exists independent of the person. It is not my truth or your truth, but the truth. Note, I did not say we need a general reaffirmation of what is true. The discovery of truth is the goal. It involves a process. That this is a common goal should be indisputable, but is not the case today. We will never have a consensus on what is true until there is a consensus that truth should be our goal.

Even with a consensus on truth as a goal, the discovery of truth is a process that cannot be reached immediately. Much of this book is about how that goal can be pursued. The basic answer is free and open discussion among those with opposing points of view. The growing polarization over the last several decades has made that increasingly difficult. A good discussion is somewhat like a tennis match, where the ball represents the arguments pro and con, going back and forth. Today's discussions are often like tennis matches with each side simultaneously hitting balls across the net, which the other side ignores.

In addition, rather than free and open discussion, censorship and suppression are growing concerns. The position of this book is solidly behind free speech. The remedy for bad speech is more speech, not suppression. Attempts to suppress errors, to only allow things that are true to spread, however well-intentioned, normally end up suppressing the truth and protecting lies. This type of free and open speech can be difficult, and at times even uncomfortable, but the alternatives are far worse.

While the book starts with a more philosophical discussion of truth, its main focus will be practical. It will emphasize the process of seeking truth, of resolving our differences, rather than the philosophical questions surrounding it. There will be a lot of examples used to make this case. Most are drawn from history, as people in various times and settings sought to understand how nature works, what happened in a particular event, or what is the best way to proceed or govern ourselves. Science, history, politics, business, all of these areas involve truth in one way or another.

Other examples are chosen to challenge conventional thinking, the mental furniture that tends to collect in our thoughts and is accepted without question. As a result, we will look at topics as varied as the Dark Ages to the origin of the terms Left and Right in politics, from a detailed analysis of the deadliest air accident in history to the origins of Chemistry and the origin of WWII. We will look at examples where people were right and where they made mistakes. All have lessons to teach us about truth and how to pursue it.

Several examples will come from the Lincoln-Douglas debates. Two serious advocates, debating at length the issue of slavery. Transcribed and printed in newspapers of the day, the Lincoln-Douglas debates are commonly seen as the prime example of political debate. Here they will provide examples of both good arguments and fallacious ones.

Why only examples from history? It is certainly possible to use more recent or even current examples. Still, historical examples have been chosen for three reasons. First, this attempts to avoid the partisan aspects of more recent disputes, disputes where issues are still hotly debated. For the Lincoln-Douglas debates, while a contentious and hotly debated issue at the time, thankfully, the issue of slavery is now settled. Thus, we can look at the arguments used by Lincoln and Douglas objectively without getting distracted by the subject matter.

The goal here is to be non-partisan. Whether I achieve that goal will be difficult to say. Some examples I planned to include were uncontroversial when I started this project. Now they are the source of significant disagreements and had to be scaled back or even dropped. What will or will not be controversial as you read this is unknown as I write. Still, I will address some more recent issues in a few places, highlighting their complexities. I will not attempt to solve them.

Another reason is that historical examples are, for the most part, finished. As such, we can get a better picture of controversies that lasted many decades. Finally, since they happened in the past, there is less temptation to 'pick a side.' These examples were chosen to highlight particular issues or problems, not for which side ultimately prevailed.

Still, when it comes to some of the bigger issues of truth and how to seek it, this book takes positions and argues for them. For example, I argue for the belief that there is an objective truth we can know, and against censorship. Those rejecting these views will undoubtedly detect a bias in favor of them. Hopefully, that bias will be kept to a minimum, and I will try to represent the various sides fairly and accurately.

As the discussion progresses, the foundations for many current disputes will become clear, leading some to conclude the reluctance to address them is somewhat disingenuous. After all, if I argue the foundations are incorrect, am I not arguing the beliefs themselves are incorrect?

There is some merit in this reasoning. However, two considerations argue against it. The first is the focus of this book is on the issues of truth, not current cultural and political disputes. Keeping them out of the discussion keeps the focus on the subject of this book.

Second, that a particular argument or foundation for a belief is wrong does not mean the belief is wrong. It only means the argument or foundation does not support it. There could be others. I do not preclude the possibility these various beliefs could be reformulated with foundations grounded on the views of truth argued for in this book.

This book is divided into three parts. The first part deals with the nature of truth and how we know what we know. When we say something is true, what are we saying? Chapter one deals with some of the various philosophical views concerning truth. Perhaps surprisingly, there is no consensus among philosophers. Still, it is possible to reach some conclusions about truth and how it is linked to reality even if philosophers still have many questions about all the details.

Chapter two looks at reality and how philosophers have tried to understand the world around us and our relation to that reality. Starting with the ancient Greeks, this development will be traced up to Postmodernism's recent emergence and growing impact. Basically, this has been a tug-of-war between two views. One is focused on what we can know. The other questions whether we can know anything at all. In this tug-of-war, the jury is still out.

Chapter three focuses on the last 250 years, seeking to understand how the philosophical theories discussed in the previous chapters have affected society. It examines the impact of science and how its changing views of our universe have affected philosophers and society as a whole. Finally, we look at the question of the self, and in particular, we will examine the issue of freewill and the complexities involved.

The first three chapters raise several questions about what, if anything, we can know. Chapter four addresses those questions and argues for an external reality and objective truth. It questions a major assumption of Materialism that has driven much of the intellectual development for the past 250 years, and its push towards skepticism. It concludes a bottom-up approach based on reason and evidence is the surest basis for truth.

With the first four chapters as background, Chapter five will tackle truth, particularly how we talk about it. What do we mean when we say something is true? How do the various types of language, such as humor, hyperbole, and metaphor, affect truth? How do judgments such as best or worse affect the truth of a statement? What about small or insignificant errors or misstatements? The chapter ends by discussing the role of ambiguous terms such as probable, likely, and safe, which can mean different things to different people. As a result, while there is truth, disagreements are inevitable.

Part two begins a more in-depth analysis of disagreement and error. Chapter six begins with a discussion of disagreement and why is it people disagree. Is it possible to disagree with someone without thinking they are in some fashion deficient? Looking at some disagreements in-depth, we see that disagreement does not mean one side is necessarily wrong. We will also look at how some disagreements come from problems with conventional wisdom.

Chapter seven takes a look at the more personal aspects of disagreement. We look at how different sides developed their views and why the disagreement occurred using some historical disagreements. We also look at the good aspects of the disagreement and some of the less desirable ones. When it comes to our differences, we can ignore them, discuss them, or enter into conflict over them. So the last part of the chapter discusses five things you should avoid when disagreeing and nine things you should do.

Chapter eight might seem odd for a book on truth, as it discusses the importance of error. Again we will look at several historical examples of error. Errors that, while wrong, resulted in expanding our knowledge of what is true. While our desire should always be to correct our errors, they serve a valuable role if handled correctly. So we will look at how to handle errors in a positive fashion.

Part Three looks at how you can improve your ability to know the truth and decide truth from error. Chapter nine is an in-depth view of our beliefs. What is it you believe? Why do you believe what you do? Have you thought things through? Do you know both the pros and cons, both long-term and short-term? Often our beliefs are a jumbled mixture; how can we organize them? How should we think about our beliefs?

Chapter ten explores the issue of openness to change. We all like to think we are open-minded but are we? How would we know? Starting with some historical examples where supposedly open-minded people were pretty closed, the chapter explores how complex real events are. An incomplete understanding of complexity can often lead to various groups thinking their view is the truth, the view supported by the evidence. In reality, all they have is an incomplete picture. The chapter ends with some suggestions on how you can be more open to the truth.

While chapter eight discussed the importance of error, it is still something to be avoided. Chapter eleven explores common sources of errors and how to avoid them. This is not always easy, and critical thinking takes effort. After looking at a couple of very common fallacies, the chapter focuses on bias, how to detect it, and how to deal with it. This discussion is followed by a discussion of common sources of information, surveys, and polls. The chapter concludes with some issues of perspective and how that can affect our thinking.

Chapter twelve brings the information of the previous chapters together under the question of how to make decisions. It starts by discussing things that can keep us from information, insulators, and those things we use to deflect evidence we don't want to deal with, blockers. Then the discussion moves to fourteen things, or red flags, to watch for when listening to advocates make their arguments. Finally, it discusses how to reach a decision.

In many places, I ask self-assessment questions, questions about your attitudes and beliefs. These are not test questions in which you will either pass or fail. A key premise of this book is no one is perfect; we all make mistakes. Rather these are questions to contemplate and help you discover your own strengths and weaknesses so you can improve.

One difficulty in writing a book like this is the various topics discussed in these chapters are not isolated. Rather they are all intertwined. As such, they do not segment themselves into nice neat chapters. For example, it is difficult to talk about truth without discussing perception. It is difficult to talk about perception without discussing the various views of reality. It is difficult to talk about reality without discussing truth. They are all interrelated. Then there is the subject of consciousness which influences all these subjects. Yet trying to talk about them all simultaneously would be very confusing. As a result, some concepts will appear several times, with brief mentions in some chapters and more complete discussions in others.

One final comment. Writing a book like this is always a bit risky in that one could see this as claiming some sort of superiority when it comes to truth. That is not correct. There are so many considerations, so many factors, no one can manage them all continuously. In a sense, seeking truth is a bit like juggling. The more you do it, the better you become. You learn to juggle three items, then four. Still, however many you learn to juggle, there are always more, some number that is too many for you. You still make mistakes.

This is why the search for truth is a group process, more than an individual one. The larger the group involved in the process, the better the result. Ideally, it should be a societal process, as this will give the best chance for discovering and preserving the knowledge of truth. Such a societal process does not require everyone to agree. It only involves them being committed to the goal of truth.

Part I
Truth and Knowledge

Chapter 1

Down the Rabbit Hole

To say of what is that it is not, or of what is not that it is, is false, while to say of what is that it is, and of what is not that it is not, is true. – Aristotle

While for many, philosophy is an esoteric and largely impractical endeavor bordering on the meaningless, philosophers are just people who think deeply about things most of us take for granted. It is by no means a meaningless exercise. Rather, most of the great advances in learning have their roots in philosophy. Some would dismiss philosophers' musings, preferring to trust scientists' more detailed analyses and investigations. They would do well to remember science is just a narrow, more specialized form of philosophy. What we now call science was originally natural philosophy.

In many respects, philosophy is like a parent conceiving of and nurturing areas of thought until they are mature to the point they can branch off on their own. Whether it be mathematics, physics, psychology, or linguistics, to name just a few, what we now call the sciences had their origins in philosophy. After philosophers have established an agreed-upon core of knowledge and a means of investigation, a portion can be carved out of philosophy. Then it can become a science in its own right.

What remains within philosophy are the children that failed to launch, the more difficult issues, issues for which there is not yet a consensus on a core of knowledge or method of investigation. These areas of investigation are not ready to branch out on their own and perhaps never will. For some of these areas, not only are the answers vague, at times, we are not yet sure we are even asking the right questions.

Even after an area branches out on its own, philosophers continue to ask the difficult and often very fundamental questions those in the sciences often ignore or just take for granted. Thus, while individual sciences have branched off from philosophy, there is still a very active philosophy of science. This continued examination is important for science changes with each discovery. Answers that seemed reasonable a hundred years ago may not fit the current state of science. Views of science developed in a Newtonian universe may not work as well in a quantum universe.

The philosophical method is basically to question those things we often take for granted. Things we all think we know, yet when asked directly about them, we suddenly find ourselves struggling for an answer. Philosophers question everything, a pursuit that sometimes seems to take them down dead ends. Still, the knowledge that a particular line of reasoning is a dead-end can be valuable. While they may end up pretty much where they started, the process will help them understand their beliefs' strengths and weaknesses. This understanding can keep them from errors to which they might otherwise fall victim. I believe this is the situation with truth.

One might think after thousands of years of pondering, discussing, and debating this most basic and fundamental of concepts, it would be pretty well understood. After all, what is there to understand? Truth is just what is, isn't it? Yet controversy and disagreement remain. One reason for this is the concept of truth is tightly intertwined with how we know what we know, which in philosophy is called epistemology. Then there is the very nature of reality itself. The uncertainty in these areas affects our concept of truth. The next two chapters will deal with epistemology. As for the issues of the nature of reality, we will address those as they come up. This chapter will focus on what we mean when we say something is "true." Is there a thing called truth, and if so, just what is it?

As philosophers have explored the concept of truth, they have found it is not quite so straightforward as it may at first seem. As such, there is a very broad range of views about truth and how we discover it, assuming there is such a thing. These views range from the fairly common and straightforward ones most would recognize to the fairly abstract.

Seeking Truth

The various philosophical views can be a daunting and, at times, bewildering maze of beliefs. One might think they have entered a land closer to Alice's Wonderland than the world of everyday existence. Many views are hybrids of the major categories of belief. I will not delve too deeply into all the nuances. Still, it will be profitable to quickly survey them, sticking to the major categories of belief.

While I think the following discussion is important, I realize philosophy is not everyone's cup of tea. Feel free to skip to the summary section at the end of the chapter, if you get disinterested or lost in the following discussion. Should you have questions in later chapters, you can always come back.

I will be outlining these various theories and raising some of the common objections to them. For the most part, I will not attempt to answer these objections, and supporters of these various theories have not left these objections unanswered. One of the problems with getting too deeply into the responses is that often there are several. Trying to treat them all fairly would only get us bogged down. Thus, we will skip the more philosophically grounded or overly technical issues. Finally, some of the more practical issues we will save for later chapters.

Still, it is important to survey these theories about truth because they often exert an influence far beyond their acceptance. It is not uncommon, for example, to find people arguing for beliefs grounded in a view of truth they would otherwise reject.

Finally, it is important to note that what follows summarizes and abbreviates what are, in reality, very complex and nuanced opinions. Some adherents are sure to think I have left out or ignored key parts or that my summarizations have resulted in a distortion. For this, I apologize in advance, as such problems are inherent in any such quick overview.

Still, gaining some understanding of the various views of truth will make it easier to recognize them when encountered. So, with that in mind, we will proceed down the rabbit hole.

TRUTH, POWER, FREEDOM AND THE LIAR'S PARADOX

By the twentieth century, many philosophers began to question whether there was ultimately anything that could be labeled truth. In contrast, others began to define it in very unconventional ways. The French Philosopher Michel Foucault famously linked truth and power. He saw truth as "a thing of this world: it is produced only by virtue of multiple forms of constraint. And it induces regular effects of power." He went on to argue "'Truth' is to be understood as a system of ordered procedures of the promotion, regulation, distribution, circulation and operation of statements." He saw "the essential political problem" as "ascertaining the possibility of constituting a new politics of truth."[3]

Richard Rorty, a leading postmodernist philosopher, questioned whether there was anything interesting about truth worth investigating. He argued,

> Our purposes would be served best by ceasing to see truth as a deep matter, as a topic of philosophical interest, or 'true' as a term which repays 'analysis.' 'The nature of truth' is an unprofitable topic, resembling in this respect 'the nature of man' and 'the nature of God.'[4]

The German philosopher Martin Heidegger took a completely different approach that other philosophers have labeled "radical and mysterious." Heidegger declared "The essence of truth is freedom" and freedom was "letting beings be."[5]

Heidegger argued the origins of the Greek word for truth, ἀλήθεια (*alētheia*), are to be found in the negation of the Greek verb meaning to forget, hide or conceal, λήθη (*lēthē*). The prefix ἀ

---

3   Foucault, M. (2001). Truth and Power. In M. P. Lynch, *The Nature of Truth* (pp. 317-319). Cambridge, Massachusetts: MIT Press. pp.318,19
4   Hicks, S. R. (2010). Explaining Postmodernism: Skepticism and Socialism from Rousseau to Foucault. Tempe, Arizona: Scholargy Publishing.
5   Heidegger, M. (2001). On the Essence of Truth. In M. P. Lynch, *The Nature of Truth* (pp. 295-316). Cambridge Massachusetts: MIT Press. pp. 302,3

Seeking Truth

in Greek acts to negate the word, similar to how "un-" works in English. So ἀ-λήθη would be un-concealment, which then became ἀληθεία. Thus, for Heidegger, truth is bound up with revealing what is. He argues if we translate ἀληθεία (*alētheia*), as 'unconcealment' rather than 'truth' this translation is not merely more literal; it contains the directive to rethink the ordinary concept of truth in the sense of the correctness of the statements.[6]

Some question this explanation of the Greek word for truth, and there is much that is mysterious in Heidegger's explanation of these concepts. Still, there is something to this view. Truth often is hidden. It must be sought after and revealed. In many cases, the truth is resisted, and it is necessary for us "to let beings be as the beings which they are."[7]

Several factors are behind the questioning of whether truth had any meaning or whether it was even legitimate to speak of 'truth.' One of these is a problem called the Liar's Paradox. There are many ways to demonstrate the Liar's Paradox; perhaps the easiest is to consider the truthfulness of the following sentence, which we will label sentence (A),

(A) This sentence is false.

This simple sentence results in the paradox that if the sentence is true, it is false, but if it is false, then it is true. While there is a temptation just to ignore such problems, ignoring problems is not what philosophers do. For philosophers, the problem is a very real one. Even if one is going to just ignore this sentence as meaningless, on what basis could one legitimately do this and yet retain as meaningful sentences such as,

(B) It is true that snow is white.

Just how is it that sentence (A) is meaningless while sentence (B) is not?

---

6 Heidegger, M. (2001). On the Essence of Truth. In M. P. Lynch, *The Nature of Truth* (pp. 295-316). Cambridge Massachusetts: MIT Press. p. 304

7 Heidegger, M. (2001). On the Essence of Truth. In M. P. Lynch, *The Nature of Truth* (pp. 295-316). Cambridge Massachusetts: MIT Press. p. 304)

The Polish mathematician Alfred Tarski set out to develop a concept of truth addressing this and other problems by putting the concept of truth into a generalized format. In doing so, he made one of the most important contributions of the twentieth century to the discussion of truth. The result is his schema T:

(T) X is true if and only if p.

Here X represents a sentence, and p is the condition under which X is true. As Tarski summarized this, "The sentence' snow is white' is true if, and only if, snow is white."[8] While this may seem obvious, generalizing this into the schematic form of (T) X is true if and only if p was an important contribution. It gave the concept of truth an almost mathematical structure. It reversed the trend away from truth as a legitimate concept. Before Tarski published his paper,

> ...there was prevalent among scientifically minded philosophers, the view that semantic notions such as the notions of truth and denotation were illegitimate: that they could not and should not be incorporated into a scientific conception of the world.[9]

Another major contribution Tarski made was developing a concept of truth immune from the Liar's Paradox. He pointed out the reason for the paradox was the sentence was self-referential; it was speaking of itself. What was needed to solve this problem was a language with an exactly specific structure, a second language. This second language could then discuss issues of truth in the first language. Tarski called the first language *'the object-language'* and the second he labeled *'the meta-language.'*

The meta-language need not be some completely different language than the object language. In fact, normally, the meta-language is just the object language with some added restrictions and

---

[8] Tarski, A. (2001). The Semantic Concept of Truth. In M. P. Lynch, *The Nature of Truth* (pp. 331-363). Cambridge, Massachusetts: MIT Press. p. 334

[9] Field, H. (2001). Tarski's Theory of Truth. In M. P. Lynch, *The Nature of Truth* (pp. 365-396). Cambridge, Massachusetts: MIT Press. p. 365

rules. One rule is that concepts such as True and False in the meta-language only apply to the object language. If you wanted to talk about the truth of a sentence in the meta-language, you would need yet another language; you would need a meta-meta-language to do so. Since you cannot discuss the truthfulness or falsehood of statements in the object language using the object language, only in the meta-language, this avoids the liar's paradox.

Again, I am only presenting the results of Tarski's work and have skipped much of his reasoning and justification. Still, what Tarski's theories did was present, formally, an understanding of truth that avoided many problems causing some to question if truth had any real meaning. But of course, Tarski did not end the discussion and, in fact, opened up new areas to consider. Before we get to those, we need to look at some of the older views of truth.

THE CORRESPONDENCE THEORY OF TRUTH

One of the oldest, most natural, and probably the most common ways of thinking about truth is it is something which corresponds to reality. In short, truth is that which is, or in the case of the past, that which was. Thus, the truthfulness of the statement, *Barack Obama was the first black President of the United States*, depends on how this statement *corresponds* to the actual events in American history.

This view is so common that normally we skip past all the language about correspondence. If asked about the truthfulness of the statement about President Obama, most would simply respond with something to the effect, *of course it is true, because he was.*

While this seems straightforward enough for most people, as we said earlier, philosophers are people who think deeply about things most of us simply take for granted. So, it should not be too surprising to find that philosophers have raised some questions about this view.

The first thing to notice in the above discussion is the difference between statements and truth. Statements are just beliefs put into language. One could write the statement above as *I believe Barack Obama was the first black President of the United States*. But we normally only include the '*I believe*' part if we want to emphasize the point or indicate some room for doubt.

As beliefs, such statements can either be true or false. Thus, they are distinct from the reality to which they are supposed to correspond. As the philosopher Bertrand Russell summarized it, "beliefs (a) depend on minds for their existence, (b) do not depend on minds for their *truth*."[10] This distinction between beliefs and the reality to which they correspond lies at the core of many problems with correspondence theory.

If belief and reality are different, then in what way do they correspond? Is it a structural correspondence that depends on the various parts lining up? How much does it depend on the conventions of the language? How does the correspondence exist, and is that even important? Philosophers ask these and many other questions.

A key component of correspondence theory is the notion of mind independence, the view that things exist apart from our minds. In other words, trees, mountains, deer, and the couch in your living room exist whether or not we are thinking about them. Because of this, most philosophers, but not all, see a link between correspondence theory and realism, i.e., the view which holds that reality exists apart from us.

Of course, for those philosophers who reject a realist view, this is a problem. As one philosopher put it, "The real objection to correspondence theories is… that there is nothing interesting or instructive to which sentences might correspond."[11] But even those who accept a realist point of view still see problems with correspondence theory. "It is sometimes said that a correspondence theory

---

10 Russell, B. (2001). Truth and Falsehood. In M. P. Lynch, *The Nature of Truth* (pp. 17-24). Cambridge, Massachusetts: MIT Press.
11 Sosa, E. (2001). Epistemology and Primitive Truth. In M. P. Lynch, *The Nature of Truth* (pp. 641-662). Cambridge, Massachusetts: MIT Press. p. 643

of truth opens up a 'gap' between our thoughts and reality – a gap that, once opened, turns out to be unbridgeable."[12]

How can there be a correspondence between them, if our beliefs about the world are separate from the world around us? More importantly, how is that correspondence to be determined? Ultimately, any explanation of these questions touches on several other concepts philosophers explore, such as the nature of reality and consciousness. These are beyond the scope of the discussion here.

Still, these are not the only questions philosophers ask about correspondence theory. If truth is that which corresponds to external reality, how do we talk about the truthfulness of statements that do not involve reality? To say that it is true that snow is white is one thing, but what about the statement "Darth Vader is the father of Luke Skywalker." Fictional characters do not exist in the real world, yet does it make sense to say the statement is false? What about the truthfulness of abstract statements like 'six is an even number' or 2 + 2 = 4? If these are true because of a correspondence, to what do they correspond? Are they true in the same sense that 'Snow is white' is true?

These issues raise the question of whether or not there are different types of truth. Is there one type of truth for the real world of rocks, trees, and couches? Another type of truth for Luke Skywalker, and another for things like math? If so, just what are those types of truth? Hopefully, you can see from this why philosophers have asked questions about truth and why some are not satisfied with correspondence theory. These philosophers have looked for different ways of thinking about truth.

THE COHERENCE THEORY OF TRUTH

In an attempt to avoid the problems with correspondence theory, some philosophers have taken a different approach. They define

---

[12] David, M. (2001). Truth as Identity and Truth as Correspondence. In M. P. Lynch, *The Nature of Truth* (pp. 683-704). Cambridge, Massachusetts: MIT Press. p. 690

truth not as correspondence with reality but as internal consistency, a coherence with the totality of belief.

Whereas correspondence theory is strongly linked to realism, the view that reality exists independent of our thoughts, coherence theory grew out of idealism. Idealism is the belief that there is an inherent link between objects and our thoughts. As Brand Blanshard put it, "The view that truth is coherence rests on a theory of the relation of thought to reality."[13]

In general, coherence theory sees reality, not as a set of facts, to which our beliefs either correspond or don't, but more as a systematic whole. When assessing any particular belief, such as *Barack Obama was the first black President of the United States,* one would see it is not just an isolated factoid. Instead, it is a statement with inherent connections. There is Obama, but there are also the concepts of the Presidency and the United States. This statement is a piece of information that fits in with numerous other pieces. In short, this fits into a much broader context of beliefs, such as humanity, race, political theory, and world history. Each of these concepts is likewise part of a much broader system of beliefs. These extend out until you get to the whole of reality. That which fits, i.e., is coherent with the totality of your beliefs is true; anything which does not is false.

Let's say you are trying to build a puzzle, but the pieces you have come from the puzzle you are trying to put together, along with several others. Coherence theory says the "truthfulness" of a piece, i.e., it is from the puzzle you are trying to build, is determined by how well it fits in with all the other pieces to make the complete picture.

Granted, like correspondence theory, most of the time, the totality of reality can be, and is, ignored in everyday life. But this notion of being part of the whole is central to coherence theory.

---

13 Blanshard, B. (2001). Coherence as the Nature of Truth. In M. P. Lynch, *The Nature of Truth* (pp. 103-121). Cambridge, Massachusetts: MIT Press. p. 103

Seeking Truth

It is one of its most attractive features. At the same time, it is also its key weakness.

It is one of its most attractive features because it closely matches how we commonly determine truth. When we hear a new bit of information or a new claim, it is common to assess it by comparing it to what we already believe to be true. Did it come from a source we believe is reliable? Does it agree or conflict with things we believe to be true? The simple fact is no one has the time or the ability to fact-check everything we hear. Thus, when we hear about a new study, if it fits well with what we already believe or want to believe, the study will often be accepted. If it conflicts, then we are far more likely to reject it. This type of response is a form of coherence theory in action.

This strength becomes a weakness when we realize we do not yet know the whole of reality. Such knowledge is not even possible. Because of this, when we compare new information to what we already believe, how do we know what we believe is true? This is not just a theoretical problem.

Alfred Lothar Wegener was a German meteorologist during the first part of the twentieth century. At that time, scientific investigation was not as specialized as now, and it was much more common for those in one discipline to contribute to another. In this vein, Wegener's interest went beyond meteorology and into geology. This interest led him to develop a theory he called Continental Displacement. Today it is called Plate Tectonics.

Yet when Wegener published his new theory, rather than being heralded, he was derided. The President of the American Philosophical Society pretty much summed up the reaction to Wegener's theory as "Utter, damned rot!" He justified this, saying, "If we are to believe this hypothesis, we must forget everything we learned in the last seventy years and start all over again."[14]

Can you hear the echoes of the coherence theory in these statements? As a result, Wegener was rejected and could not even

---

14 Winchester, S. (2003). *Krakatoa, The Day the World Exploded. August 27, 1883*. New York: HarperCollins. p. 74

get a teaching position in his own country. He died, never knowing acceptance would come within a few decades of his death. Today, his theory is not only accepted; it is central to our understanding of the formation of the earth's surface.

There is an important distinction between a test for truth and a description of the nature of truth. A strength of coherence theory is it parallels how we commonly determine truth. Still, coherence theory is making a somewhat different claim. Coherence theory is not just a method for determining truth but a description of what is truth. Blanshard put the problem as "nor does there seem to be any direct path from the acceptance of coherence as the test for truth to its acceptance as the nature of truth."[15]

Viewed as a theory for the nature of truth, coherence theory has several problems. The first is that if truth is grounded in coherence, what exactly is this coherence? All seem to agree it is broader than simple correspondence. Thus, there must be a much richer set of relationships in its set of interrelations. Still, unfortunately, there is no agreement on this, and coherence theorists have various explanations.

There are deeper problems. Coherence theory avoids the problems of correspondence theory by being based on idealism, which has an implicit link between our ideas of reality and that reality. But doesn't this then argue truth changes as our understanding of reality changes? A similar objection is that since truth is based on coherence with the whole, and we do not know the whole and probably never will, we can never know the truth. Because of this, coherence theory leads to skepticism, which is fine for those who are skeptics. For those who aren't, this is a problem.

Probably the most serious objection to coherence theory is it leads to multiple truths. Phrased another way, a system can be a coherent system and yet not be true. For example, one could conceive a coherent thought system where Darth Vader was really

---

15 Blanshard, B. (2001). Coherence as the Nature of Truth. In M. P. Lynch, *The Nature of Truth* (pp. 103-121). Cambridge, Massachusetts: MIT Press. p. 110

Luke Skywalker's father. But would we want to believe this because the statement was part of a coherent whole? Would it be true in the same way as Lincoln was the 16th President of the United States? Coherence Theorists counter by claiming it is not just any belief system, but "that truth is coherence with a certain particular set of beliefs."[16]

This objection may be good "common sense;" after all, does anyone claim Darth Vader or Luke Skywalker really exist in some other reality? Still, it avoids a deeper issue. How do we know the system we are comparing with is the correct system? As a method for determining reality's truthfulness, these flaws could be written off as simply part of the process. Coherence with current beliefs is a good description of how human knowledge has progressed. But for a theory of the nature of truth grounded on an inherent link with our ideals about reality itself, these are more serious objections.

PRAGMATISM AS A THEORY OF TRUTH

The next theory of truth we will look at is a distinctly American one. This is not to say only Americans accept this view or that all Americans accept it. Still, it is a theory developed primarily by American philosophers and grew out of a particularly American way of looking at things. At the core of pragmatism is the idea that what is important about a belief is its practical effects. In these practical effects, truth is to be found. As Charles Peirce, the founder of the pragmatist movement, put it, "Our idea of anything is our idea of its sensible effects."[17]

This linking of truth to its practical value, which "is primarily derived from the practical importance of their objects to us"[18] is

---

16 Walker, R. C. (2001). The Coherence Theory. In M. P. Lynch, *The Nature of Truth* (pp. 123-158). Cambridge, Massachusetts: MIT Press. p. 129

17 Peirce, C. S. (2001). How to Make Our Ideas Clear. In M. P. Lynch, *The Nature of Truth* (pp. 193-210). Cambridge, Massachusetts: MIT Press. p. 202

18 James, W. (2001). Pragmatism's Conception of Truth. In M. P. Lynch, *The Nature of Truth* (pp. 211 - 228). Cambridge, Massachusetts: MIT Press. p. 214

at the core of pragmatism. If something has no importance, if it is irrelevant, does it matter if it is true?

Another aspect of pragmatism is for something to be true, it must be verifiable.

> True ideas are those that we can assimilate, validate, corroborate and verify. False ideas are those that we can not." However, since ideas need to be verified before they are true, truth *happens* to an idea. It *becomes* true, is *made* true by events.[19] [emphasis in the original]

This view is a distinctly different one from correspondence theory. In correspondence theory, something is true if it corresponds to reality. The ability to verify something or its practical effects is irrelevant, for something is true or false regardless of anything we do. While in correspondence theory, we might discover a truth, there is no concept of an idea becoming true, of truth happening, or something being made truth. In correspondence theory, truth is ultimately determined by reality rather than our view of its practicality.

To see the difference between these views, consider the question of whether the earth circles the sun. Was this view true before the Copernican theory was verified? Did the theory only become true once it was verified and its practical effects understood? It became true for the pragmatist only when the Copernican Theory showed it worked better than the earlier Ptolemaic system. Before that, the earlier Ptolemaic system was true.

While this might seem to be a surprising statement, remember the Ptolemaic system, while much more complex and cumbersome, did work pretty well. It did allow one to predict where the known planets would appear as they moved among the stars at night. Since it worked in a very practical way, the Ptolemaic system was, at least in some sense, true.

---

19 James, W. (2001). Pragmatism's Conception of Truth. In M. P. Lynch, *The Nature of Truth* (pp. 211 - 228). Cambridge, Massachusetts: MIT Press. pp. 212-3

From this, we see truth is not a fixed property a statement has for pragmatism. Truth is a more flexible and variable concept. Things are true only in the sense they are practical and are only true to the extent we can verify them. As James put it, "truth lives, in fact, for the most part on a credit system. Our thoughts and beliefs' pass', so long as nothing challenges them, just as banknotes pass so long as nobody refuses them."[20]

Paper money has value only because everyone accepts that it does; likewise, things are true because people accept they are. Even if we ultimately reject pragmatism as a theory of truth, in a very practical sense, this is a good description of how truth works in the culture.

Still, even some pragmatists see a problem in this flexibility of reality. To address such problems, some pragmatists see truth as more forward-looking. Peirce wrote, "The opinion which is fated to be ultimately agreed to by all who investigate, is what we mean by the truth, and the object represented in this opinion is the real. That is the way I would explain reality."[21]

This does not solve all the problems. We would normally see some things as having a truth but which are beyond any ability to investigate. Included in this would be any number of historical questions for which there is simply not enough evidence to conclude one way or another, such as Jack the Ripper's identity. Yet, for pragmatism, such unknown truths can have little if any practical value simply because they are unknown. As such, they "concern much more the arrangement of our language than they do the meaning of our ideas."[22]

---

20 James, W. (2001). Pragmatism's Conception of Truth. In M. P. Lynch, *The Nature of Truth* (pp. 211 - 228). Cambridge, Massachusetts: MIT Press. p. 215

21 Peirce, C. S. (2001). How to Make Our Ideas Clear. In M. P. Lynch, *The Nature of Truth* (pp. 193-210). Cambridge, Massachusetts: MIT Press. p. 206

22 Peirce, C. S. (2001). How to Make Our Ideas Clear. In M. P. Lynch, *The Nature of Truth* (pp. 193-210). Cambridge, Massachusetts: MIT Press. p. 208

Thus, pragmatism is, in a sense, cut off from the real world. It moves the foundation of truth away from direct correspondence with reality and to the closely related but distinct concept of verification. As a result, pragmatists are split over the question of realism, i.e., does the world exist independent of us or our minds? The realist answer is pretty straightforward, yes. Still, there remains a great deal of difference between how we understand and know the world in which we exist and how we can say something about the world is true.

For those who reject realism, the answer is far more complex. Hilary Putman rejected realism or the "*externalist* perspective" for something he called internalism. He argues,

> Internalism is not a facile relativism that says, 'Anything goes.' Denying that it makes sense to ask whether our concepts 'match' something totally uncontaminated by conceptualizations is one thing; but to hold that every conceptual system is therefore just as good as every other would be something else... Internalism does not deny that there are experiential *inputs* to knowledge.[23] [emphasis in the original]

For many of these issues, pragmatism returns to the question, what is the practical difference? If all you know is the Ptolemaic system and it does what you need it to do, is it not "true" for you? If something cannot be known, such as Jack the Ripper's identity, does that have any practical effect on us? And if not, why should it affect our view of truth?

Deflationary Views

Another group of philosophers take a vastly different approach. Instead of seeking to understand the nature of truth, they question whether truth has any nature to discover. Rather than seeking some sort of nature, deflationary views see truth as something so obvious

---

23   Peirce, C. S. (2001). How to Make Our Ideas Clear. In M. P. Lynch, The Nature of Truth (pp. 193-210). Cambridge, Massachusetts: MIT Press. p. 256

Seeking Truth

it needs no explanation. It is when we attempt to try that we run into problems. One of the earliest of these was Frank Ramsey, who wrote,

> what *is* the meaning of 'true'? It seems to me that the answer is really perfectly obvious, that anyone can *see* what it is and that the difficulty only arise when we try to *say* what it is, because it is something which ordinary language is rather ill-adapted to express.[24] [emphasis in the original]

For Ramsey to say something is true is redundant. For example, to say 'The earth is round' and to say 'It is true the earth is round' is to say the same thing. As such, we can just drop the 'It is true' part without losing anything. As Ramsey put it, true "is generally added not to alter the meaning but for what in a wide sense are reasons of style."[25] Since it adds nothing, it has no nature to discover.

P.F. Strawson also sees a problem in attempting to explain truth. He writes, "it would be futile to attempt to do it in terms of the words 'fact,' 'statement,' 'true,' for these words contain problems, not its solution."[26] From this point of view, when correspondence theory uses language to explain how language relates to the world, it suffers from the very problem it is trying to solve.

Drawing on the work of Alfred Tarski mentioned earlier, and the sentence, *'Snow is white' is true if and only if snow is white*, W.V.O. Quine noted, "ascription of truth just cancels the quotation marks. True is disquotation. So the truth predicate is superfluous when ascribed to a given sentence; you could just utter the sentence."[27] In short, you could just say, "Snow is white." For Quine,

---

24 Ramsey, F. P. (2001). The Nature of Truth. In Lynch, *The Nature of Truth* (pp. 433-445). Cambridge, Massachusetts: MIT Press. p 436-7
25 Ramsey, F. P. (2001). The Nature of Truth. In Lynch, *The Nature of Truth* (pp. 433-445). Cambridge, Massachusetts: MIT Press. pp. 440-441
26 Strawson, P. F. (2001). Truth. In M. P. Lynch, *The Nature of Truth* (pp. 447-471). Cambridge, Massachusetts: MIT Press. p. 457
27 Quine, W. V. (2001). Truth. In M. P. Lynch, *The Nature of Truth* (pp. 473-481). Cambridge, Massachuetts: MIT Press. p.475

"What is true is the sentence, but its truth consists in the world's being as the sentence says."[28]

To some, this may sound a lot like correspondence theory, and there are some similarities. However, there are some key differences. Quine writes, "The disquotational account of truth does not define the truth predicate – not in the strict sense."[29] Yet, defining the truth predicate is exactly what correspondence theory is attempting to do. Instead of defining the nature of 'true,' one "should puzzle rather over the sentence to which he ascribes it. 'True' is transparent."[30] By transparent, he means when you focus on the nature of truth in the sentence 'It is true that snow is white,' you will not see anything in 'true,' you will only see that snow is white.

Dorothy Grover takes a somewhat different approach that sees words like 'true' functioning in sentences much like pronouns do for nouns. We use pronouns as a shorthand way of referring to nouns. Thus, instead of saying, "Sam caught the ball and Sam threw it to first base," we could replace the second occurrence of 'Sam' with the pronoun 'he,' resulting in "Sam caught the ball and he threw it to first base." In the second sentence, 'he' is simply a linguistic device for referring to Sam.

In the same way pronouns refer to nouns, Grover sees words like 'true' as a shorthand way of referring to sentences, a sort of pro-sentences. Thus the name, prosentential theory. She writes, "The basic claim of the prosentential theory is 'it is true' and 'that is true' function as pro-sentences in English."[31] This theory would mean words like 'true' are more a feature of language than a concept requiring investigation.

---

28 Quine, W. V. (2001). Truth. In M. P. Lynch, *The Nature of Truth* (pp. 473-481). Cambridge, Massachuetts: MIT Press. p. 476
29 Quine, W. V. (2001). Truth. In M. P. Lynch, *The Nature of Truth* (pp. 473-481). Cambridge, Massachuetts: MIT Press. p. 476
30 Quine, W. V. (2001). Truth. In M. P. Lynch, *The Nature of Truth* (pp. 473-481). Cambridge, Massachuetts: MIT Press. p. 476
31 Grover, D. (2001). The Prosentential Theory. In M. P. Lynch, *The Nature of Truth* (pp. 505-526). Cambridge, Massachuetts: MIT Press. p. 506

Much of this difference turns on the issue of whether or not truth is a property. To understand this, consider something simple like a shirt. It could have a property of color (red, green, blue, yellow) and sleeves (long, short, none), to name two. Likewise, a sentence could have a truth property (true, false). While this seems easy at first, the problem comes when we attempt to determine what this property is? For the shirt, one could ask what is a color or what is a sleeve. We can provide the definitions for these properties.

The problem for the truth property then becomes just what is this thing called truth. Thus, concerning prosentential theory, Grover states it "has been classified as a deflationary theory, a theory that denies there is (a need for) a truth property."[32]

At one level, this all seems to make sense. Of course, 'snow is white' is true if and only if snow is white; still, deflationary theories are not without their own problems. For example, concerning Ramsey's claim saying something is 'true' is redundant, Michael P Lynch asks, "why we would have the word 'true' in our language if it is as gratuitous as the generalized redundancy account suggests."[33] Another is not all uses of "true" fit neatly into the explanations of the deflationists.

A deeper problem is deflation theories are vague on exactly what is meant by truth being obvious and/or transparent. So, for example, if 'Snow is white' does not correspond to physical reality as in correspondence theory, exactly what is 'true' saying about a sentence. Put another way, how does it actually differ from correspondence theory?

One of the difficulties here was pointed out by Michael Devitt. "Whereas the focus of the correspondence theory is on the nature and role of *truth*, the focus of the deflationary theory is on the

---

[32] Grover, D. (2001). The Prosentential Theory. In M. P. Lynch, *The Nature of Truth* (pp. 505-526). Cambridge, Massachusetts: MIT Press. p. 508

[33] Lynch, M. P. (2001). Deflationary Views and Their Critics: Introduction. In M. P. Lynch, *The Nature of Truth* (pp. 103-121). Cambridge, Massachusetts: MIT Press. p. 423

nature and role of *the truth term.*"³⁴ [emphasis in the original]. In short, correspondence theory focuses on the supposed nature of truth. In contrast, deflationary views focus on how the word 'true' functions in our language. Ultimately these are different things. Another problem is although deflationary theorists deny a nature to truth, a metaphysics of truth, they still often speak in those terms.

These two factors result in confusion. The more one tries to pin it down, the more deflation either moves toward correspondence theory or into antirealism, antirealism being the view that reality is determined in some fashion by what we think. Again, consider the statement: 'Snow is white is true.' Correspondence theory says 'true' here refers to a correspondence to reality, i.e., the physical world. There exists something called snow, and it is white. Some deflationary views say this is redundant or obvious. Yet, this still leaves the correspondence to reality.

Other deflationists stress the empty nature of truth. There is no correspondence to the physical world, and 'true' is merely a linguistic device with no connection to reality. If this is so, how is this different from a rejection of reality?

> The typical realist thinks that there is a reality to truth that, like any other reality, has a nature and causal role, and that this nature and role needs explanations. The deflationist reveals her antirealism by rejecting the need for, and possibility of, such an explanation.[35]

Thus, deflationary theories exist on a knife-edge. On the one side, they are ready to fall into correspondence theory, and on the other, antirealism. Its key problem is maintaining 'true' has no nature while maintaining statements like 'Snow is white' are statements about the world.

---

34 Devitt, M. (2001). The Metaphysics of Truth. In M. P. Lynch, *The Nature of Truth* (pp. 579-611). Cambridge, Massachusetts: MIT Press. p. 580
35 Devitt, M. (2001). The Metaphysics of Truth. In M. P. Lynch, *The Nature of Truth* (pp. 579-611). Cambridge, Massachusetts: MIT Press. p 591

OTHER VIEWS OF TRUTH

The difficulties with all these various attempts to understand truth have led other philosophers to conclude the attempts to define truth are folly. Donald Davidson argues truth is "an indefinable concept"[36] Truth, like other basic concepts, is elementary. Such elementary concepts are

> concepts without which (I am inclined to say) we would have no concepts at all. Why then should we expect to be able to reduce these concepts definitionally to other concepts that are simpler, clearer, and more basic."[37]

In short, truth is a basic or primitive concept that cannot be defined. These theories fall under the heading of Primitivism.

While at first glance, this may seem yet another deflationary view, there is a key difference. Deflationary views see truth like a balloon with all the air let out, as a basically empty concept, and thus not all that important, other than perhaps as a linguistic device. Thus, truth has little or no role beyond a linguistic one; it is not important when considering other philosophical concepts such as meaning.

Primitivism, on the other hand, sees truth as a very important concept. While important, it is so basic it cannot be defined. In fact, Donald Davidson sees it as so important that "I do not think we can understand meaning or any of the propositional attitudes without the concept of truth."[38]

Ernest Sosa likewise sees truth as a primitive concept beyond our ability to define. However, he sees primitive truth as "consistent

---

36 Davidson, D. (2001). The Folly of Trying to Define Truth. In M. P. Lynch, *The Nature of Truth* (pp. 623-640). Cambridge, Massachusetts: MIT Press. p. 625

37 Davidson, D. (2001). The Folly of Trying to Define Truth. In M. P. Lynch, *The Nature of Truth* (pp. 623-640). Cambridge, Massachusetts: MIT Press. p. 624

38 Davidson, D. (2001). The Folly of Trying to Define Truth. In M. P. Lynch, *The Nature of Truth* (pp. 623-640). Cambridge, Massachusetts: MIT Press. p. 635

with a substantive metaphysical theory that takes truth as involving correspondence with reality – so long as the theory is not seen as implying anything about the concept of truth."[39] Thus while Davidson and Sosa agree truth is primitive and defies definition, they disagree on exactly what truth is and its role.

Another approach attempts to understand truth by identifying truth as facts. As Jennifer Hornsby describes it, "The identity theory is encapsulated in the simple statement that true thinkables are the same as facts"[40]. For Hornsby, a "thinkable" is anything we might think about or any statement, including "beliefs, hopes and fears"[41]. This view makes sense in one respect for the statement "it is true that snow is white" is basically the same as "it is a fact that snow is white."

However, when we consider the uses of the words 'true' and 'fact,' while there is a great deal of overlap, they do not quite have the same meaning, at least in normal usage. While 'true' can almost always replace 'fact,' the reverse is not the case. Thus, as we will see in chapter five, there are places where it would be proper to use the word 'true,' but not really correct to use the word 'fact.'

We normally use 'fact' to refer to things that are objectively true and easily verifiable. We use true to refer to things that, in some sense, could be considered a fact but are usually more in the realm of a correct judgment. As Marian David summarized this "truth talk and fact talk do not go together as smoothly as identity theorists might like."[42]

39　Lynch, M. P. (2001). Primitivism, Identity Theory, and Alethic Pluralism. In M. P. Lynch, *The Nature of Truth* (pp. 615-621). Cambridge, Massachusetts: MIT Press. p. 616

40　Hornsby, J. (2001). Truth: The Identity Theory. In M. P. Lynch, *The Nature of Truth* (pp. 663-681). Cambridge, Massachusetts: MIT Press. p. 664

41　Hornsby, J. (2001). Truth: The Identity Theory. In M. P. Lynch, *The Nature of Truth* (pp. 663-681). Cambridge, Massachusetts: MIT Press. p. 672

42　David, M. (2001). Truth as Identity and Truth as Correspondence. In M. P. Lynch, *The Nature of Truth* (pp. 683-704). Cambridge, Massachusetts: MIT Press. p 696

Seeking Truth

One could, of course, expand the meaning of fact to include all the uses of true, but then this would change its basic meaning. On the other hand, if it retained the connection to the physical reality normally connected with the concept of fact, it would basically result in correspondence theory.

Finally, still other philosophers have noted all of these theories have something important to say about truth. Yet, all run into problems at some point. As Michael Lynch summarized the problem:

> A theory of truth is proposed and argued for by appeal to propositions of a certain domain, the truth of which the theory seems to explain quite nicely. The theory is then extended to cover propositions of every domain. But this extension runs up against counterexamples; that is, the theory does not explain how propositions from certain domains can be true.[43]

In short, theories of truth work well in some areas, but none seem to cover all the various ways we use the term truth. Moreover, Lynch sees a key problem with all these approaches in that they all assume "that the question 'What is truth?' has a single answer."[44]

One approach that does not make this assumption is pluralism, the idea "truth may consist of different things in different… areas."[45] Crispin Wright sees truth more as a series of propositions, or what he calls platitudes, things "that chimes with ordinary *a priori* thinking about truth."[46] Most of these are drawn from, or related to, the other theories of truth discussed earlier. For example, from

---

43 Lynch, M. P. (2001). A Functionalist Theory of Truth. In M. P. Lynch, *The Nature of Truth* (pp. 723-749). Cambridge, Massachusetts: MIT Press. p 723
44 Lynch, M. P. (2001). A Functionalist Theory of Truth. In M. P. Lynch, *The Nature of Truth* (pp. 723-749). Cambridge, Massachusetts: MIT Press. p. 725
45 Wright, C. (2001). Minimalism, Deflationsim, Pragmatism, Pluralism. In M. P. Lynch, *The Nature of Truth* (pp. 751-787). Cambridge, Massachusetts: MIT Press. p. 761
46 Wright, C. (2001). Minimalism, Deflationsim, Pragmatism, Pluralism. In M. P. Lynch, *The Nature of Truth* (pp. 751-787). Cambridge, Massachusetts: MIT Press. p. 759

correspondence theory, "The Correspondence Platitude – for a proposition to be true it for it to correspond to reality, accurately reflect how matters stand, 'tell it like it is,' etc."[47]

In addition to correspondence, Wright also has platitudes for transparency, opacity, absoluteness, among others. While these platitudes describe the range of the meaning of truth, when judging the truthfulness of particular statements, "truth may consist in different things in different such areas: in the possession of one property in one area, and in that of a different property in another."[48]

While this would certainly help explain the difficulties the other theories face, by now, it should not be surprising this is not without its own problems, the foremost being that if different things have different ways of being judged to be true, in what way are they all 'true.' If truth is in some fashion ambiguous, meaning different things in different contexts, this will pose major problems in areas such as logic, which assumes that things that are true are true in the same way.

Lynch attempts to avoid this problem with what he calls a functional theory of truth. A functional theory of truth works similarly to modern theories of consciousness. These theories of consciousness say the brain has different areas responsible for different things. These areas deal with memory, language, etc.. Conscious states, such as pain, consist of different combinations of these areas. Another analogy Lynch uses is that of a head of state. These can be "presidents, prime ministers, kings, queens, and even religious figures." There will be a common pool of duties (functions) which describes their role as head of state. None will match all of these, as the exact nature of their duties "will vary from country to country."

---

47 Wright, C. (2001). Minimalism, Deflationsim, Pragmatism, Pluralism. In M. P. Lynch, *The Nature of Truth* (pp. 751-787). Cambridge, Massachusetts: MIT Press. p. 760

48 Wright, C. (2001). Minimalism, Deflationsim, Pragmatism, Pluralism. In M. P. Lynch, *The Nature of Truth* (pp. 751-787). Cambridge, Massachusetts: MIT Press. p. 761

Seeking Truth

Yet these differences in details do not keep us from saying "both Fidel Castro and Bill Clinton [were] heads of state."[49]

Summary

What can we make of all this? Hopefully, it is clear why the study of truth has not yet branched out on its own in the same fashion as physics or chemistry. Yet do all these different views and alternate ways of viewing truth mean the rest of the book is doomed from the start? No, or at least I hope not.

Regardless of where one may come down on all these theories, we all grasp there is something to truth, even if we cannot clearly specify exactly what it is. While the notion of truth may be perplexing to philosophers, it is something we learned as children. While very young children may not clearly understand the difference between the imaginary and the real world, it is something they learn. Over time, they come to realize questions like, "Did you take that cookie?" are in some way different from the questions that come out of play, such as, "Are you a princess?" They grow to understand there is a difference between imagination and make-believe on the one hand and reality on the other. It is in this realization truth is found.

In many respects, we return to the statements of Aristotle that started this chapter. "To say of what is that it is not, or of what is not that it is, is false, while to say of what is that it is, and of what is not that it is not, is true"[50] There is, at least in some fashion, a correspondence to the physical world, even if the exact nature of that correspondence cannot be clearly specified. Philosophical nuances aside, there is a reality about which we can say some propositions are true while others are false.

To say this does not remove all the issues. One that remains is the question, if this reality is separate from us and our thoughts,

---

49 Lynch, M. P. (2001). A Functionalist Theory of Truth. In M. P. Lynch, *The Nature of Truth* (pp. 723-749). Cambridge, Massachusetts: MIT Press. p 728
50 Aristotle. (n.d.). *Metaphysics*. p. 1011b25

how can we know anything about it? That is the subject of the next chapter.

Chapter 2

I Think;
Therefore I Am, I Think

Reality is what we take to be true. What we take to be true is what we believe. What we believe is based upon our perceptions. What we perceive depends upon what we look for. What we look for depends upon what we think. What we think depends upon what we perceive. What we perceive determines what we believe. What we believe determines what we take to be true. What we take to be true is our reality. – Gary Zukav

There are two key questions, when it comes to knowledge. What do you know? How did you come to know it? Before we get too far, I need to clarify which meaning for knowledge I am using. Philosophers, when speaking of knowledge, usually refer to a technical definition for knowledge combining truth and justification. To be knowledge in a philosophical sense, a belief must be both true and justified. A false belief can never be knowledge. A true belief can only be knowledge if there is good reason to hold that belief. If I believe that Dave's car is blue because I mistakenly believe the blue car in the parking lot is Dave's, that is not knowledge, even if Dave's car happens to be blue. For philosophers, to be knowledge, a belief must be both true and held for valid reasons.

I am using the more common and generic meaning of knowledge, something you believe to be true despite the philosophical definition. Using this definition, we all know or perhaps more accurately think we know a lot of things. Some of this is complex and specialized, such as the knowledge you need to do your job.

The knowledge needed to be an engineer is different from a carpenter, different from a chef, and different from a nurse. Much of our knowledge is just the mundane facts of life we take for granted, allowing us to live our normal day-to-day existence. We only really become aware of them when, for example, we must teach our children their address, or when we travel to a different country and suddenly have to learn new ways to do common things, such as which side of the road to drive on or how to number the floors of a multi-story building, (e.g., first, second, third, vs. ground, first, second).

There is also, how we come to know what we know. The foundations of our knowledge come first from our family and then from our culture. Much of this is taken for granted by the time one is an adult. It is just the way things are done. Families and cultures are different, and so we all learn somewhat different things. A good metaphor here is food. Each family has different ways of cooking. While families from the same regions tend to have similar foods, there are still some differences from family to family.

What we know can be thought of as a basic food. Different areas will have different base ingredients. Some areas will use rice, other areas grains, others potatoes. Added to this will be various fish, meats, vegetables, and spices common in that area. The result will be basic dishes for each region customized for each family. While families near you will have similar basic dishes, the farther you travel from home, the more different the basic food.

Granted, this metaphor, like all metaphors, breaks down if pushed too far. It also works better for earlier periods in history, when there was not such a wide variety of foods to choose from, and people were more dependent on what existed nearby. Even here, though, it does not break down completely. Just as people have become more exposed to different foods, they have also become more exposed to different ideas and ways of doing things, which also goes into their basic knowledge.

As we enter adulthood, we take this basic knowledge that we have acquired and add to it. Some go to college or technical school; others learn a trade. Some continue to add to their knowledge deliberately, reading books or watching documentaries. Some effectively stop reading as soon as school ends and simply pick up knowledge as it presents itself as they live life. Everything we do as we live our lives shapes us.

In many respects, we are the sum of what we believe and know, what we think is true, right, and correct. As what we know changes, we change. What we know is shaped by everything we do. It is shaped by the books we read, the movies we watch, whether we travel or not, how much time we spend in nature. Everything we do affects us, some a little, some a lot. It all impacts our views, either changing what we believe or confirming and reinforcing what we already believe.

Since we do not all do the same things, we will not all believe the same things. For example, a person who reads will have knowledge unknown to a person who doesn't. A do-it-yourself hobbyist will acquire knowledge that a person who never picks up a hammer does not have. A person who spends a lot of time fishing will have knowledge unknown to someone who has never fished.

Often this knowledge will go beyond the mere facts or skills acquired. It will shape their overall perspective in subtle ways. People will often draw parallels, valid or invalid, to other things they know.

This shaping of our perspective is a particular issue with movies and TV. They give us a view of reality that is, by definition, not real. Things happen, not because of reality, but because it was written in the script or improvised by the actor. Still, the shows we watch shape our view of reality in subtle ways. The "normal" ways things are depicted on screen becomes, to some extent, our normal. As a result, we expect murders to be solved, the good guys will win, the guilty to confess, and that in the end, the outcome will be happy.

A study by Julia Lippman, L. Monique Ward, and Rita Seabrook at the University of Michigan researched the ways movies and TV shaped our views of love. They found a strong belief that "love finds a way" was correlated with romantic movies. Those who watch marriage-themed programming were more likely to believe in "love at first sight" and "true love." However, those watching content that featured multiple dating partners were less likely to believe in "true love" or a soul mate for people. As Lippman put it, "It is possible that frequent exposure to romance and courtship in this idealized form could lead viewers to adopt equally idealized notions about relationships in the real world."[51]

The sum of all we know and all that has happened to us will shape our perspective. As a result, we all are unique. We all know different things. Still, even with this, few ever go far from the foundations of the broader culture instilled in them as they grew to adulthood.

How Do We Know

There is a more basic issue to this question of how you know what you know. We all learn from the experiences we have had, either focused as in reading or less so such as pursuing a hobby or watching a movie. However, this more basic issue can be summed up in how do you experience something?

Look around you. What do you see? Perhaps it is early morning, and you are sitting on a soft couch in your home. Around you are furniture, walls with pictures, perhaps a window looking out onto your yard. You are drinking some warm coffee or tea as you smell breakfast cooking in the kitchen, all the while the radio plays your favorite music. Maybe it is a bright sunny day, and you are relaxing on the warm sands of a beach. You can hear the sound of the surf, the smell of the ocean as you sip your favorite tropical drink. However, this latter possibility might call into question your choice of relaxing reading material.

Whatever is around you, you take it for granted because you are experiencing it. Or are you? Long before the movie, *The Matrix*, philosophers had questioned the nature of our experiences. How do we know anything? Take something as mundane as a dog. We all know what a dog is; a dog is a dog! But how do we know that?

---

51 Wadley, J. (2014, June 20). *Isn't it romantic? Movies, TV shows strongly shape how we view love.* Retrieved from Michigan News: https://news.umich.edu/isn-t-it-romantic-movies-tv-shows-strongly-shape-how-we-view-love/

When we see a friend's pet for the first time, how do we instantly know it is a dog? There are numerous breeds, and even within a breed, each dog is unique. Add to this all the pure-bred mutts. So how do we know the animal in our friend's house is a dog, even if we have never seen it before, and we may not have even known our friend had a pet?

This issue is not just an ancient problem, as it goes to the heart of our consciousness and thinking. What are consciousness and thinking? Are we just biological information processors, computers made from carbon rather than silicone? Is our brain, as some philosophers have put it, just a meat machine? This second question is not an easy one to answer, and we will return to it later.

As for the first question, actually, that is an easy question to answer. No, we are not just biological computers as there are too many differences. Things computers do well, like processing large lists of numbers, we struggle with. Things we take for granted are difficult, if not impossible, for computers, such as recognizing a dog. Whatever we are, we are distinctly different from the binary computers we build today. What makes them so useful is that they are strongest where we are weakest.

CAN COMPUTERS KNOW

Returning to how we can recognize a dog, it is one of the many differences in how we think and how computers work. Recognizing a dog as a dog is something children learn at an early age. Still, it is something very difficult, if even possible, for a computer. Because of this difference, many websites have a security check based on pictures. You are shown various pictures and asked to check those containing an object, such as a crosswalk or a chimney—child's play for human beings, extremely difficult for computers.

Even if you had a very complex computer algorithm that could process a picture and determine if there was a dog in the picture, can the algorithm be said to know it is a dog? Is this knowledge, or is this just the output of an algorithm?

Consider something as simple as the following to understand the difference: You have groups of symbols consisting of * and @. You combine these groups column by column with the following two rules: @ and @ stay @; @ and * become *. With these two rules, you can combine the following two groups column by column, *@@@, and @@@*; you would get *@@*. You do not have to understand what you are doing to do this. You just follow the rules. exposure

If you have had any exposure to binary operations, the basis for how computers operate, you may have recognized this as * is 1 and @ is 0. If we do the corresponding replacements, *@@@ becomes binary 1000, which for us is 8. @@@* would be 0001 binary or just 1. The operation then was 8 + 1 = 9.

It's okay, if this is your first exposure to binary, and this is still a bit confusing. The point here is that you do not have to know the groups of symbols represent numbers or you are adding 8 and 1. You just apply the two rules to the groups of symbols, and you can add two numbers without knowing what the numbers are, what the answer is, or even that you are adding.

Of course, computers can do more than just add numbers and thus have more than just these two rules built into them. The philosopher, John Searle, published a more elaborate example of this problem in 1980. Called the *Chinese Room Argument*, Searle proposed the following thought experiment. A person is in a room who knows nothing about the Chinese language, but the person has a rule book on how to process the symbols coming into the room. This person follows the rules perfectly, sending back the corresponding symbols as indicated in the rules.

Those outside the room are asking questions in Chinese and are getting back the correct answers in Chinese. So they conclude whoever is in the room knows the Chinese language. Yet, the person in the room does not know Chinese. They are simply following a rule book to process the symbols that come in without knowing what they, or the symbols they send back, mean. They can follow an algorithm, but they do not know Chinese.

The problem with a computer recognizing a dog in a picture is developing a set of rules the computer could use. These rules would not just have to detect a dog where the dog is the only thing in the picture and clearly shown. It would have to cover all the possible situations and angles where people can see a dog. It would even have to find dogs that were not actually dogs, such as the silhouette of a dog on a sign.

Even if a set of rules could be developed to accomplish this, the difference would remain. We do not need to consult a list of rules to know what it is when we see a dog. We just know. We might suggest a few rules, if questioned, such as a small four-legged animal with fur and a tail, but such a list would cover far more animals than dogs. It would even cover cats. How is it we can look at a picture and instantly know a dog is a dog and not a cat? What is this knowledge of dogs that allows the child to do what is so difficult for a computer?

CLASSICAL ANSWERS

While the computer part of this question is new, the rest is very old and was asked long before computers. For Plato, the physical world was but a mere shadow of the true reality of ideas. What Plato noticed is we seem to have an idea of things independent of the real world, what he called Forms. In this case, the Form of a Dog independent of any actual dog. We can speak of dogs in abstract terms. In fact, we can think of a perfect dog, the idealized dog, or the Dog Form. When we look at dogs in the real world, even the top dog at a dog show, they all fall short of the idea of a dog. There are no perfect dogs.

For Plato, at best, the dogs we see in everyday life are pale imitations, the Form corrupted by the encounter with the material world. The Form is what is important; physical reality is but a shadow of the Form. As such, he believed the Forms were more real than the physical world around us. Our senses were deceiving us.

Aristotle, though a student of Plato, took a somewhat different view. While accepting the concept of the Forms, he believed the Forms were not independent of things. Aristotle was much more interested in the physical world, thus in observation and empirical evidence than Plato. These two different ways of looking at reality, the ideal and the physical, have shaped Western thought down to the present day. When combined with Christianity, they greatly influenced thought during the Middle Ages, with Augustine and the early Medieval period tending toward Plato. Aquinas and the later Medieval period tended toward Aristotle.

THE MIDDLE AGES

Contrary to popular belief, the so-called Dark Ages never occurred. If they did, they only lasted for a few years following the collapse of the Western Roman empire. The term Dark Ages was used by those who saw the demise of classical Greek and Roman culture as a disaster. They saw its re-discovery as a "Renaissance" resulting in an "Enlightenment." More recent historians have realized how value-laden these terms were. Worse for the term Dark Ages, it was incredibly inaccurate. The Middle Ages, as they are now more commonly referred to, were a time of considerable activity both culturally and intellectually.

Rather than a disaster, Rodney Stark argues in *How The West Won: The Neglected Story of the Triumph of Modernity* that Rome's collapse was beneficial. By its end, the Roman Empire had become a stifling bureaucracy limiting development and innovation. The decline of cities such as Rome, resulting from the empire's collapse, mainly affected the governmental centers, which had no other reason for existing. They had no means of support without the empire.

Regardless of the pros and cons resulting from the Fall of the Western Roman Empire, the Middle Ages saw tremendous intellectual development and the birth of Scholasticism. Today, Scholasticism is seen negatively, but like all knowledge, it played an important role in laying a foundation for much of the later advances that replaced it. A key intellectual problem in the Middle Ages was understanding the knowledge passed down to them. This knowledge came both from Christian and classical writers. What did it all mean, and how did it all fit together?

Scholasticism developed as a solution. It approached issues with rigorous analysis using reason, breaking them down into their component parts. A similar analysis would be used on these component parts to reach core truths. The results of all this analysis would then be harmonized and systematized to create a summation, a Summa, of knowledge. The greatest of these was the *Summa Theologica*, written by Thomas Aquinas.

As Scholasticism developed, it saw the creation of many intellectual methods and tools, ways of approaching issues, and arguing in defense of a position. Long after Scholasticism was eventually replaced, many of these continued to be used and valued. Not the least of these creations was the university system. Scholasticism's use of reason to answer questions set the standard to the point few questioned reason or its usefulness. Still, there was a serious flaw in Scholasticism. The more Scholasticism sought to systemize; the more problems appeared.

THE END OF SCHOLASTICISM

By the 16th century, the Scholasticism of the Middle Ages had run its course. The common view is the Middle Ages were a time of faith, and reason replaced faith in the modern era. Sometimes, the modern era is defined as the triumph of reason over faith. There are several problems with this view. As we just saw, the first is reason played a central and defining role in Scholasticism. There would have been no need for intellectual development or the creation of universities, if the Middle Ages were simply faith instead of reason. There would have been no need for Scholasticism.

Second, faith and reason are not either/or concepts. They are different concepts that do not have a lot of overlap. At the core of faith is trust and confidence. Faith is simply the trust or confidence you have in something leading you to act or not act upon it. It is fundamentally a confidence that what you believe is correct. Its importance to religion is clear. One can intellectually hold a belief, which has no impact on one's life and what one does. Or one can trust that belief and change how one lives accordingly.

Faith is, when one trusts something to the point that they act. As one author, writing about the Enlightenment put it, "confidence in the power of reason underlay all of their achievements."[52] Yet this is basically the same as saying faith in the power of reason underlay all of their achievements. We will have more to say on this in the next chapter.

To define Modernity as reason instead of faith is little better than calling the Middle Ages dark. Both eras valued reason, and both eras exhibited faith in some things. What changed from the Middle Ages to the Enlightenment was the framework in which reason was applied.

Scholasticism's use of reason had reached a dead end. Scholasticism sought to solve the problem of systematizing knowledge, either from God in the Bible or classical authors such as Plato and Aristotle. But this was proving to be increasingly problematic. Different people could start from the same premises and reach vastly different conclusions. Even worse, some, like Galileo, increasingly used empirical observation to show the classical authors, including even Aristotle, were wrong.

The result was a growing skepticism, a concern that nothing could be trusted, that questioned if we could know anything at all. At this point, two major thinkers of the modern era began to address the state of knowledge they found. Both proposed major changes and, as a result, helped create the modern world.

BACON

The first was Francis Bacon. His major work, *Novum Organum (New Method)*, was a direct challenge to Aristotle. Bacon surveyed

---

52 Hicks, S. R. (2010). *Explaining Postmodernism: Skepticism and Socialism from Rousseau to Foucault.* Tempe, Arizona: Scholargy Publishing.

the intellectual landscape in which he lived and saw four major sources for error.

> The idols and false notions which have already preoccupied the human understanding, and are deeply rooted in it, not only so beset men's minds that they become difficult of access, but even when access is obtained will again meet and trouble us in the instauration of the sciences, unless mankind when forewarned guard themselves with all possible care against them.

The four idols Bacon identified were the idols of the Tribe, the Cave, the Market, and the Theatre. The Idols of the Tribe are those assumptions we make as a whole grounded in our nature because we think we are the measure of things. In reality, Bacon argued, "the human mind resembles those uneven mirrors" with their distortions.

The Idols of the Cave are those errors we make as individuals. A person's mind,

> intercepts and corrupts the light of nature, either from his own peculiar and singular disposition, or from his education and intercourse with others, or from his reading, and the authority acquired by those whom he reverences and admires, or from the different impressions produced on the mind, as it happens to be preoccupied and predisposed, or equable and tranquil, and the like.

The Idol of the Marketplace emerges from the fact that we "converse by means of language." While a wonderful tool of communication, "there arises from a bad and unapt formation of words a wonderful obstruction to the mind."

Finally, there is the Idol of the Theatre, "various dogmas of peculiar systems of philosophy." All of the idols that Bacon lays out are still with us today in one form or another.

Bacon then rejected the scholastic approach based on the classical authors and argued instead for a process of observation of the natural world and induction based on those observations. For Bacon, you start with what you perceive and reason from that to build knowledge. In doing so, Bacon laid the foundation of modern science.

Descartes

At about the same time, René Descartes sought to answer the question, can we know anything at all? Rather than Bacon's emphasis on induction, Descartes focused more on deduction. Similar to Scholasticism, deduction starts with what is known and reasons from that. Rather than start with classical authors, Descartes sought a more firm foundation. By Descartes' time, it was clear classical authors were not always correct. They could be doubted. What couldn't you doubt? Our senses sometimes deceive us. What can we trust if we cannot trust them?

Descartes started considering what he could doubt. Quickly he realized this was pretty much everything. If there was even the smallest doubt, Descartes rejected it. "There is neither God, nor sky, nor bodies, and that we ourselves even have neither hands nor feet, nor, finally, a body." Thus, in the end, there was only one thing Descartes could not doubt; he could not doubt that he doubted. From this realization came his famous line, "Cogito, ergo sum," Latin for "I think, therefore I am."

On this proposition was a foundation that Descartes could be certain. It was a foundation he could build on, and build he did. Step by step, he reconstructed much of what was believed to be known at the time. Later philosophers would critique much of this rebuilding. As we will see, even the foundation Descartes lay for it with his famous phrase came to be criticized.

While revolutionary in approach, Descartes' reconstructions remained very conventional for the time, supporting the belief in God and an objective existence for reality. For example, a key intellectual principle accepted by Descartes was that for two things to be the same, they must share all the same properties. Thus, Descartes could doubt his body existed, but he could not doubt his thoughts existed.

Descartes also argued physical reality consisted of things that could occupy space and be detected with our senses. Yet, our thoughts do not occupy space, and while clear to us, they are not accessible to others' sense perception. As a result, Descartes concluded the mind and body could not be the same thing. This position has come to be called mind-body dualism, or Cartesian dualism. The mind and body are different substances. This view fits in very well with the religious view of the time that we are body and spirit.

THE ENLIGHTENMENT

Many intellectual leaders of the age such as Baruch Spinoza, Gottfried Leibniz, John Locke, Isaac Newton, and others would build on the foundations laid by Bacon and Descartes. Others would find problems with them. In some ways, Bacon and Descartes took different approaches to the problems of Scholasticism. Nevertheless, together they formed the foundation for the modern era; they transformed the way people looked at the world around them.

Again, it was not the use of reason that changed; it was the framework in which reason was applied. The Scholastic approach had been top-down based on authority. Now it would be a bottom-up approach based on evidence.

The new view also emphasizes the individual and their ability to reason and make decisions. Individuals had reason and should think for themselves instead of letting others think for them. Thus, the Enlightenment quickly became about individuals and freedom, freedom to think, and freedom to act.

For those in traditional positions of leadership and power, either political, religious, or intellectual, this was a very scary proposition. Could people be trusted to make such decisions? During the Middle Ages, not only was intellectual life based on authority, so was society. The government, with the rule of monarchs, was authoritarian by nature. So was religion, with the church headed by the Pope, though that was already being challenged. Medieval life was grounded in authority defended by Scholasticism.

Replace authority with a brand-new view based on evidence and one emphasizing the individual's freedom, what does that do to the status quo? At the beginning of the Enlightenment, nobody could really say with any certainty. It was clear there would be changes. Still, no one could say what those changes would be. However, if you were the one in control, it was pretty clear they would not be good for you.

The results are now known. For the government, Enlightenment ideas revolutionized the political thinking of Thomas Hobbs, John Locke and others. These views played a role in the largely bloodless Glorious Revolution of 1688 in England. Their writing spurred an actual revolution 126 years after Descartes' death with the American Revolution. The American Revolution was hardly over before revolution broke out in France. With the Reign of Terror ending in Napoleon's dictatorship, that one did not go as well. Still, today, governments founded on Enlightenment political ideas dominate the Western world.

Religion was already in turmoil by Bacon and Descartes' time, with the Reformation starting about 100 years earlier. In fact, the disruption caused by the Reformation was one, but not the only, factor leading to the Enlightenment. Prior to Martin Luther and the Reformation, the focus had been on the role of the Church and Priests. Luther's Ninety-Five Theses were a challenge to the authority of the Church. When he said he had to follow his conscience instead of the Church Leaders, he was saying the individual is more important than the church hierarchy. In doing so, Luther initiated a change that elevated the importance of the individual in understanding the Bible.

Still, in the beginning, the Reformation largely accepted the general scholastic view of the time. While Christianity in Europe was split between Catholic and Protestant, both looked to authority. The authority was the Pope for Catholics, and the Bible for Protestantism, even if interpreted by the individual. If you toss out

Scholasticism, what of religion? What about morality grounded in religion? Some did toss out God and religion. Others sought to re-establish Christianity within the new framework of the Enlightenment. Overall, religion survived far better than monarchy, particularly in the United States.

MATERIALISM AND IDEALISM

As might be expected, some did not accept Descartes' reconstructions. Based on the work of Bacon and others, they increasingly saw perception not as just a good or even the best source for knowledge but as the only source. This view came to be called materialism, and it rejected any notion of the spiritual. If you could not detect something with the senses, it did not exist. Away went the notions of God and the supernatural.

Materialism fit in very well with the new science's growing list of successes, and the two views were often linked. In fact, sometimes materialism is reduced down to scientism, the view that science is the only source of knowledge. Just as the materialists questioned Descartes, others questioned the materialists. One of those was the Irish philosopher and cleric George Berkeley. Berkeley took the materialist's premise, i.e., if you cannot directly experience something through sense perception, it does not exist, one step further. Berkeley pointed out you do not directly experience objects through your senses. According to materialists, we can see a table but cannot see God; therefore, the table exists, but God does not. What Berkeley asked was, do you actually see the table?

Berkeley argued that when we see an object in the distance, such as a table, that which we call "seeing" is not a direct impression of the object in our mind but a complex process. This process involves light coming to our eye, which is translated into signals sent to the brain. There they are translated into ideas, such as the idea of a table. We only experience the result of this process. If the materialists are correct that the only things we can know are those we directly experience, then the only things we directly experience are the ideas formed in our minds. As a result, Berkely concluded the material world does not exist; only our ideas exist.

Few were willing to follow Berkeley's argument to a rejection of the material world. After all, the new sciences seem to be discovering rules for a natural world that was real. Still, his arguments were a powerful counter to the core argument of materialism. There was also a growing unease with the attempts to reduce everything to a mechanical, Newtonian worldview. There was a growing sense there was more to life than just mechanics and laws of nature despite all the successes of science. Out of this sense of unease, Romanticism was born at the beginning of the nineteenth century.

Hume and Kant

Another group, however, was far more skeptical of the enlightenment claims concerning the importance of reason or the importance of the individual. In the 18th century, David Hume questioned both our ability to learn about nature using reason and whether induction, central to Bacon's views, was a viable method for knowledge. The major work in this area was done by Immanuel Kant in his *Critique of Pure Reason* (1781). Kant took the challenges of Berkeley and Hume and expanded them into a gulf between objects in the real world (noumenon) and our perceptions (phenomena). This was a gap, Kant argued, that reason could not cross. Reason could only work on phenomena; it was cut off from the objects themselves.

Kant transformed the way philosophers thought about some of the central questions of philosophy in ways far beyond the discussion here. Kant's main purpose was to defend traditional religious and moral beliefs along with the new Newtonian science from the attacks by skeptics. Kant's reasoning was involved and often difficult to follow, but it was convincing.

In terms of his intentions, Kant failed. His attempts to safeguard traditional religion and morality against reason's attacks only work if you accept an objective reality where such concepts make sense. Newtonian science works because reason can be applied to phenomena. Again, this assumes a noumenon, a real-world object producing phenomena, our perception. The link between the noumenon and the phenomena, what Kant called transcendental idealism, is central to his maintaining a connection to the real world. But even if accepted, the connection is tenuous at best; reason is still cut off from noumenon, i.e., the real world. Transcendental idealism was also one of his most controversial proposals.

REACTIONS TO KANT

Since Kant, philosophers have attempted to work through the implications of his theories. Georg Hegel marks one path. Where Kant placed a gulf between the subject (us) and object (reality), Hegel said there was just subject. And not just any subject, but the Subject, which was the universe as a whole. He saw reality as completely subjective, not at the individual level but at the collective level. As a result of the subjective nature of reality, he embraced contradiction as inherent and the resolution of those contradictions as the means by which truth is created. This resolution was done through a dialectical process of conflict. As a result, truth was relative to the time and place one was at in the dialectical process.

Another group took a different approach. Considering Kant's views on reason and reality and Hegel's acceptance of contradictions, they concluded reason could not be trusted and must be abandoned or at least diminished in importance. Real truth was to be found by other means, by emotions or faith. In these non-rational or irrational means was the actual reality to be found. Kierkegaard, for example, argued a rational approach to Christianity was the wrong way to approach God. Religion should be about a transformational experience, not rational disputes about doctrine.

In the early twentieth century, Martin Heidegger brought the various ways of understanding the implications of Kant together. In chapter one, we discussed Heidegger's view of truth as unconcealment and letting being be. Very controversial, and in notoriously difficult prose, Heidegger sought to answer the very basic question of why anything exists instead of nothing. He argued one could not answer this question with reason, for the answer will inevitably end up in absurdity.

In Hegelian fashion, conflict is to be embraced as the path to real truth. Logic and reason must be set aside. The true path is found in the emotions, particularly negative emotions, such as anxiety. One's sense of being must dissolve into nothing, to understand reality. As this happens, as you sense the reality of becoming nothing, this will result in anxiety. In this anxiety is to be found the essence of being, that Being and Nothing are identical. In this unity is Becoming.

While this intellectual development was going on amongst philosophers in Europe, philosophers in the United States took a somewhat different path, but with similar results in the end. Whereas philosophers like Kant and Hegel had tried to protect religion and morality, those in the United States focused on protecting science from the gulf Kant had left between reality and reason. Their basic approach was to recast philosophy away from the traditional questions and more onto an analysis of the tools of science. This included things like perception, language, logic, and math.

While there was a lot of diversity, there was a general agreement regarding the main points of concern. Perception is theory-laden, so what you experience with perceptions is what your theory of reality expects. As for logic and math, these were necessarily true but are distinct from the real world. The result was devastating for science and the belief in an objective reality that could be known.

Counter-Enlightenment Becomes Postmodernism

During this development, much of Western Society, particularly in the United States, still followed Enlightenment principles. Principles that held there was an objective reality that could be dis-

Seeking Truth

covered using perception and reason. That truth was universal, and the focus was on the individual, individuals who had rights. Yet, philosophers starting with Kant had by the mid-twentieth century rejected all of that. The later twentieth century would mark the emergence of these counter-enlightenment views into the broader society with the growth of postmodernism.

Postmodernism grew out of the various attempts to understand philosophy post-Kant. It stands in almost complete opposition to the Enlightenment. As Stephen Hicks summarized it, "Postmodernism is the first ruthlessly consistent statement of the consequences of rejecting reason, those consequences being necessary given the history of epistemology since Kant."[53] From the perspective of Postmodernism, reality is subjective, reason unreliable, or even misleading. Returning to the quote from chapter one where the Postmodernist Richard Rorty summarized the situation,

> Our purposes would be served best by ceasing to see truth as a deep matter, as a topic of philosophical interest, or 'true' as a term which repays 'analysis.' 'The nature of truth' is an unprofitable topic, resembling in this respect 'the nature of man' and 'the nature of God.'[54]

Michael Foucault rejected we can know reality claiming "it is meaningless to speak in the name of – or against – Reason, Truth, or Knowledge."[55] With reason and truth meaningless, there can be no objective statements about reality. This view is behind Foucault's linking of truth and power discussed in chapter one, particularly political power. If there is a real-world, it is unknowable. What is important is our view of the world, which must be deconstructed to reveal the power structures underlying our beliefs. Picking up from Hegel and Heidegger, contradictions are part of the creative

---

53   Hicks, S. R. (2010). *Explaining Postmodernism: Skepticism and Socialism from Rousseau to Foucault*. Tempe, Arizona: Scholargy Publishing.
54   Hicks, S. R. (2010). *Explaining Postmodernism: Skepticism and Socialism from Rousseau to Foucault*. Tempe, Arizona: Scholargy Publishing.
55   Hicks, S. R. (2010). *Explaining Postmodernism: Skepticism and Socialism from Rousseau to Foucault*. Tempe, Arizona: Scholargy Publishing.

process. They are at the core of the process of discovering reality and embraced, not rejected. All truth is relative, and the focus is on the collective, the group, not the individual.

Having abandoned the need to seek truth or the nature of reality, Postmodernism turns more political, a source for social change. Frank Lentricchia summarized postmodernist's goal as one that "seeks not to find the foundation and conditions of truth but to exercise power for the purpose of social change."[56] Rather than a lens of truth, reality is viewed through a lens of power, of oppressors and oppressed.

Many of the disparate movements stemming from Postmodernism see western civilization, particularly that portion based on Enlightenment principles, not just as a competing intellectual theory, but also as a culture to be destroyed. Reason and logic, for them, are tools of an oppressive system. As the French philosopher, Jean-Francois Lyotard put it, "reason and power are one and the same."[57] That the various oppressed groups make different and contradictory claims is rejected. Trying to point out these contradictions is merely an example of an oppressive system using reason to oppress.

At the beginning of the 21st century, philosophy's search for the answer to the question, how do you know what you know, ended with the answer there is nothing objective to know. Knowledge is subjective, truth at best, an illusion. Can this really be correct?

---

56 Hicks, S. R. (2010). *Explaining Postmodernism: Skepticism and Socialism from Rousseau to Foucault*. Tempe, Arizona: Scholargy Publishing.
57 Hicks, S. R. (2010). *Explaining Postmodernism: Skepticism and Socialism from Rousseau to Foucault*. Tempe, Arizona: Scholargy Publishing.

Chapter 3

I Exist, You Exist, Maybe

For the great enemy of truth is very often not the lie — deliberate, contrived and dishonest — but the myth — persistent, persuasive, and unrealistic. Too often we hold fast to the clichés of our forebears. We subject all facts to a prefabricated set of interpretations. We enjoy the comfort of opinion without the discomfort of thought.
— John F Kennedy

The last two hundred and fifty years have seen the ideas discussed in the last chapter play out, not just in intellectual circles but in the broader society. The materialist position, aided by the ever-growing importance and success of science, grew steadily. On the other side, idealism and antirealism saw renewed interest with the discoveries in Quantum Mechanics and the growing understanding of how the brain works. A vast middle ground exists between these alternatives; this is not either/or, rather a blending of both.

During the nineteenth and early twentieth centuries, one significant difference between various camps centered around God's existence and the need for religion. Materialists tended to see both as pre-scientific concepts. As science learned more and more, the need for these would decline. Materialists envisioned a time when science would answer all the important questions to the point there was no more need for God or religion. A time when people would live lives governed solely by scientific principles.

This view looked much more promising in the nineteenth-century view of science governed by Newtonian mechanics. It was a century that saw the Industrial Revolution and great scientific advances resulting in great improvements for humanity. But the disruptions caused by the Industrial Revolution and its resulting transformation of the labor market also caused great suffering, suffering that spawned a reaction. The Romantic movement resisted materialism and science. In response to the Enlightenment's individualism came a growing collectivism. This collectivism, by the 1830s, would formalize into the beginning of socialism.

In the middle of the century, Karl Marx would take materialism and socialism and blend in the ideas of Hegel, creating Communism. As we saw in the last chapter, Hegel saw reality as the conflict or dialectic of ideas. Marx embraced the concept of the dialectic but with a materialist view, creating historical materialism. Here the dialectic conflict works itself out, not in the realm of ideas, but history, particularly in economic history.

The Impact of WWI

The twentieth century saw several changes. Perhaps the biggest was WWI. It is important to note that the beginning of the twentieth century was a time of great optimism. For materialists, science was well on its way to taming the world and ushering in Utopia. At the beginning of the nineteenth century, the world was powered as it always had been, by muscle, either man or animal. There was also fire, water, and wind to a limited extent, but most work required muscle. By the twentieth century, that had changed. Steam power had been harnessed, factories built, and the concept of mass production was creating a growing middle class and supplying them with a growing list of goods.

In addition to the trains and steam-powered ships that made transportation easier and more regular than ever, there were new gasoline-powered vehicles. Even the air had been conquered. Just as nature had been tamed, the new "scientific principles" were being focused by progressives on society and government issues. By 1910, Utopia seemed just over the horizon.

The "War to End All Wars" shattered these notions. In the war, the new science that had improved life was brought to bear to improve killing efficiency, increasing it to what had before been unimaginable levels. On the first day of the battle of the Somme, the British alone suffered 57,470 casualties, with nearly 20,000 killed. In addition to the many improvements to guns, machine guns, and cannons were added poison gas, airplanes, and tanks.

This was not supposed to have happened; science was supposed to be a force for good; it was supposed to improve things. Later in the century, this was further compounded with WWII and its refinement in technology to further "improve" killing power, its addition of atomic bombs to humanity's arsenal, and applying the principles of mass production to killing in the concentration camps. Thus, in the twentieth century, science was shown to have a very dark side. Rather than ushering in Utopia, with the creation of nuclear weapons, science now threatened humanity's existence.

Early Twentieth-Century Science

Then there was the disruption to science itself. Einstein cracked the notion of the mechanical world which dominated the nineteenth century, and quantum mechanics destroyed that view. The Newtonian universe was predictable. You could predict anything with certainty if you knew the variables. The laws of physics were exact and precise. Tell me where an object is and its momentum, and I can tell you where it has been and where it will be. The more you know, the better you can predict. Strictly mechanical; a universe that has always existed and will always exist. No room for miracles. No need for God.

The Quantum universe changed that. You cannot know a range of things. For example, you cannot know both the position and momentum of a particle beyond a certain limit. After that limit, the more accurately you know one, the less you can know the other. You can know a particle's momentum exactly, but then you have no idea where it is.

Rather than the certain knowledge found in a Newtonian universe, you have probability in a quantum universe. During the nineteenth century, a major question was whether light was a particle, a small object acting at a single point, or a wave, the movement of energy along a line. This was definitively settled in a series of experiments showing light was clearly a wave by the end of the nineteenth century.

Then Einstein definitively showed that light was a particle. Somehow, it seemed to be both, but how could that be? The concept of a wave and a particle seemed to be mutually exclusive. Worse yet, from a Newtonian point of view, there might even be a role for thought. Whether light was observed as a particle or a wave seemed to be determined by what the experimenter wanted to find. In short, rather than a Newtonian universe that could be understood and known exactly, the twentieth century gave us a quantum universe that seemed to defy common sense and was based on probability.

Other factors came into play. Whereas in nineteenth-century science, the universe always existed, observations by Edwin Hubble in the early part of the twentieth century eventually showed the universe is expanding. In turn, this view led to the Big Bang Theory and the belief the universe had a beginning. This discovery was extremely unsettling for the materialists that dominated science. It instantly raises the question of what, or even who, created the universe? The attempt to find a suitable natural answer to this question, which avoids even the possible need for God, continues to dominate research in the area.

Another trend was the research into the mind. The nineteenth and early twentieth centuries saw a growth in materialism questioning the need for God. As the twentieth century progressed, many of the same questions and lines of reasoning were turned toward the question of the self. As mentioned earlier, philosophers question Descartes' assumption there was an I, in his famous statement, I think, therefore I am.

DETERMINISM VS. FREEWILL

A lot of the discussion is centered around the issue of freewill. Much of who we are as individuals are the choices we make. In many ways, we are defined by our choices. But can we even make a choice? The question is not can you choose everything. Supporters of freewill accept that not everything is a matter of choice. You cannot jump off a building and decide if you are going to fall. That "choice" is constrained by natural law, in this case, the law of gravity. Many of our choices are constrained in one fashion or another. You may choose to vacation in Paris, but you will have to settle for someplace cheaper if your budget does not permit it. Virtually all choices have some degree and number of constraints.

The question of freewill asks whether or not, after all the constraints, is there any room for choice left? Perhaps the best way to understand the question is to imagine that you encounter a genie at the end of your life who will grant you a wish. You choose to have a second chance to live your life again. Of course, you will not know you are living it a second time. Still, you will have a chance to redo all the decisions you made and hopefully correct some of the bad ones without undoing the good ones. The question for us is, could anything change? Could you make different choices, or will your life unfold exactly as it did before?

Things would unfold exactly as before in the materialist's universe. If there were any differences, these would be traced back to the universe's probabilistic nature, not to you making a different choice. This is because, in a materialist universe, just as there was no room for God, there is no room for you either. In a materialist universe, everything comes down to natural processes. All your thoughts and actions, emotions and beliefs, the sum total of who you are, are simply the result of electrical and chemical processes happening in the brain. In short, your "decisions" don't come from you; they are simply the result of these natural processes. Therefore, there is no place within the materialistic universe for a concept of choice, for an intellect or will that could choose.

For some, this questions the belief there is a thing called 'I,' and that this 'I' makes choices is, at best, an illusion. You only think you exist. Others accept there is an 'I' and only rejected the 'I' could actually choose. While you may think you make choices, that is still just an illusion. It is as if you are watching the movie of your life and thinking you have some say in the outcome. You don't. You only think you do. If the mythical genie grants you a second chance to live your life, there would be no more ability to change the outcome than when you watch a movie with an ending you do not like. In short, you have no more ability to affect the choices you will make in the future than you can change the choices you think you made in the past. Both are equally out of your control.

THE PROBLEMS OF CONSCIOUSNESS

As for the denial that we exist, there are, of course, several problems with this view. For one, the view upon which it is based, materialism, is no longer the new kid on the block. It has been around long enough that, rather than challenging the status quo, it has, in many respects, become the status quo. As a result, it has come under increasing scrutiny, and like all views, has its own problems and questions.

One of those problems is the concept of consciousness. What is it? We touched on this a bit at the beginning of chapter two when discussing whether computers can know. We concluded they could not, at least not in the way we know what a dog is. Still, what is the knowledge of a dog we have that computers do not? What is going on when we actively think about a dog or remember a dog we once had? We can not only think about a dog; we can know we are thinking about a dog. In short, what is conscious thought?

At the moment, the nature of consciousness remains a mystery. There are, as one might expect, many theories, but all have problems. A discussion of consciousness would be a book, in and of itself. Still, here we will highlight just two of the problems that have been raised, the zombie problem and the Mary's room argument.

The zombie problem is not one of the zombie apocalypses found in the movies. Before the movies, zombies were people who had supposedly died and been brought back to life using voodoo. They were alive, but the essence of the person was gone. Philosophers took this concept with a few modifications to imagine a zombie as a person without consciousness. These zombies would look and act like everyone else but without any real self-awareness. They would be like robots, processing information and nothing more. They would act and talk like everyone else, but they would not have the internal subjective experience we have.

If such a conception is possible, consciousness is an unnecessary addition that adds nothing. So why do our perceptions of it exist? More to the point here is if philosophical zombies are logically possible, then any attempts to explain consciousness by purely physical means would only apply to zombies. Put differently, all the attempts to explain consciousness by physical mechanisms would not explain our sense of consciousness. Consciousness would be beyond physical explanation. Of course, all this hinges on the question of whether or not zombies are at least logically possible. It does not require they actually exist, only the concept is logically possible. The debate is ongoing.

The Mary's Room argument is a similar line of reasoning reaching the same goal, rejecting the idea everything is physical. The Australian philosopher Frank Jackson put forth this argument in his 1982 paper *Epiphenomenal Qualia*.[58] In the paper, Jackson postulates a brilliant scientist, Mary. Mary lives and works in a black and white room. Her only visual access to the outside world is utilizing a black and white television monitor.

> She specializes in the neurophysiology of vision and acquires, let us suppose, all the physical information there is to obtain about what goes on when we see ripe tomatoes, or the sky, and use terms like 'red', 'blue', and so on.[59]

As a result of her investigation, Mary knows all there is to know about the physical nature of light and color. Jackson then asks, "What will happen when Mary is released from her black and white

---

58 Jackson, F. (1982, April). *Epiphenomenal Qualia*. Retrieved from JSTOR: https://www.jstor.org/stable/2960077
59 Jackson, F. (1982, April). *Epiphenomenal Qualia*. Retrieved from JSTOR: https://www.jstor.org/stable/2960077

room or is given a color television monitor? Will she learn anything or not?" Of course she will. She will know the redness of red and the blueness of blue. Yet, she had all the physical knowledge when she was in the room. Therefore, the redness of red and blueness of blue are not physical information, and purely physical explanations will not suffice. This additional information that we know subjectively through the conscious experience of things like color is called Qualia.

As with the previous example, this is an ongoing debate with philosophers on both sides. Still, the very debate calls into question the idea that materialism is a given. If you adhere to materialism, then, of course, qualia have a physical explanation. How could it be otherwise? If all things have a physical explanation, and qualia is a thing, then qualia must have a physical explanation. This deductive argument is valid, so if the premises are true, the conclusion must be accepted. Likewise, any doubt in the conclusion casts doubt on the premises, particularly the premise that all things have a physical explanation.

Other Problems With Materialism

There are other problems. How can we trust anything, if this view is correct, and the concept of the self and freewill are but an illusion? Perhaps our strongest and most basic perception is we exist as entities with a will, with the ability to choose. While sometimes our choices are little more than a whim, we agonize over them at other times. We weigh the various alternatives, examine all the costs, play out the various scenarios in our minds.

Sure, the materialist would say this is just the brain processing all the information, like some computer solving a large equation. Those who accept the self but still reject freewill argue this agonizing does not come from indecision. Instead, it is just an emotional response resulting from an inability to predict the future. Either way that is hardly our perception.

Because of our perception, we are invested in this "decision" in a way a computer could never be. We agonize over the choice because we believe we exist. In short, we think in a way a computer cannot. Yet if materialists are correct, this is all because of an illusion, an illusion that we actually can make a decision. In reality, it is beyond your ability to control. You are, in reality, a biological machine processing inputs and giving outputs. You are like a biological computer. Your program may be dynamic and change over time, but in the end, you have no more say in what you think and do than a computer running a program.

This is where the problem comes in; how do we know this? The materialist claims this is based on perception, and the things that can be perceived are the only things that exist. But as a result of this view, they claim our most basic perception cannot be trusted. It is only an illusion. If our most basic perception is unreliable, what does that say about all our other perceptions?

There is an additional problem. To see it, let's assume for a moment the materialist is correct. How should we change so we are no longer living the illusion but living reality as it is? That is impossible to do. If, for nothing else, there is the illusion of the self getting in the way. In fact, the vast majority of what we call the human experience would not make any sense. This is because the entire structure of society is grounded in the illusion of self-existence and choice.

Poor George

Consider a rock coming loose due to rain. It falls down the hill, bouncing here and there until it reaches the bottom, where it strikes and kills George, who happened to be walking at the bottom of the cliff. Now consider someone picking up a rock and killing George. Why do we consider these to be different types of events? The first event is a tragedy; the other is murder. The first event is tragic because no choice was involved for the hill, rain, and rock. It was just the interaction of the laws of nature. It just happened.

The second is murder because the person chose to pick up the rock and use it as a weapon. Still, what does this sentence mean if there is no choice? There is no difference between the two events if the materialist is correct. Both are nothing more than the interaction of the laws of nature. The first was a series of physical interactions beginning with the rain loosening the rock, Then it went through a series of additional physical interactions as it bounced down the hill until it struck and killed George.

In the other case, physical reactions in the brain caused the body to pick up a rock, strike George, and kill him. Perhaps the causal chain of the murder is more complex. Still, from a materialist point of view, there is no fundamental difference between these two actions. Both were purely physical, neither involved any choice.

One might claim that the person who kills shows a tendency to do so and must be stopped from doing so. There are three problems with this line of reasoning. The first is that it implies a choice in how to treat them. But if there is no choice, then there is no choice in how we react to these events. The second is this reasoning could be applied to the cliff. The cliff dislodged the rock, and there might very well be other rocks that could fall. Thus it could be said the cliff killed and might kill again. The third problem is this still does not address the core issue, which is our perceptions of these are still vastly different. Even if someone were to say the cliff killed, it could hardly be understood in the same sense as the person killed.

In our normal understanding, the presence of choice in the person and the lack thereof in the cliff separates these two. Even if actions are taken to deal with the threat, such as putting the person in prison or cutting the cliff further back, the reasons and rationale for these will be different. There is no concept of a trial for the cliff, no rights that need to be protected.

Still, this just scratches the surface of the problem. Our language and our very way of thinking are inextricably linked to our concept of self. After all, just look at the pronouns in the last sentence. What does 'our' mean if there is no 'we.' Then there is the whole absurdity of the debate itself.

What does the concept of debate about choice even mean if there is no choice? What is the purpose of an article or book arguing that choice is an illusion? No one can be convinced because no one has a choice. But then the author had no choice in writing it. Thus, even if true, the materialist view fails because it is completely unworkable and is ultimately absurd. Even if it is true, it can be ignored, as it can have no impact on us or what we do. Things will be what they will be, and we are just passengers along for the ride with no say in the matter.

This last line of reasoning brings us to an important consideration. Any view of reality, to be viable, must be livable. It must explain the world around us in a way we can put into practice, a view that we can use to understand our lives. It is useless, if it does not do that.

We saw at the end of the last chapter that philosophy ended by questioning the notion of truth. In this chapter, now even our ability to know we exist is questioned. Is there anything we can know? Is there anything to know? I would argue yes.

Chapter 4

Can We Know Anything?

I am wiser than this man; for neither of us really knows anything fine and good, but this man thinks he knows something when he does not, whereas I, as I do not know anything, do not think I do either. I seem, then, in just this little thing to be wiser than this man at any rate, that what I do not know I do not think I know either. – Socrates quoted in Apology by Plato

Our experience is the history of our perception. If a view of reality is not grounded in experience, it conflicts with our perception and raises the question of why we would accept it. Of course, our experience is fallible. In later chapters, we will discuss some important qualifications and exceptions to the statements that our view of reality must be based on experience. Still, our view of reality should not completely invalidate it. In short, the view of reality must be livable and conform to our experience. As simple as these two principles are, they call into question much of the discussion in the last two chapters.

We have a clear perception we exist and exist in an objective world, one existing independently of us and that others like us share the world. It is a world we can discover. That we can learn about it has been amply demonstrated over the last 250+ years of science.

Just consider the effort to go to the moon. The understanding of science it took, and the thousands of people working toward a common goal. The millions of people who followed the progress and then watched it on television as it happened. What does this all mean if there is not an objective reality apart from us? What then of the last 250 years of intellectual development calling all of this into question?

I think where materialists go wrong is in a confusion between knowledge and explanation. This situation is similar to what we saw in the first chapter and the definition of truth. There were a lot of very good ways of understanding truth. Considering them gives one a better understanding of truth. We know a lot about truth. Still, none of the theories of truth gave a complete explanation without problems. The common view that truth is what corresponds to reality stumbles on the inability to explain exactly how that correspondence works. Despite this, that truth is that which corresponds at least in some fashion to reality, is a very clear perception and what we live by daily.

Most of our waking hours are spent interacting with the world around us. It is a world that is real. If we step out in front of a bus, the reality of that bus could end our life very quickly. At least, that is our perception, and that is how we live. Here philosophy has stumbled on the inability to explain how it all could work. Still, our inability to explain is not the same as a lack of knowledge that it exists. If reality exists independent of us, it also must exist independent of our explanations.

The Core Assumption of Materialists

For the last 250 years, philosophers have attempted to either preserve room for religion and morality from materialist critiques or preserve science from the various reactions to materialism. However, these all stem from a key assumption made by materialists, which I believe is unwarranted. Materialists argue that matter and energy, things that can be perceived, are the only things that exist. I believe that claim to be unwarranted and unsupportable.

It looked far more supportable in the Newtonian Universe of mechanical interactions. It is only a small step from a Newtonian view of the universe to a deterministic view. With determinism, the future is determined by the present. To see this, imagine the trajectory of a cannonball midway through its flight. With Newtonian physics, you can work out its past, its entire path, from when it left the cannon until now. You can also calculate its future, precisely where it will go and where and when it will land. It is all deterministic, governed by the laws of physics. The more you know, the more accurately you can predict.

It is likewise for the entire universe, if you knew everything about the universe at any instant, you could work out both the past and the future completely. Everything would be just matter and energy, reacting within certain natural laws. This is why materialists did not see a place for miracles or God. Everything was deterministic.

Still, while it was a small step, it was a step. Nothing mandated that just because the flight of a cannonball was deterministic, everything, including people, were deterministic. So while materialists took that step, not everyone followed them.

It is less supportable in the probabilistic universe of Quantum Mechanics. Unlike the precise answers given by Newtonian physics, Quantum Mechanics can only give probabilities. An electron may go in a certain path, but then it might follow a different one. Quantum Mechanics has no explanation for why it would do one over the other. Even if you knew everything about the universe at a given instant, you could not predict what would happen next, except at the macro level, the level of cannonballs. Even worse, because of the uncertainty principle, you cannot even know everything. The step to determinism is a much larger one, if not a questionable one. While it does not automatically mean there is something else, it makes the conclusion there is nothing else harder to maintain.

Often this claim is met, with a challenge to prove something else does exist. Yet this starts us down the road of the last 250 years again. This road ends, not with the materialists' claims demonstrated, but with subjective reality and the denial of reason and objective truth.

An important consideration is that complete answers and certainty, while desirable, are not expected when dealing with such fundamental questions. Perhaps someday we will have these, but at the moment, they are a long way off and might even be impossible. It may literally be beyond our ability to understand. It appears that we are missing some pieces of the puzzle to make sense of it all, but what those may be and if we will ever be able to find them is unknown. As a result, universal statements appear unwarranted and unsupportable. Universal statements such as the things we can confirm empirically are the only things that exist.

These considerations do not mean we should toss out the last 250 years of philosophy. For one, we have only looked at a small and focused portion, and a lot of good and valuable work has been done. Second, even working through the particular issues here provided a lot of valuable insights and lessons. Things were learned. For example, perception is theory-laden, and as a result, we do tend to see what we expect to see, at least to some extent. Later, we will see how this view helped investigators understand a crash and how that led to safer air travel.

Still, that perception is theory-laden is a real problem for science. Scientists approach issues with theories. They construct experiments based on those theories and examine their finding in light of those theories. In addition, there have been many times in the history of science where new theories were rejected because they did not fit the old ones, did not fit what was expected, only to be accepted later.

The example of Alfred Wegener mentioned in the first chapter is an example of this problem. There have also been times when theories ran into problems due to deeper philosophical considerations concerning science's very nature. This issue was a problem that Georg Ohm faced with the acceptance of his book *The Galvanic Circuit Investigated Mathematically*, which is the origin of the electrical law that bears his name.

How Science Should be Done

Ohm's Law says the current flowing through a conductor is proportional to the voltage, that proportionality being the resistance of the conductor. While basic to our understanding of electricity today, its initial reception was mixed. While some accepted his theory, Ohm's critics called it "a web of naked fancies" and

Seeking Truth

"the result of an incurable delusion." In his country, Ohm's critics had sway with Johannes Schulze, the Minister of Education, and he ruled about Ohm, "a physicist who professed such heresies was unworthy to teach science."[60]

One of Ohm's critics was Georg Friedrich Pohl, a physics professor at the Friedrich Wilhelm University in Berlin, now known as Humboldt University. He and Ohm had fundamentally different views on how electricity worked. Pohl saw Ohms' view as "the most innumerable confusions in physics."[61]

The reasons Ohm's theory faced resistance are complex. Part of the problem was political. Ohm's brother Martin had made a name for himself by criticizing the education system, which did not make him popular with the Minister of Education. To make matters worse, as part of his reforms, Martin had pushed a geometry text written by Georg.

There were also some conflicts with earlier experiments, due largely to the evolving nature of the science and the lack of good tools and techniques needed to investigate electricity. Still, Ohm's real problem was actually in his title. His book was a *mathematical* investigation. For many of his critics, that is just not how one does science.

For many of the older scientists of the period, physics was an experimental science. Experiments, not theory and analysis, are what matters. Thus, while Ohm had published the results of his experiments in earlier papers, he relied on mathematical analysis in his book. As a result, for many of his critics, the detailed analysis in his book "was viewed as a pleasant exercise in mathematics but utterly without relevance to the phenomena."[62]

---

60 Hart, I. B. (1923). *Makers of Science, Mathematics, Physics, Astronomy*. London: Oxford University Press.
61 Page, B. R. (n.d.). *G. S. Ohm and the mathematization of physics*. Retrieved from Amateur Radio: http://n4trb.com/Publications/Ohm%20and%20the%20Mathematization%20of%20Physics.pdf
62 Page, B. R. (n.d.). *G. S. Ohm and the mathematization of physics*. Retrieved from Amateur Radio: http://n4trb.com/Publications/Ohm%20and%20the%20Mathematization%20of%20Physics.pdf

MATH AND REALITY

The issue of the proper role of mathematical analysis in science goes back as far as the ancient Greeks and is still with us today. Over a hundred years before Plato, Pythagorean philosophers saw the world as defined by numbers. The number of pebbles, the number of men, the number of animals. Numbers or fractions of numbers, one number divided by another, defined everything. Today these are called the rational numbers. Rational numbers will define a rational world.

While a good start, problems developed very early with the discovery of irrational numbers such as π. What do you do with these? Thus, since the early Greeks, a fundamental question has been the relationship of science to math. Ohm was at the beginning of a major shift toward mathematical analysis. It is why his work found much more acceptance among the younger scientists of his day. Eventually, Ohm's work was accepted. Unlike Wegener, Ohm received recognition for his work during his lifetime. Still, the question remains with us even today.

The fundamental question is, why does math relate to reality? It is easy to see why the Pythagoreans saw a link. Things you can count lend themselves to numbers. You can add, subtract, multiply and divide them in the real world and math. Things get a bit more difficult when you get to irrational numbers like π and later e. The number π shows up, not just in circles, but in a large number of areas. Why should these numbers be so important and so useful?

Still, mathematicians did not stop there and developed even more abstract concepts, such as imaginary numbers -- the square root of negative numbers. While you can take one cow and add another to get two, you cannot take the square root of a negative number. At least you couldn't until mathematics invented imaginary numbers for that purpose.

The name imaginary comes from Descartes, who used it as a derogatory term. He thought these numbers were useless for describing anything in the real world. Descartes had a point. How could a mathematical concept created solely to allow mathematicians to do something that otherwise cannot be done have any bearing on the real world? Yet, as it turns out, they are incredibly useful in science and engineering. Why is that?

This question was asked by Eugene Wigner in his 1960 paper, *The Unreasonable Effectiveness of Mathematics in the Natural Sciences*. In this paper, Wigner argues

> that the enormous usefulness of mathematics in the natural sciences is something bordering on the mysterious and that there is no rational explanation for it.

Mathematicians develop and explore mathematical concepts, not because they are useful but because they can. Normally, it is more for an aesthetic sense of beauty than any sort of practicality. In doing so, they come up with concepts that, while mathematically beautiful, don't seem to make sense in the real world, like imaginary numbers.

Physicists, on the other hand, explore the functioning of the real world. Their focus is entirely on the real world, what works, and on discovering the laws of nature. So why do these two different endeavors line up so well? Why are the advancements in physics so often tied to advancement in mathematics? In the end, Wigner concludes

> the miracle of the appropriateness of the language of mathematics for the formulation of the laws of physics is a wonderful gift which we neither understand nor deserve. We should be grateful for it.[63]

Scientists have made tremendous advancements since the major shift to mathematical analysis starting in the early nineteenth century. Recently they have sought a grand unified theory, a complete mathematical description of reality. So far, the search for this

---

63 Wigner, E. (1960, Feb). *The Unreasonable Effectiveness of Mathematics in the Natural Sciences*. Retrieved from High Energy Physics Experimental Group Univesity of Pennsylvania : http://www.hep.upenn.edu/~johnda/Papers/wignerUnreasonableEffectiveness.pdf

theory has not been successful. This lack of success has led some to question if science is even on the right track. Has the mathematical analysis approach to science run its course? Is this just another example of theory-laden perception? Does mathematical analysis work because we made it work and don't see its problems? Or is this just an example that we do not yet know everything, and these questions will work themselves out in time?

Ultimately, perception is theory-laden, but it is not completely theory-laden. There are examples of good theories being rejected. There are also many times in the history of science where accepted theories failed. Ohm's Law and Plate Tectonics were eventually accepted. At one time, the accepted theory was that light was a wave. The question was thought to have been a definitively settled issue until Einstein showed light was also a particle.

In many of these issues, it is not either-or. Perception shows us reality, or perception is unreliable. It is somewhere in between. Using our perception, we can learn about the world. Of course, our perception is not perfect, and there are some problems, but if we are careful, we can advance our knowledge.

One of the helpful views in life is the Pareto Principle, aka, the 80-20 rule. Created by the economist Vilfredo Pareto, it deals with the imbalance between inputs and outputs in economic situations, but it has grown into an almost universal principle. It is almost certainly not exactly 80 and 20 percent, but it does capture the general sense. While the exact percentages are mere guidelines, there are such imbalances everywhere. The same here; our perception is quite good. Still, sometimes it misleads us.

Return to the Enlightenment

This approach basically brings us back to the Enlightenment views based on the thinking of Bacon and Descartes, but without the demand that everything be material. Why this view and not some other? First, it is based on realism: the belief an external world exists apart from us. Granted some have cast doubt on this view over the last 250 years, but it remains the dominant view and with good reason.

While some philosophers were asking good and relevant questions, scientists were also making significant progress in understanding a world that does seem to exist. This last statement takes us to the second point: we can learn about the external world. The enlightenment's view of a bottom-up framework based on evidence shows there is a real world. We can make objective statements about that world that best fits the evidence.

The reasoning is very pragmatic; historically, it seems to have worked the best. Based on these views, we had the emergence of liberal Democracy, the growth of science, and the start of the Industrial Revolution. It launched an unprecedented period in the growth of liberty and prosperity that continues to this day. The competing views that have come since have tended to cause far more problems than they have solved. This is particularly true for competitors in the twentieth century that rejected individualism for the group and liberal Democracy for totalitarianism. Views such as Communism and Fascism.

What about the problems that later philosophers were attempting to solve? The main problem for some, like Kant, was to try and protect religion and morality as foundations for society. For others, it was to protect science from the ramifications of Kant. All ultimately failed, as we saw in the last chapter. Nor, I would argue, was such protection needed. For science is quite at home in the enlightenment view that gave it birth. The view that we exist and exist in an objective reality and through our perceptions can learn about the world around us, even if they are not perfect, is not a problem for science.

MORALITY?

As for religion and objective morality, one could, of course, argue these are false concepts anyway. We are better without them. Yet, there is a problem. While some might want to discard notions of morality, still, most have a very strong sense of right and wrong. To see this, consider the following two people. The first is Josef Mengele, aka, the Angel of Death. Mengele was an SS doctor who conducted many experiments on the prisoners at Auschwitz. Many of these experiments completely disregarded notions of health and safety. As a result, they ended in death, and many amounted to torture. The second is Mary Teresa Bojaxhiu, aka, Mother Teresa or St. Theresa of Calcutta. St. Theresa of Calcutta spent most of her life in poverty, dedicated to serving the poorest of the poor, treating the sick, hungry, and dying.

The question is, why do we look at these two people differently. They were born about 900 miles and seven months apart into the Europe of the early twentieth century. Why do we admire Mother Teresa and denounce Mengele? Is it only a matter of subjective preference or societal conditioning that leads to our view? Or is there something more, some objective moral consideration that leads to our different views of these two people?

I would argue the latter. Only an objective morality can draw such a distinction. Without objective morality, this becomes a matter of preference. I consider any morality that leaves the horrors of the Concentration Camps and the Holocaust as matters of preference to be seriously lacking.

Religion?

Kant's other major concern was religion. Religion in general and Christianity in specific did indeed take a beating in the Enlightenment. Yet this was only temporary and tied more to materialism than the Enlightenment itself.

During the Middle Ages, authority was foundational. Christian thinkers looked to authority for justification along with everyone else for over a thousand years. The Enlightenment moved away from a top-down approach based on authority to a bottom-up approach based on evidence. So it is no wonder some worried about how this would affect religion.

Initially, the response was not good, and Christian intellectuals were not prepared. How could they be? In a sense, they had spent a thousand years preparing for one debate, and now the ground rules for the discussion had changed. Making matters worse, some parts of Christianity still clung to authority and questioned the Enlightenment. There was also the rise of materialism, with its *a priori* exclusion of anything non-material, which means God. So Kant's concern was not completely unwarranted.

Still, looking back after 250 years, it is easier to see that Kant's concerns were not justified. Christianity did just fine in a framework based on reason and evidence. While some resisted, many Christian intellectuals quickly adapted to the new framework. Sure, there were periods of decline, but there were also periods of revival. As has always been true, Christianity was more threatened by wealth and prosperity than reason and evidence.

An Enlightenment view of reason and evidence is compatible with religion and morality. The key here is compatible. There is room for theism. There is also room for atheism. In this sense, an Enlightenment view is neutral on this question, and I would argue it should be. Some Christians are uncomfortable with this approach. They want an *a priori* belief in God. Some atheists are likewise uncomfortable with this. They want strict materialism with its *a priori* rejection of God. Still, the framework we use to seek knowledge should not demand or preclude particular answers. If it does, it cannot be trusted on those questions.

PROOF AND CERTAINTY

There remains a final problem with the Enlightenment approach; it does not lead to certainty. This is a problem. Philosophers want complete explanations that are certain. Theists want certain knowledge of God, while atheists demand proof God exists. We all want proof we are wrong before we change our minds when we are challenged. This is a standard the enlightenment approach will often fail to meet.

Outside of mathematics, proof is a somewhat subjective term. Generally, it is the amount of evidence required to conclude something is true. That the amount varies from person to person is demonstrated by the problem of hung juries. Even for an individual, it varies from issue to issue.

In a courtroom, there are different standards depending on the case. Criminal trials require proof beyond a reasonable doubt. Civil trials require just a preponderance of the evidence. Because of the flexibility in the standard, demands for proof are suspect. Skepticism can always be justified by raising the amount of evidence needed slightly higher than the evidence available.

If the last 250 years of intellectual and scientific development have shown us anything, it is that certainty is hard to come by. In the end, we cannot even prove we exist, much less anything else. This should not be a surprise. Uncertainty is a part of daily life, so much so that we have an aphorism for it; nothing is certain but death and taxes. In this sense, our lives are more akin to Quantum Mechanic's probabilities than the mechanical universe of Newton. Much of life is making choices where we are not certain of the outcome.

Life is made up of a series of choices, and each choice involves risk. The risk can be large or small, such as walking around the block versus walking on the edge of a tall cliff. The risk can vary in its significance. It can be insignificant. You ordered a meal at a restaurant, but it ended up not being what you expected. On the other hand, it can be very significant. Every time we get in a car and go somewhere, there is a chance we will be killed in an accident. Large or small, significant or insignificant, uncertainty is part of almost everything we do.

Sometimes the uncertainty is so great, the risk so significant that we are paralyzed by it. Yet, most of the time, we ignore it completely. For example, most people ignore the risk involved in driving unless the conditions are hazardous. On the other hand, for the parents of new teenage drivers, all these risks suddenly become

Seeking Truth

very apparent. Still, most of the time, we just make our decisions and act based on them.

Problems in a Word

This ability to act based on the choices we make in the face of uncertainty is called faith. As discussed earlier, some do not like this term because of its association with religion. Here we need to make a short diversion to introduce a problem we will frequently encounter in this book. The problem is with language. Words have meanings. But these meanings are not static, nor are they value free. They change over time from usage and bias, which is the case with the word faith.

It is clearly an important term for Christianity. In the Greek of the New Testament period, the word translated faith is *pistis* (πίστις) and can also mean trust. It is a trust and a commitment leading one to act based on that trust. Hebrew 11 has been called the faith chapter of the New Testament. In that chapter, the word is defined and a long list of examples given. All the examples of faith listed there follow the same general pattern: by faith, someone did something. Faith (*pistis*) is simply the trust and commitment in something leading us to act.

In Latin, the word for faith is *fides* from which we get fidelity: a strict observance of promises and duties. In short, doing what you say you will do. We can see similar roots in the word faithful. Again, doing what you say you will do. An unfaithful spouse has broken their marriage vows. In all of these meanings is the concept of doing something or of failing to do something. Faith is primarily a word of action, not of belief. This connection to action is why in his New Testament epistle, James, the brother of Jesus, wrote, "faith by itself, if it does not prove itself with actions, is dead." (James 2:17, ISV)

Yet, because of its religious connection, faith and belief were often used interchangeably. Saying one had faith in God was synonymous with stating one had belief in God. As a result, faith came to be seen as belief rather than a trust leading to action for some. From this, it was a short leap for faith to become a description of a belief system as in "the Christian faith." For others, it became a reason for belief or a means of belief. From this faith came to be seen in opposition to reason. Thus as one atheist, Nolan Dalla summarized it,

> In fact, FAITH and TRUST are two entirely different things. One may even argue convincingly, faith and trust are contradictory… Faith requires no evidence for belief nor practice. The very nature of faith surmises that tangible evidence doesn't exist.[64]

This definition is completely opposite to the common meaning of *pistis* during the first century. To be clear, I am not saying that Dalla is wrong to use 'faith' this way. He is not, and this is one of the common ways 'faith' is used. Still, there are several other legitimate meanings, and this is one of the problems with language. Words come with meanings, often several, but they also come with baggage.

As an author, I am confronted with a problem at this point. There is a common word for something that I want to say, in this case, 'faith.' Its meaning of trust and commitment leading to action expresses what I mean. Yet, it also has several other meanings and uses. In short, it carries a lot of baggage, so I have four options, five if I include just ignoring the problem.

I could choose another common word. The main problem here is that faith is the closest to the meaning I intend, though trust would be a good alternative. As such, any other word will have similar problems. Second, I could invent a new word or adapt an obscure word, a word not commonly used and thus with little baggage. I could then give it the meaning I want. Third, since the first century meaning of *pistis* is pretty much the meaning I intend, I could use *pistis*. This is an approach commonly used in philosophy.

---

64 Dalla, N. (2014, May 19). *The Difference Between Faith and Trust*. Retrieved from Nolan Dalla: https://www.nolandalla.com/difference-faith-trust/

Rather than translating a key term, translators will often leave it in the original language. While tempting, it is also one of the reasons reading philosophy can be difficult. Finally, I can use 'faith' and clearly define exactly how I am using it.

All the options have their pros and cons. I am choosing the final option, as I believe it is the best despite the problems. The meaning I am using is also a common meaning with a very long history, and I am reluctant to surrender it. Abandoning the term in favor of one of the other options would introduce other problems. So here, when using the term faith, I mean it as trust and confidence leading one to act.

While a religious concept, it is not just a religious one. Faith is not restricted to religion. This is another reason for using this term, as it removes distortion from our thinking. Some want to make religious thoughts some special type of thinking. Some do this to protect religion, others to attack it. Religious thought is not different. It is just thinking. It differs from other types of thought only in the subject matter; in the same way, there is a difference between thinking about history and thinking about sports.

While we can have faith in a religious belief, we can also have faith in a person, such as a spouse or a friend. Given the risks of driving, we have faith they will get us there safely when we let someone drive us. We can have faith in a process or method. We can have faith in a medicine, an institution, or even a government.

An important point about faith is it is a trust in a belief leading to action. It says nothing about the reason or basis for the trust. Your faith in something can be well placed or misplaced. You can have good reasons for your faith or have no reason or even reasons against your faith. The latter two are special cases referred to as blind faith. Note the fact we have a particular category of blind faith implies not all faith is blind.

A person may come to a bridge and simply assume it will support them. A structural engineer can come to the same bridge, thoroughly investigate it, and conclude it would support them.

Still, only when they cross the bridge do they demonstrate they have faith it will support them.

This view of faith also allows us to distinguish between what people profess and what they do, or even when we believe one thing but do another. What we do demonstrates our faith much better than what we say or even what we think we believe.

Not all beliefs require faith. Beliefs that ask nothing of us and have no impact on what we do or our decisions require no faith. No faith is required, if you tell me that there is oil on my property, but I do not care one way or the other. The same claim when I desire to exploit the riches on my property requires faith if I am to invest the money needed to drill.

Finally, there is the relationship between faith and reason. There is some tension in that faith is a trust leading to action while reason is, to some extent, a distrust. Rather than trust, reason wants demonstration. Still, there need be no conflict. Reason must operate within a framework. As we saw earlier, the major change from the Middle Ages to the Enlightenment was not a transition from faith to reason. Reason was important in both periods.

Rather, what changed was the framework in which reason was applied. During the Middle Ages, the framework was top-down based on authority. During the Enlightenment, it was bottom-up based on evidence. Both reason and faith are important. Reason is important for testing, which eliminates error and helps discover what truth is. Faith is important, for reason cannot give us all the answers. If nothing else, one must have faith in reason to benefit from it.

Summary So Far

The uncertainty inherent in the Enlightenment's emphasis on reason and evidence is neither new nor uncommon. It is built into our daily life. So is the faith required to act on our belief. I hope I have shown to this point we exist, that we exist in an objective reality, and we can learn about that reality using evidence and reason.

I have also briefly argued for the existence of an objective morality. Yet, I have said little about what that morality might be, except in the broadest terms. I also argued the Enlightenment's bottom-up approach based on reason and evidence is not synonymous with materialism's insistence that only a material world exists. As such, it does not automatically preclude religious belief, but neither does it demand it.

Beyond this point, I will not discuss morality or religion in this book other than to say the questions in these areas are not fundamentally different from those in other areas of life. Some want to segment these questions as a completely different type of knowledge exempt from the normal rules. While they can be more difficult to discuss, that is not because they are a different type of thinking. Rather it is because people tend to be more invested in these views. Still, there are plenty of other issues to discuss without going into those areas. I will only say the rules and principles discussed here apply to religion and morality as well.

Chapter 5

What is Truth?

Everything we hear is an opinion, not a fact.
Everything we see is a perspective, not the truth. – Marcus Aurelius

What is truth? – Pontius Pilate

Disagreements surround us. Recent Presidential elections are hotly contested and won by the narrowest of margins. Opinion polls show declining levels of confidence in our public institutions and our information sources. Charges of misinformation, fake news, and bias abound. Even fact-checks are not without controversy. Everyone claims they are correct; they have the truth.

So far, I have argued that we exist in a reality that is at least in some fashion independent of us and what we think about it. To the extent our beliefs correspond to that independent reality, they are true. The extent to which they differ they are false. This view is good in theory, but it leaves many unanswered questions regarding how we normally talk about truth on a day-to-day level.

For example, consider the following three statements. (A) Abraham Lincoln was the President of the United States. (B) Abraham Lincoln was the *sixteenth* President of the United States. (C) Abraham Lincoln was the *greatest* President of the United States. These statements differ by only one word; (B) adds 'sixteenth' and (C) adds 'greatest.'

Even most who believe that all three sentences are true will distinguish between the first two statements and the last. Statements (A) and (B) are easily verifiable. It is a simple matter to look at a chronological listing of the Presidents to see that Lincoln was indeed a president and the sixteenth. As a result, statements (A) and (B) are considered facts.

There is another characteristic to statements (A) and (B) in addition to their being easily verifiable which is not as easy to specify. There is a definitiveness to these statements that gives a clear binary quality to their truthfulness. There is little ambiguity; the statement will either be correct or incorrect, true or false. Even when we do not know a particular statement is true, we know it has a clear truth value.

For example, few probably know if the statement (D) "Millard Fillmore was the twelfth President of the United States" is true or false without looking it up. Yet even without knowing, they know it is one or the other. (A), (B) and (D) are statements of being that will correspond directly with reality or will not. This correspondence will exist independent of our ability to verify it.

Consider some far distant time in the future, where all knowledge of the United States has long since been lost and forgotten. If some future archeologists unearthed a page where statement (D) was the only legible part, they would know it had a binary truth value, even if they had no way to determine what it was.

The statement is just a factual claim when the truth of such a statement is unknown. Once the claim's truthfulness has been determined, the factual claim becomes either a fact or an error. As it turns out, statement (A) is a fact. Statement (D) is an error. Millard Fillmore was the thirteenth President. Zachary Taylor was the twelfth.

Statement (C), Abraham Lincoln was the greatest President of the United States, could be as true as (A) and (B). Still, it differs in the binary nature of its claim. For statement (A), Lincoln either was or was not a President of the United States. For (B), 'sixteenth' implies a chronological sequence. Lincoln either was the sixteenth, or he was not. 'Greatest' is ambiguous. Greatest in what way? How do you measure greatness?

A quick search will find lots of lists ranking presidents, and not all of them agree.[65] There is a broad consensus, but there are

---

65 *Historical rankings of presidents of the United States.* (n.d.). Retrieved from Wikipedia: https://en.wikipedia.org/wiki/Historical_rankings_of_presidents_of_the_United_States

also significant differences. There is a strong consensus on who should be in the top three: Washington, Lincoln, and Franklin D. Roosevelt, though a few rankings place Washington fourth, putting Jefferson or Theodore Roosevelt instead into the top three.

A key issue is how you define greatness. Is it who was best at the job? Who had the most impact? The most successful? These terms are themselves ambiguous. The most popular? What time frame, if the latter? The assessment of a President changes with time. Truman's popularity was very low, when he left office. Now he is viewed much more favorably and is normally included among the top ten.

There is a temptation to look at all these differences and write them off as simply opinions, closer to preferences than truth. While this might explain the differences, you then have a greater problem accounting for all the agreements. For example, if it were just a matter of preference, why is there a strong consensus on the top three and near-universal agreement Lincoln and Franklin Roosevelt belong in the top three?

The question of best seems to be a mixture of preference and fact. Given the complexity of the modern presidency, this should not be surprising. Stating a person was president is to state a single fact. Stating a president's ranking in terms of greatness is to assess many factual issues and then rank their totality.

There will be at least three major points of concern and many minor ones, when assessing the greatness of a president. The first is the criteria by which greatness is assessed. This will include questions of what factors will be considered and the importance they each have. One common factor is impact. How did they change the office in a way affecting those who came after them? Impact is probably the main factor that places Washington, Lincoln, and Franklin Roosevelt consistently in the top three. Each shaped the office in ways that continue to affect Presidents today.

Washington, as the first president, defined the office. Before Washington, the Presidency was just words on the pages of the Constitution. He gave those words meaning. He set the standard for what it means to be President. For example, he served only two-terms, instead of serving for life. In doing so, he set a standard that remained unbroken until FDR. Following Roosevelt's death, the two-term limit was added to the Constitution. Just consider how different the presidency, and the country, would be if the norm had been that Presidents, once elected, served for life unless voted out by the people. How different would American history have been?

Lincoln's actions during the Civil War not only saved the Union but, in many ways, defined what the Federal Government would be. Likewise, Franklin D Roosevelt significantly redefined the relationship between the people and the Federal government. A key aspect here is that impact does not mean approval. One can disagree with what Washington established or how Lincoln and Roosevelt changed the presidency and still see them in the top three for impact.

In addition to impact, other factors would include how they handled major decisions that had long-lasting effects on the country. How well they manage the government, the relationship with Congress, domestic vs. foreign policy, the economy, relations with the states, and a range of other policy and management issues. Each of these areas is then made up of numerous considerations. Just determining how you will judge the various presidents is quite a task in and of itself.

Second comes the evaluation. History does not repeat itself. Each president is confronted with different situations, different conditions, and different challenges. Add to this, except for Harrison and Garfield, who died during their first year in office, presidential terms last years. Some years are better than others. In short, there is a huge amount of data that must be considered when making such rankings.

Finally, there is the problem of preference. Objectively ranking presidents in this fashion would be very difficult to do even if one was completely dispassionate and objective. It becomes even harder for the later presidents, presidents who one may have voted for or opposed.

These considerations help us understand the differences. The latter two are particularly true for some of the changes seen in presidential rankings over time. For example, Reagan's rankings following his term up until 2000 put him in the low twenties. As time passed, political concerns faded, and more information came out. Rankings since 2000 tend to put him in the top ten.

Simple, Compound, and Complex Truth

Thus, the real difference between the statements (A) and (B) on the one hand and (C) is not truth versus preference. Statement (A) is a simple factual claim. Statement (B) is a compound claim, two or more factual claims bundled together. It claims he was both President and he was the sixteenth. Like (B), a statement about being 'best' is also a compound factual claim. Yet, it is more than just compound; it is complex. It involved ranking many factual claims into a hierarchy involving both judgment and values. We will talk more about values in the next chapter. The key point, for now, is that difference between 'sixteenth' and 'best' is one of complexity.

While we could, in theory, say it was true Lincoln was the best president, it would be better to say it was a valid, reasonable, or correct point of view. Given the complexity, it would even be correct to say concerning Lincoln and Washington being best; both were reasonable views to hold. Even though logically there can be only one best, there is enough flexibility in how one makes such determination that they could each be best given different criteria.

This difference between simple, compound, and complex truth is often simplified into fact vs. opinion. Again, this is one of those areas where the looseness of everyday language is a problem. Opinion often implies a subjective preference, like my opinion that chocolate ice cream tastes better than vanilla. Yet, there is more here than just subjective preference.

There is an objective truth to the statement 'Lincoln was the best president' that does not exist in the statement 'chocolate ice cream tastes better than vanilla.' The latter is a subjective statement.

It would not be wrong for someone else to say they like vanilla better because these are subjective views. On the other hand, it would be incorrect to say James Buchanan was the best President as a general statement. Buchanan is generally considered the worst President in American history, as he badly handled the issue of slavery, leading to the civil war. As such, judgment, the rational evaluation of all the evidence, is probably a better term to use than opinion.

Normally, when it comes to common disputes, they are not over single truth claims, though these sometimes happen. Rather, most disputes involve compound and complex truth claims. For example, to say one car is better than another could involve hundreds of truth claims and judgments concerning them. Likewise, to say one car company is better than another would involve evaluating many cars, in addition to many other factors.

In reality, many of these truth claims would be shared in common and could be effectively ignored. These would form the common ground upon which any discussion is based. Still, there would remain a large number of disagreements, both in factual claims and judgments. Because of this complexity, rarely is one side going to be completely correct or completely wrong. Instead, both sides are a mixture of truth and error, good and bad judgments.

Rather than which position is true and false, it is an issue of which side is the most correct or the least in error. This is where discussions are so valuable. Done correctly, they can help correct the problems on both sides and build a consensus. At the end of a good discussion, there may not be agreement, but hopefully, both sides have moved closer to the truth.

CONTEXT

All this assumes we talk precisely like scientists; we don't. Normal, everyday speech is casual, imprecise, even sloppy at times. As we have already seen in a few places, everyday language can lead to problems. One area where this occurs is with simplification.

It is common to say things like Republicans support X or Democrats believe Y. Technically, these should be qualified with words such as some or most. Yet normally, these are left off with the implied understanding that there will be some disagreement in such large groups of people. I make many similar statements throughout this book, even though some in the groups mentioned would disagree. Qualifying every such statement with most or some would only become cumbersome.

Then there is the problem that these groups are not monolithic. There are a wide range of views and opinions. Because of this, large groups are normally better represented by bell curves, with a large central grouping, but small fringes on both sides. For large countries like the United States, you can find an extremely wide range of opinions. In fact, it is probably safe to say that most every view is held by someone. Still there is a broad agreement on a number of ideas, and this broad agreement could be different from the broad agreement among the peoples of other countries like France. These broad agreements could then be labeled an American view and a French view, despite the fact that they are not held by every American or everyone in France.

This also shows up in historical comparisons. In the Introduction, I mentioned C. S. Lewis' concern about the decline in truth. This is not to say that everyone in the past was completely rational or logical, or that everyone now has abandoned the notion of truth. Rather, it means the bell curves have shifted, away from an objective truth and towards a subjective view of truth.

Another area would be precision. For example, often, we would shorten statements like (A) and say that Lincoln was President. This is fine, but now we assume the person we are talking to knows we are referring to Abraham Lincoln. We are also assuming they know the presidency referred to was the United States. In short, the truthfulness of the statement depends on the context in which the statement occurs.

If the statement "Lincoln was President" was in response to the question, "What was Sarah Lincoln's position in our club last year?" The statement could still be true but would be completely different than statement (A). Normally this is not an issue, but the specific context does become an issue at times.

A more recent dispute highlights many of the difficulties of this problem. Some may find even the mention of this dispute disturbing, but the focus here is to outline why such problems can be so difficult, not take sides. The dispute concerned whether President Biden called President Trump's travel ban from China to slow the spread of the COVID-19 virus xenophobic during the 2020 presidential campaign. On January 31, 2020, President Trump announced a travel ban for non-US citizens coming from China.[66] Later that day in Fort Madison, Iowa, while campaigning for his party's nomination, Biden said,

> We have, right now, a crisis with the coronavirus. This is no time for Donald Trump's record of hysteria and xenophobia - hysterical xenophobia - and fearmongering to lead the way instead of science.[67]

The next day Biden tweeted,

> We are in the midst of a crisis with the coronavirus. We need to lead the way with science — not Donald Trump's record of hysteria, xenophobia, and fear-mongering. He is the worst possible person to lead our country through a global health emergency.[68]

In late January, the Coronavirus outbreak was still relatively new. It would be nearly a month before the U.S. had its first death.

---

66 Werner, E., Abutaleb, Y., Bernstein, L., & Sun, L. H. (2020, January 31). *Trump administration announces mandatory quarantines in Response to coronavirus.* Retrieved from The Washington Post: https://www.washingtonpost.com/us-policy/2020/01/31/trump-weighs-tighter-china-travel-restrictions-response-coronavirus/

67 Hunnicutt, T. (2020, January 31). *Biden slams Trump for cutting health programs before coronavirus outbreak.* Retrieved from Reuters: https://www.reuters.com/article/us-usa-election-coronavirus-idUSKBN1ZV38M

68 Biden, J. (2020, March 18). *Tweet.* Retrieved from Twitter: https://twitter.com/JoeBiden/status/1240361258957897728

In March, Trump tweeted, "I always treated the Chinese Virus very seriously, and have done a very good job from the beginning, including my very early decision to close the 'borders' from China - against the wishes of almost all. Many lives were saved."[69] Biden replied to this tweet with "Stop the xenophobic fear-mongering. Be honest. Take responsibility. Do your job."

A few months after the travel ban, when the country was shut down and deaths increasing, this became a dispute. Trump claimed Biden opposed his travel ban, calling it xenophobic. Biden denied the claim and said he had supported the President's China travel ban.[70] Did Biden claim the travel ban was xenophobic?

Which side is correct depends completely on the context of Biden's statements. Just exactly what was Biden referring to when he said, "Donald Trump's record of hysteria and xenophobia - hysterical xenophobia - and fearmongering to lead the way instead of science." According to an article written the day of Biden's comments, the main focus of his criticism was Trump's "reducing U.S. oversight of global health issues before the coronavirus outbreak."[71] While the main focus, "xenophobic fear-mongering," is a strange way of referring to a proposed budget cut. In the weeks following the travel ban, there was much criticism from Democrats about travel bans. Still, it was not clear these included or excluded the China travel ban.

Biden's comments in March to "Stop the xenophobic fear-mongering" would seem a little clearer. Biden was responding to a tweet by Trump. The only specific policy measure mentioned in Trump's

---

69 Valverde, M. (2020, March 27). *Fact-checking whether Biden called Trump 'xenophobic' for restrictions on travel from China*. Retrieved from Politifact: https://www.politifact.com/factchecks/2020/mar/27/donald-trump/fact-checking-whether-biden-called-trump-xenophobi/

70 Tapper, J. (2020, April 3). *Biden campaign says he backs Trump's China travel ban*. Retrieved from CNN: https://www.cnn.com/2020/04/03/politics/joe-biden-trump-china-coronavirus/index.html

71 Hunnicutt, T. (2020, January 31). *Biden slams Trump for cutting health programs before coronavirus outbreak*. Retrieved from Reuters: https://www.reuters.com/article/us-usa-election-coronavirus-idUSKBN1ZV38M

tweet was the travel ban. It would not be a big leap to conclude that Biden was referring to the travel ban. Yet, was he reacting to this particular tweet, or was he using this tweet to make a more general attack on Trump's policies?

Given the timing and ambiguity, it is easy to see why Trump and his supporters think Biden's comments referred to the travel ban. Biden did call Trump's COVID response xenophobic. Part of Trump's COVID response was the travel ban announced earlier in the day of the first comments and in the tweet in March, to which Biden replied.

It is also easy to see why Biden supporters would accept he did not include the travel ban in his comments about xenophobia. Biden never explicitly linked the comments about xenophobia to the travel ban. The links, if they exist, all depend on the context. Biden said he supported the travel ban.[72] Still, this was in April over two months later and well into the controversy. There does not appear to be any record of this support before April.

What is the truth here? Were Biden's "xenophobic" comments directed at the travel ban? Were they directed at Trump's policies in general, including the travel ban? Were they directed at Trump's policies in general without any actual thought about the travel ban, one way or the other? Were they directed at Trump's policies in general but excluded the travel ban? Ultimately, at this point, it is impossible to say with certainty. A good case could be made for each of these options.

This is the problem with language. While normally, this is not a problem, it can be very difficult, if not impossible, to settle the matter when there is a contentious disagreement. This is particularly true for politicians, who are often very practiced at being ambiguous but not sounding ambiguous.

This controversy also highlights a deeper issue: the difference between what is true and what we can know is true. There is a truth

---

72   Tapper, J. (2020, April 3). *Biden campaign says he backs Trump's China travel ban.* Retrieved from CNN: https://www.cnn.com/2020/04/03/politics/joe-biden-trump-china-coronavirus/index.html

here. Biden either did or did not include the travel ban in his comments. Still, that there is a truth does not mean we can know that truth with any certainty. In this case, plausible arguments can be made either way. None of them can be ruled out with any degree of certainty. In the end, we just do not know, as a matter of fact, one way or another. We can have our beliefs. We may choose to believe Trump or Biden. Still, that belief is just as likely to reflect pre-existing bias than any objective evaluation of the evidence.

It is possible more evidence exists, which could be revealed to settle the issue. For example, we could uncover records or statements from January 31st where Biden directly said the travel ban was or was not included. Until such evidence is uncovered, the truth is unknowable.

The only one who might know for sure would be Biden. Still, it is even possible Biden does not really know. This is not a negative comment on Biden. Memory is just not that accurate or precise. While we all like to think we have perfect memory, our memories are not fixed. They can be, and often are, shaped by our current beliefs. Many studies have shown we can have very clear memories of things that never happened.

CERTAINTY

The difference between what is true and what we can know is true is a major factor in our beliefs. While the truth is binary, true or false, our knowledge of the truth is more like a spectrum of certainty. This spectrum is somewhat different from the one mentioned earlier concerning the mixture of beliefs, some true, some false. This spectrum focuses on how certain you are of a particular belief. At one end of the spectrum, you are completely certain. On the other end, you are really unsure—a lot of what we believe is somewhere in the middle. There is nothing unusual in this. It is very common for people to include some percentage with their statements of belief, such as "I am 90% certain."

Thus, when thinking about what we believe, there are facts and more complex beliefs. In terms of our complex beliefs, there are those beliefs we are certain are true and those we are less sure about. Like which President is best, given the complexity and uncertainty, both true and false can sometimes be reasonable positions to hold for some beliefs. Good cases can be made either way. This is not to say both are correct positions; only both are reasonable given the available evidence.

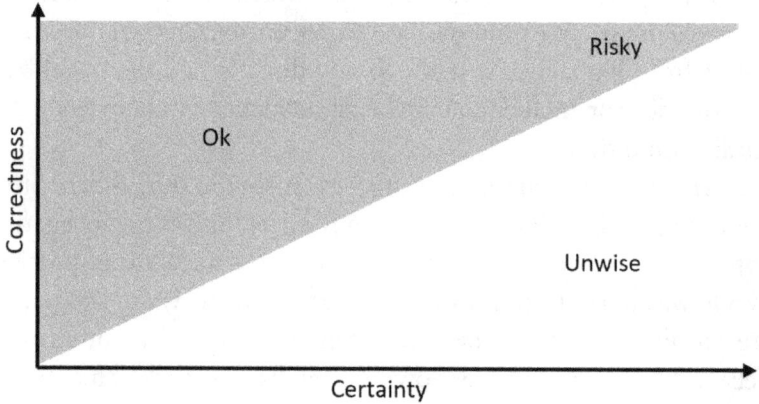

Figure 1 Correctness and Certainty in Complex Views

Figure 1 can help visualize how correctness and certainty relate when considering complex views. Initially, the best place would seem to be the upper right-hand corner, where you are the most certain of what is completely true. Yet, that position also has the greatest risk. It is preferable to be certain and correct. Still, it is better to be correct and uncertain than incorrect and certain. Being uncertain leads to more investigation, which can lead to a better understanding and better knowledge. Being certain tends to settle an issue. No new information is needed. If you are certain and correct, this is fine. However, if you are certain and incorrect, correction becomes very difficult. Being less certain is preferable to being less correct than you should be. The latter leads to dogmatism, and dogmatism should be avoided.

COMMUNICATION

If this was not enough complexity, then there are all the issues of communication. So far, we have looked at communication as if it consisted only of straightforward declarative sentences. However, there are many different ways to look at communication. There are several things to consider, whenever you communicate with someone. You have the sender, the sending instrument, the transmission, the receiving instrument, and the receiver.

This outline can be broken down in many different ways. You can have the speaker, their mouth, the air, the listener's ear, and the listener. Problems can occur at each stage. Perhaps the speaker has just been to the dentist, and their mouth is numb, or the room is noisy, or perhaps the listener is not paying attention. At each stage, things can happen impeding communication.

There are also other ways this can be broken down. For example, when using a cellphone, there is you, your cell phone, the transmission network, the recipient's cell phone, and the recipient. This general outline could be applied to many different types of communication. All must work, for effective communication to take place. In the example concerning the claim of xenophobia above, a major issue was the initial communication was unclear.

Even in normal conversation, people can and do misspeak just as people can and do mishear. In written conversations, we do not always type what we planned. Sometimes "helpful" software will change what we type to what the software calculates we should have typed. Most of the time, the suggestions are helpful. Still, at times they significantly change the meaning from what was intended.

Even then, given the black and white nature of the written word, someone can easily misunderstand a message's tone. For example, in an online discussion once, I wrote what I thought was a complimentary message to a person I normally disagreed with. I thought they had made a really good point and said so. Unfortunately, they mistook my message as sarcasm, and I received a flaming reply. It took several messages and the intervention of a few others on the forum to straighten out the situation.

LANGUAGE

Add to this all the various figures of speech. Effective communication can use a range of styles. Hyperbole, humor, metaphors, irony, to name just a few, are all legitimate ways to make or drive home a point. So how do we assess the truth value of such statements? There is, of course, the classic exchange.

"You object to everything I say!"

"No, I don't."

The first statement was almost certainly hyperbole. In fact, a great majority of absolute claims, claims using words such as all, none, every, never, etc., are hyperbolic. When we say 'all,' we do not mean absolutely every single one. This is shown by saying things like, "the exception proves the rule," which would only make sense if the initial claim was not absolute.

Figures of speech such as hyperbole present a problem for truth. In a strict sense, they are false. Yet their purpose is often to make a point the speaker believes to be true. Thus, there is a difference between the literal meaning and the intended meaning of hyperbole. In short, there is a difference between what a person is trying to communicate and what they are literally saying.

What they are saying might literally be impossible but still be very effective in communicating the truth of a situation. For example, sometimes large amounts of money are described as how high a corresponding stack of bills would be. You take the thickness of a dollar bill (.0043 inches) and multiply it by the amount in question.

When doing this for one trillion dollars, the stack would reach a quarter of the way to the moon. It is a good picture of how much money one trillion dollars is. Still, you could not put that much money into a single stack of bills. All sorts of practical issues would come into play, such as compressing the bills at the bottom by all

Seeking Truth

the bills above them and the stability of the stack. In short, creating such a stack would be impossible, but does this make it untrue?

When dealing with such figures of speech, it is best to take them for what they are. Their truth would be based on the main point they are trying to make and not on a literal reading. Taking a figure of speech as a literal statement would be a hyper-literal understanding that should be rejected.

Untruth

The difference between what someone literally says and what they are trying to communicate cuts both ways. It is possible to say something that is literally true and yet intend to deceive. If someone asks, did you go to the bar, you could respond with, 'I went to the grocery store.' This statement would be true if you did go to the grocery store. It would also be a lie if you had gone to the grocery store after the bar so that you would have an alibi. These are often called lies of omission, lying by not saying something or saying something different and not giving the full truth.

This concept of deception is a key distinction of a lie. Often a lie is seen as anything not true, but not all untruths are lies. Many are simply mistakes or errors. On the other hand, it is possible to lie by saying things that are true. Given this, rather than things that are untrue, a better definition of a lie is anything said with the intent to deceive.

Even when it comes to error, not all errors are of equal import. Some errors are more significant than others. Some errors are an issue of scale. Say there is a dispute over a $213.23 charge on a bill. Mis-stating the charge as $213.32 would not be incredibly significant to the overall dispute.

Another example would be minor errors not amounting to much. The statement, 'John F Kennedy became President in 1960' would technically be false. Kennedy was elected President in 1960; he became President in 1961. But rarely would this difference be significant in a discussion. Stressing an insignificant error or mistake is called quibbling and is to be avoided.

Common vs. Technical

Another source of problems is using terms having both a common meaning and a technical one. Consider the statement, "the President's policies caused a recession." Setting aside for the moment the whole issue of how much a president can actually affect the economy, there is still an issue with the term recession. In common usage, it can refer to any economic slowdown. On the other hand, the term has several technical definitions. The most common is two consecutive quarters where the Gross National Product declines. The National Bureau of Economic Research defines a recession as a decline lasting several months.

As a result of these various definitions, it is easy to envision a disagreement over the question, "Did the President's policies cause a recession?" A supporter of the President could argue they did not. An opponent could argue they did. Both could be completely correct depending on which definition they were using. This flexibility of definitions is behind a large number of disputes, as we will see in later chapters. In fact, at times, people will change the definition they are using in the middle of an argument, creating the fallacy of equivocation.

Ambiguity

Vague terminology in communications causes other problems. Even when we are all using the same words, we may not be using the same understanding. One exercise in my critical thinking classes drove this point home. I would put the following list of common words up.

Seeking Truth

Likely	Unlikely
Probable	Doubtful
Certain	Questionable
Possible	Liable
Feasible	Remote

I would then ask everyone to write down the words and put a number next to each word representing the chance something will happen in terms of a percentage. Once everyone was done, we would go to each word, and I would ask what the highest and lowest numbers were for each of them.

Not too surprisingly, there was a significant difference between the low and high numbers on many of these terms. This difference can lead to problems. For example, imagine you tell your boss you think a project is *possible*, meaning a 30 percent chance. However, your boss hears *possible*, meaning an 80 percent chance. Could this end up in a problem?

This type of ambiguity became a huge issue during the COVID-19 pandemic, centering on the issue of what is "safe?" In the early months of the pandemic, little was known since this was a new disease. Assessing risk was difficult. No one knew how easily it spread or how deadly it was. Would it affect all groups equally or hit some groups harder than others? As the data got better, a difference began to develop around the question of safety.

For example, at the time that I am writing this, my state of Wisconsin reports there have been 790,282 cases, with 8483 deaths, or 1.07 percent. On the other hand, roughly 98 percent have survived. Furthermore, of those who died, 89.4 percent were older than 59 years. Only 1.2 percent were younger than 40. This difference due to age becomes even starker when comparing cases by age to death by age. Thus, whereas those 60 and above had a fatality rate of 4.98% or roughly a one in twenty chance of dying if they caught COVID, for those under 40, the fatality rate was only 0.04% or one chance in 2500. Given these statistics, it is easy to see why a person in their early twenties might have a vastly different view of the risks of COVID-19 given a fatality rate for their age of only 0.023% compared to a person in their eighties looking at a fatality rate of 12.52%, which is 544 times greater.

It is a question of what is safe. Different people have different circumstances, different risk factors, and different tolerances for risk. Two people can look at the same risk and have vastly different reactions. The only objective standard would be zero, but that is an impossible standard to reach. There will always be some possibility of COVID-19 coming back or of some new disease breaking out. While zero is impossible, any other standard will be a matter of judgment.

Some argue such judgment calls should be left to the experts; but which experts? Even among epidemiologists, there are various views of what is safe. Even if there were a single view, there would still be problems, for whatever steps are taken will have side effects. While epidemiologists are experts in infectious diseases, they are not experts on the side effects of shutdowns. These other areas would involve experts in public health, distinct from epidemiology and other areas such as economics.

Before long, such decisions become very complex, like which President is best that we looked at earlier in the chapter. It is not just a matter of "following the science" but a very complex issue of ranking and evaluating the vast number of considerations. At the time of this writing, COVID-19 was a deadly disease that killed over 741,135 people in the United States alone, but the shutdowns killed people as well.

For example, with doctor visits canceled, some cancers that would have been discovered and treated went undetected. We know increased unemployment has various physical and physiological issues, including increased drug and alcohol abuse, domestic abuse, and suicide. As the shutdown disrupts the food distribution system around the world, the World Health Organization estimates that up to 132 million may go hungry as a result.[73]

Ultimately, these are very complex considerations involving a lot of data and a lot of judgments. There are no experts on everything. Truth may be binary, but how we evaluate and judge real-life situations will often involve a lot of gray, with conflicting and even contradictory concerns. Whether trying to decide who was the best president or what exactly was meant by a statement is not always easy. Real-life is messy. What is the truth can be very difficult to determine when the situation is unclear. With issues such as a global pandemic, there often will not be a clear-cut answer; the actual data can be sparse and conflicting. Judgments between competing claims and concerns will have to be made. Disagreements will be inevitable. How you deal with these disagreements will be important, and that is where we go in the next section.

---

73 WHO. (2020, July 12). *As more go hungry and malnutrition persists, achieving Zero Hunger by 2030 in doubt, UN report warns.* Retrieved from www.who.int: https://www.who.int/news/item/13-07-2020-as-more-go-hungry-and-malnutrition-persists-achieving-zero-hunger-by-2030-in-doubt-un-report-warns

Part II
Disagreement and Error

Chapter 6

Agreeing to Disagree

Love is wise; hatred is foolish. In this world, which is getting more and more closely interconnected, we have to learn to tolerate each other, we have to learn to put up with the fact that some people say things that we don't like. We can only live together in that way. – Bertrand Russell

An initial question might be, why a section on disagreement? It is a fair question, but in many respects, this is a book about disagreements and how to resolve them. Think about everything you believe to be true. Now realize that for each belief, you could find someone who disagrees. You probably do not have to go very far. One neighbor might have a different religious belief; another might support a different political party; yet another might support a different sports team. There are two or more sides to virtually everything we believe. We are surrounded by people who disagree with us. It is safe to say that for everyone you know, there is something about which you disagree.

Disagreements come in two basic forms: objective and subjective. Subjective disagreements are about things like style and taste. You may like a certain food; someone else can't stand it. While a disagreement, they are not really issues of right and wrong, true or false, thus not the focus here. Objective disagreements are about issues involving right and wrong, true and false. I say 'involve' because often, these discussions are about very complex issues.

When it comes to disagreement, here is the core problem. Consider a person just like you, just as smart, just as well informed, just as concerned, just as compassionate. You're equal in whatever positive adjective you wish to specify. There is only one difference. They disagree with you on a particular issue. How can that be? There must be something wrong with them or their position. Correct?

This question is set up this way for a reason. It is very tempting to reject someone who disagrees by finding some fault with them. You may, in fact, reach that as a conclusion after some discussion. For example, say you disagree with someone over the significance of a Civil War battle. In discussing this, it quickly becomes clear they know very little about the Civil War. On the other hand, you have done considerable reading on the subject. In this case, you may rightly conclude their position is due to their ignorance. While legitimate as a conclusion, you do not want to start with that as an assumption.

Starting with the assumption that those who disagree are in some manner deficient often ends any consideration of the truth. After all, if they are _____ (Fill in a negative adjective), why should you bother listening to them? It is not a problem if you are correct. Still, can you guarantee you are? Is there no room for even the slightest misunderstanding or lack of information on your part? Is there no room for a better, more complete understanding of the matter?

It would be a very difficult claim to maintain, given how we come to know what we know. It would mean you have perfect knowledge, but is such a thing even humanly possible? Consider the Civil War example above; unless you are *The Expert*, there are others who know more than you do about the Civil War. Even if you just happen to be the one person who knows the most, there will be people who specialize in certain aspects of the Civil War who know more about their area of specialization than you.

In short, nobody knows everything there is to know, even about one subject, much less all subjects. Even if you are the most knowledgeable, you still have things you could learn. It is still possible the person knows something you don't, assuming everything you know is correct. It almost certainly isn't—some of what you believe is certainly false. How could it not be?

The relationship between reality and knowledge can be seen in Figure 2. Again, this is using the common understanding of knowledge, not the philosophical definition. There is reality, which is true, some of which we know, and some we don't. There is what we know, or at least think we know. Where the two overlap, we are correct. That part of our knowledge not overlapping with reality is in error. It can be very difficult to tell where we are correct from where we are incorrect. It is just knowledge to us.

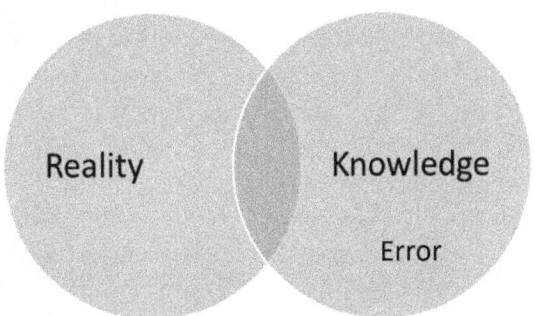

Figure 2 Reality and Knowledge

SOURCES OF KNOWLEDGE

We get what we know from a variety of sources and methods. At one end of the spectrum are things you have studied and researched carefully. At the other are things you picked up in passing. We get what we know from our parents, teachers, friends, and casual acquaintances. Our knowledge is affected by what we read, watch on TV, and see in movies. The music we listen to affects how we see things. Then there is all the cultural knowledge, beliefs, and ways of thinking about things you acquired because of the time and place you lived. Even the language you speak and whether or not you speak more than one affects how you think about things.

Now it is certainly possible to disagree when one side is factually wrong while the other is right. Still, because of the complexity of many issues, as we saw in the last chapter, this is rarely black and white. In addition to judgments, most views contain all sorts of assumptions and claims mixed together. In such cases, normally, neither side is completely right or wrong, and what is true or false needs to be untangled and clarified. Even when the claim seems clear-cut, hidden assumptions can cloud the matter.

Defining Tax

A similar but more difficult issue occurs when people think they are talking about the same thing but are really talking about two related but different concepts. A great example of this is found in an older article in the Washington Post.

The headline frames the issue, "*Tax Burden Shifts to the Middle.*" It was a fairly standard and common political dispute. One party claimed recent changes to the income tax law had shifted the tax burden to the middle class. The other party, the party responsible for the tax change, argued the opposite. The Post article concerned a Congressional Budget Office (CBO) study of the dispute. According to the article,

> The CBO study, due to be released today, found that the wealthiest 20 percent, whose incomes averaged $182,700 in 2001, saw their share of federal taxes drop from 64.4 percent of total tax payments in 2001 to 63.5 percent this year. The top 1 percent, earning $1.1 million, saw their share fall to 20.1 percent of the total, from 22.2 percent. Over that same period, taxpayers with incomes from around $51,500 to around $75,600 saw their share of federal tax payments increase. Households earning around $75,600 saw their tax burden jump the most, from 18.7 percent of all taxes to 19.5 percent.[74]

It seems clear enough. However, not too surprisingly, members of the other party disagreed. As the article went on to detail, they also pointed to the same CBO report claiming it showed the wealthiest households were actually paying a greater percentage of the tax burden, not less. They argued the wealthiest 20 percent saw their share of income taxes go from 78.4 percent to 82.1 percent. "In contrast, the middle-class share of income taxes dropped to 5.4 percent, from 6.4 percent."

Again this news article represents a pretty typical Washington dispute, with the two sides making seemingly opposite claims. It

---

74 Weisman, J. (2004, August 13). Tax Burden Shifts to the Middle. *Washington Post*, p. A04.

Seeking Truth

is easy to see why people in the middle often just throw up their hands at the bickering, while the more partisan assume the other side is just lying.

In my critical thinking classes, I would often use this as an example of disputes and, at this point, would ask, which side is right? Given the claims and counterclaims, the normal response was that it was hard to tell. I would then ask; how would you find out? Eventually, someone would suggest looking at the CBO report quoted in the article. At that point, I would produce copies of the report, break them into groups and have them go at it.

While such reports are not exactly exciting reading, they are a wealth of data. Before long, the groups could answer the question of which side was correct; they both were. The dispute was not about facts, which way the burden shifted; it was about definitions. What exactly do you mean by tax burden?

Those claiming the burden shifted to the middle class defined tax burden as including federal taxes in general and thus included not only income taxes but other taxes as well, such as payroll taxes. As such, their numbers came from the section in Table 2 of the report, which showed the "Share of Total Federal Tax Liabilities."[75] Those numbers are there, and they show the tax burden did shift to the middle class.

The other party, noting the tax change in question was a change to the income tax, used a different section of Table 2, which referred to the "Share of Individual Income Tax Liabilities." They then compared these to the values recorded in Table 3, which estimate what the liabilities would have been had there not been a change in the law. Again, those numbers are there as reported, and they show the burden shifted to the wealthiest households.

The actual dispute was not one of fact but of definition, something not brought out in the reporting. When considering a change to the income tax, which is more important, the shift in the burden of the income tax or the shift in the burden of total Federal taxes?

---

75   CBO. (2004). *Effective Federal Tax Rates Under Current Law, 2001 to 2014*. Washington, DC: The Congress of the United States. p. 10

Then there is the issue of tax burden vs. tax dollars paid. If both go up or both go down, the matter is pretty straightforward. Yet what about when they move in opposite directions? What about when the dollar amount in taxes you pay goes down but the percentage of your tax burden compared to others goes up? What about the reverse when you pay more in dollars but your percentage of the overall burden goes down?

This example reveals another source of disagreement: values. It is pretty easy to envision someone who only cares about the actual dollars paid and for whom the percentage of the burden does not matter at all. On the other hand, it is also easy to envision someone for whom the burden's percentage was extremely important, perhaps more important than the actual amount. It is not that one person or the other is right or wrong. This is a question of what is important for them. Do you seek lower taxes, or is your primary focus a more equitable distribution of the tax burden?

People with different values will reach different conclusions. This is particularly clear with the values of selflessness and self-serving. People can and do support government policies, such as taxes, because of personal interest. Someone could support a tax cut or a government spending program because it will benefit them. At the same time, someone else opposes these for selfless reasons. A quick survey of political debates would lead one to think this was the primary factor, with all sides claiming to be selfless while their opponents are focused on self-interest.

The Political Spectrum

The previous example was yet another instance of the ambiguity in language. Other factors lead to disagreements as well. Existing beliefs influence how we process new information. Errors can enter into the culture. They can shape the flow of information. Because they are accepted as true, these errors shape events to the point they take on a sense of truth. An example of this is the common political spectrum of Right vs. Left.

Convention sees the political spectrum as the polarization of two extremes, Fascism and Communism, with democracy in the middle. Given the political spectrum is an artificial construct in many respects, there is nothing inherently wrong with it, at least as long as it remains a construct. The problem comes in when you try to take this and map it to real-world politics. The governments of Fascist Italy and Nazi Germany go on the right. The Soviet Union and Communist China are on the left. The democracies go in the middle. So far, so good.

In a broad sense, this works, but it is also arbitrary and tells us little. For example, why are the Fascists on the right and the Communists on the left? Why not the reverse, with the Communists on the right and the Fascists on the left? What is it about the Left making it left and the Right that makes it right?

The terms Left and Right, have their origin in the French Revolution, where the national assembly split. Those who supported the King sat on the right; those who supported the Revolution sat on the left. Nice and clear. Still, what does that mean nearly 250 years later and for countries outside of France?

It is possible to trace these movements' development since then up to modern times, but still not without problems. Both sides have changed and developed over the years. The Right no longer supports kings. The Left is no longer synonymous with revolution, particularly when they are in power. Over the last 250 years, liberty and equality have become key features of both the Right and the Left, but not to the same degree.

A TALE OF TWO REVOLUTIONS

The difference between the political Left and Right can be traced back to the differences in the two revolutions of the period and the intellectual foundations that drove them. Thirteen years before the French Revolution, the American Revolution was marked by resistance to new taxes and laws imposed on the colonies to recover the cost of the 7-years War.

Until that time, the British government had largely left the colonies alone. Left alone, they developed into a series of thirteen separate colonies, each with its own government. These governments were grounded in the intellectual theories of the day, primarily the enlightenment. The main guiding thinkers were John Locke and Montesquieu. Individual liberty and reason were the guiding principles.

Then came the 7-years war. From Britain's point of view, the colonies had dragged them into a costly war, leaving them with huge debts. Making matters worse, because they had largely been left to fend for themselves until then, they did not pay as much in taxes as the average person in Britain.

From Great Britain's viewpoint, they had ignored the colonies for too long. It was time to bring some order and control to the situation. The colonies should also pay more taxes to help cover the costs of the war fought on their behalf.

It was not so simple for the colonies. They had grown used to governing themselves. They also saw the 7-years war as between two European powers, France and England. As a result, they resisted the new restrictions being imposed on them. Particularly the new taxes imposed on them without any say in the matter.

Their governments based on enlightenment thinking worked for them. Now they were being asked to follow the dictates of a King without any ability to provide input. Thus the slogan, no taxation without representation. When they objected, rather than seeking to work out a compromise, the British Government doubled down, which eventually led to revolution. It was a revolution grounded in the enlightenment principles of liberty and the rights of the individual. The result was a new country founded on those principles.

The French Revolution started with enlightenment principles and went through several phases, with different historians breaking the revolution into different numbers. For the purposes of contrast, we will look at four. The first phase was an attempt by the nobles to increase their power at the expense of the King. The Nobles, however, could not control the people, and the revolution quickly entered a second phase when they lost control.

The second phase was a better expression of enlightenment values with its Declaration of the Rights of Man. Whereas the American colonies had a history of self-rule, that did not exist in France. The second phase also broke down, resulting in the rise of the Jacobins.

Rather than followers of the enlightenment, the Jacobin leaders such as Robespierre and Saint-Just drew inspiration from the French philosopher Jean-Jacques Rousseau. While a later enlightenment philosopher, Rousseau rejected the enlightenment views of reason and the individual. Rousseau did agree with other enlightenment thinkers that reason was the basis for civilization. The problem was he did not like civilization, preferring the state of nature instead. Rousseau wrote in *Discourse on the Origin of Inequality*, in the state of nature,

> [pity] is a natural sentiment, which, by moderating in every individual the activity of self-love, contributes to the mutual preservation of the whole species. It is this pity which hurries us without reflection to the assistance of those we see in distress; it is this pity which, in a state of nature, stands for laws, for manners, for virtue, with this advantage, that no one is tempted to disobey her sweet and gentle voice: it is this pity which will always hinder a robust savage from plundering a feeble child, or infirm old man, of the subsistence they have acquired with pain and difficulty.[76]

In the state of nature, the only inequalities were "the difference of age, health, bodily strength, and the qualities of the mind, or of the soul." For Rousseau, these were "almost imperceivable." The real problem of inequality is a problem of civilization, which is built upon reason.

> It is reason that engenders self-love, and reflection that strengthens it; it is reason that makes man shrink into himself;

---

76 Rousseau, J.-J. (1755). *Discourse on The Origin of Inequality*.

it is reason that makes him keep aloof from everything that can trouble or afflict him: it is philosophy that destroys his connections with other men; it is in consequence of her dictates that he mutters to himself at the sight of another in distress, You may perish for aught I care, nothing can hurt me. Nothing less than those evils, which threaten the whole species, can disturb the calm sleep of the philosopher, and force him from his bed. One man may with impunity murder another under his windows; he has nothing to do but clap his hands to his ears, argue a little with himself to hinder nature, that startles within him, from identifying him with the unhappy sufferer.[77]

For Rousseau, the individual, with their selfish desires, was the problem, and these came with civilization. His attitude is summed up when he wrote,

> Metallurgy and agriculture were the two arts whose invention produced this great revolution. With the poet, it is gold and silver, but with the philosopher it is iron and corn, which have civilized men, and ruined mankind.[78]

It is impossible to go back to the state of nature. The only path forward was the Social Compact.

> If then we discard from the social compact what is not of its essence, we shall find that it reduces itself to the following terms— "Each of us puts his person and all his power in common under the supreme direction of the general will, and, in our corporate capacity, we receive each member as an indivisible part of the whole." At once, in place of the individual personality of each contracting party, this act of association creates a moral and collective body, composed of as many members as the assembly contains votes, and receiving from this act its unity, its common identity, its life and its will.[79]

Rousseau went on to say that, "Those who are associated in it take collectively the name of people, and severally are called cit-

---

77 Rousseau, J.-J. (1755). *Discourse on The Origin of Inequality.*
78 Rousseau, J.-J. (1755). *Discourse on The Origin of Inequality.*
79 Rousseau, J.-J. (1762). *The Social Contract.*

Seeking Truth

izens." When it came to the power of the state, for Rousseau, the matter was straightforward.

> If the State is a moral person whose life is in the union of its members, and if the most important of its cares is the care for its own preservation, it must have a universal and compelling force, in order to move and dispose each part as may be most advantageous to the whole. As nature gives each man absolute power over all his members, the social compact gives the body politic absolute power over all its members also; and it is this power which, under the direction of the general will, bears, as I have said, the name of Sovereignty.

This centralization of power led to the fourth and final phase. As part of a group that overthrew the directorate, Napoleon became First Consul on November 10, 1799. On May 18, 1804, he crowned himself Emperor.

As a result, the French Revolution differed significantly from the American Revolution. Rather than a rebellion against new laws and taxes, the French Revolution opposed an overburdensome social structure with strong class distinctions. Rather than the individual and liberty, the main focus for the French Revolution was the people as a whole and equality. Everyone was the same; everyone was simply called Citizen. Finally, where the American Revolution saw government as a threat to liberty, the French Revolution saw the government as sovereign.

LIBERTY VS. EQUALITY

Both revolutions valued liberty and equality, but both emphasized one over the other. They had to. Liberty and equality are mutually exclusive. The more you get of one, the less you will have of the other. This is because given the liberty to make choices, not everyone will make the same choice. Some choices will be better, or perhaps just luckier than others, and thus, inequality will result over time.

The only way to preserve equality is to limit liberty. Since the French revolution's supporters sat on the left side of the chamber, and the French revolution tended to support equality, the Left has historically supported equality over liberty. Those who supported liberty over equality have gravitated to the right.

This difference between liberty and equality resulted in more differences over the years. Liberty tends more towards an individual choice. One can be completely free when one is alone. Liberty is individualistic.

The concept of equality makes no sense for a single individual; it requires others for comparison. There must be at least two people before the concept can even be considered. Following Rousseau, normally, it is thought of in terms of groups, not individuals.

As a result, another difference that emerged over the nineteenth century is the Right focused more on the individual, the Left more on the collective, the group. In the 1830s, this focus on the group led to the emergence of socialism.

The main threat to individual liberties is the government; the main solution to group inequalities is the government. So different views of government developed between Left and Right. The Left wanted a larger, more powerful central government, while the Right wanted a smaller, less intrusive government.

All of these trends have developed over the last 250 years. They define the difference between Left and Right. The Left values equality, sees society as a collection of groups, and wants a larger government to solve society's problems. The Right values liberty, sees society as a collection of individuals and wants a smaller government, one just large enough to protect the individual's rights.

There are three key aspects here. The first is neither of these is absolute. It is not that the Right rejects equality or the Left, liberty. On the contrary, except at their extremes, both values are important to both groups. However, when the two come into conflict, something has to give. When there is a conflict, the Right will tend towards liberty, the Left towards equality.

Seeking Truth

The second thing to notice is these are not right and wrong questions but value and judgment. Both liberty and equality are important. In a perfect world, we would want both. When there is a conflict between liberty and equality, it is not always easy to say with any certainty which should be more important. There is room for legitimate disagreement.

This brings us to the third aspect, which is when there is a disagreement, it does not require one side or the other to be in some way deficient. Two people who are just as smart, just as well informed, just as concerned, just as compassionate, equal in whatever positive adjective you wish to specify can still disagree. They only have to differ on the question of liberty vs. equality.

While a core difference between the left and the right, it is a difference that gets very little notice, much less discussion. Both sides have reasons for why their value should have priority. Still, political disagreements are rarely discussed at that level. Instead, current political discussions get fought out on a number of different fronts, with charges and countercharges thrown back and forth, both sides demonizing the other. These battles often occur, cut off from the fundamental differences driving them.

In the tax discussion above, which is more important? Lower taxes? Lower taxes certainly means more liberty, as every dollar saved in taxes is a dollar you are free to spend as you see fit. Every dollar paid in taxes is a dollar you no longer control. Equality? Equality is a major consideration when looking at the distribution of the tax burden. Is it good to have lower taxes if the burden is not distributed equally?

OTHER VALUES

Nor are liberty and equality the only two values in conflict. There are many such conflicts. Justice and mercy conflict. Justice demands getting what you deserve. In a court of law, this could mean a long prison sentence. Mercy would argue against that. Which is more important? For many, mercy is more important, but it comes at the expense of Justice. Thus the saying, compassion for the guilty is cruelty to the innocent. What is the right balance?

Consider the question of the importance of blood relations. For some, it is extremely important. For others, it is close to irrelevant. You can see this in the issue of adoptions at birth. Are your parents the two people who conceived you and the mother who gave birth to you? Are your parents the ones who raised you to adulthood? Which is most important? Which are your "real" parents? Different people answer these questions in different ways.

Another example is the conflict between the importance of following the rules and getting the correct outcome. In our court system, we put following the rules first. At times, this will mean that the guilty go free. Some think justice is more important than following the rules, but can you have justice if you don't follow them?

A similar disagreement occurred in the Lincoln-Douglas debate over whether it was ok to oppose a ruling of the Supreme Court. The Lincoln-Douglas debates were a series of seven debates between Abraham Lincoln and Steven Douglas when they ran for Senator in Illinois. The structure of the debates was one candidate would speak for one hour. The second candidate would then speak for one and a half hours, followed by a half-hour rebuttal by the first candidate.

The case in question was the Dred Scott case, where the Supreme Court ruled 7-2 against Scott. In the first part of the majority opinion written by Chief Justice Roger Taney, the Court ruled that Scott, as "one of the African race," could not be a citizen. This statement was not grounded in the Declaration of Independence or the Constitution. Taney used his racism rather than these documents to reach this decision. In his dissent, Justice Curtis rejected the claim the Constitution was a document for the white race.

> It has already been shown that in five of the thirteen original States, colored persons then possessed the elective franchise, and were among those by whom the Constitution was ordained and established. If so, it is not true, in point of fact, that the Constitution was made exclusively by the white race.

And that it was made exclusively for the white race is, in my opinion, not only an assumption not warranted by anything in the Constitution, but contradicted by its opening declaration, that it was ordained and established by the people of the United States, for themselves and their posterity.

This part of the ruling should have ended the case. This case was only in the Supreme Court because Scott and Sanford, his owner, were citizens of different states. Yet, if Scott was not a citizen as Taney ruled, the Court had no basis upon which to proceed, still, proceed Taney did. Taney ruled that Scott, as a slave, was mere property, and Congress had no power to restrict slavery. By doing so, Taney effectively invalidated the earlier compromises. Today, legal scholars consider Dred Scott and a related ruling, Plessy v. Ferguson, to be anti-canon, mistakes by the court.

Still, at the time of the Lincoln-Douglas Debates, the Dred Scott decision was only a year old and a major issue. Douglas argued that as the highest court in the land, the Supreme Court's rulings were, to use a current phrase, settled law and could not be questioned. Speaking of Lincoln in the sixth debate, Douglas said,

> He tells you that he does not like the Dred Scott decision. Suppose he does not, how is he going to help himself? He says that he will reverse it. How will he reverse it? I know of but one mode of reversing judicial decisions, and that is by appealing from the inferior to the superior court. But I have never yet learned how or where an appeal could be taken from the Supreme Court of the United States! The Dred Scott decision was pronounced by the highest tribunal on earth. From that decision there is no appeal this side of Heaven. Yet, Mr. Lincoln says he is going to reverse that decision. By what tribunal will he reverse it? Will he appeal to a mob? Does he intend to appeal to violence, to Lynch law? Will he stir up strife and rebellion in the land and overthrow the court by violence? He does not deign to tell you how he will reverse the Dred Scott decision, but keeps appealing each day from the Supreme Court of the United States to political meetings in the country. He wants me to argue with you the merits of each point of that decision

before this political meeting. I say to you, with all due respect, that I choose to abide by the decisions of the Supreme Court as they are pronounced. It is not for me to inquire after a decision is made whether I like it in all the points or not.[80]

Lincoln, not surprisingly, argued against the court's ruling. Earlier in the debate, Lincoln said,

> We oppose the Dred Scott decision in a certain way, upon which I ought perhaps to address you a few words. We do not propose that when Dred Scott has been decided to be a slave by the court, we, as a mob, will decide him to be free. We do not propose that, when any other one, or one thousand, shall be decided by that court to be slaves, we will in any violent way disturb the rights of property thus settled, but we nevertheless do oppose that decision as a political rule, which shall be binding on the voter to vote for nobody who thinks it wrong, which shall be binding on the members of Congress or the President to favor no measure that does not actually concur with the principles of that decision. We do not propose to be bound by it as a political rule in that way, because we think it lays the foundation not merely of enlarging and spreading out what we consider an evil, but it lays the foundation for spreading that evil into the States themselves. We propose so resisting it as to have it reversed if we can, and a new judicial rule established upon this subject.[81]

Douglas argued that Supreme Court decisions were final and must be followed. Lincoln argued that while they would not oppose the decision with violence, they would still oppose it politically because it supported slavery, which "we consider an evil." In the end, the Dred Scott decision was formally overturned with the ratification of the 13th amendment. While it is over in this case, the

---

80 Douglas, S. (1858, October 13). *Sixth Debate: Quincy, Illinois*. Retrieved from Lincoln Home: https://www.nps.gov/liho/learn/historyculture/debate6.htm

81 Lincoln, A. (1858, October 13). *Sixth Debate: Quincy, Illinois*. Retrieved from Lincoln Home: https://www.nps.gov/liho/learn/historyculture/debate6.htm

Seeking Truth

issue of when to accept a ruling by the Supreme Court, or if it is proper to argue against it, remains with us on many other rulings by the court.

In addition to all these conflicting values, there is a hierarchy of values. Not everything can be number one. There is no problem when all the various principles agree, but a choice must be made when there is a conflict. One value will have to take precedence over the other.

This is sometimes a problem with advocacy groups. They see their particular cause as the most important thing. So important that a few have put it ahead of the truth. You see this in their claims about how big the problem is or how many people are affected. Yet, when you look closely at their definitions, you see they are playing fast and loose with them, thereby including many things under the heading of their issue that most people would not.

This book argues, as a general rule, truth should be our primary value. True, in rare and highly unlikely situations, life would take priority. If I hid someone from a murderer, and the murderer asked me where they were, I would not be truthful. Baring such situations that involve an immediate threat to life, truth should be paramount.

MAPPING PROBLEMS

Unfortunately, the Left-Right spectrum based on liberty and equality has a problem. While it is possible, and I believe helpful, to see the spectrum this way, it does not map to the traditional spectrum of Communists on the Left, Fascists on the Right, and Democracies in the middle. Thus the traditional spectrum is a source of discord when it comes to discussions.

An increasing emphasis on equality, groups, and big government fits the left half of the spectrum. At the far Left would be a Communist totalitarian government free of class. All property is shared, and everyone is equal, at least equal in theory. The individual, and thus liberty, do not matter; the group, i.e., the state, is all that is important.

The middle of the spectrum works as various democracies seek to balance the competing values of equality and liberty. On the right, liberty, and thus the individual, are paramount. On the far-right, equality is irrelevant, as the group does not matter. Only the individual is important. As you get to the extreme-right end of the spectrum, you eventually get to people who want complete liberty and recognize no government authority over them.

However, this presents a problem; the right simply does not make sense. How do you take increasing individuality, liberty, and small government and end up with Fascism? The problem stems from a societal misunderstanding concerning Fascism.

In terms of historical movements, Fascism is a left-wing movement. Its origins are on the left. It came from leftists trying to address problems in socialism/communism. Marx saw history as an economic struggle centered around class. The working class would rise up and overthrow their oppressors, because of the inequality. Yet, as the decades passed, that was not happening.

To make matters worse, during WWI, workers in one country fought workers in another. It seemed Marx got something wrong. As a result, some leftists branched off from traditional Marxism, making several changes in the process.

Marx had seen a universal aspect of the class struggle that went beyond borders. He wrote in *The Communist Manifesto* that "Communists everywhere support every revolutionary movement against the existing social and political order of things." He ended the Manifesto with its now-famous call for "Workers of the world unite!"

Yet, it seemed that workers would not fight for their class. Still, they would fight for their nation, so the first change was to reduce the universal aspects of class and emphasize the nation. Second, in place of class conflict, they sought more cooperation among the classes. As a result of this focus on cooperation, they also took a step back from state ownership of the means of production and merely sought total state control.

This new type of government was still socialist. They continued to reject individualism, capitalism, and liberty. However, this new form of government was a national form of socialism centered on class cooperation rather than conflict. This cooperation was aimed at building the power of the state.

Mussolini was one of the socialists who became disenchanted with what he saw as "orthodox socialism" during WWI. He wanted a new form of socialism. As a result, Mussolini formed the first fascist government, the term fascist coming from the Italian word for a bundle of sticks, symbolizing the strength of the many becoming one, i.e., the state. This is not an individualistic notion. Hitler called it National Socialism as he formed his party; the German name was soon commonly abbreviated to Nazi.

F.A. Hayek noted the similarities between Communism and Fascism in his book written during the war.

> Everyone who has watched the growth of these movements in Italy or in Germany has been struck by the number of leading men, from Mussolini downward… who began as socialist and ended as Fascist or Nazis. And what is true of the leader is even more true of the rank and file of the movements. The relative ease with which a young communist could be converted into a Nazi or vice versa was generally known in Germany, best of all to the propagandists of the two parties. Many a university teacher during the 1930's has seen English and American students return from the Continent uncertain whether they were communist or Nazis and certain only that they hated Western liberal civilization.[82]

Hayek's reference to "Western liberal civilization" is the traditional liberalism of the enlightenment, based on individualism and liberty. So how did this movement created by leftists seeking to address problems in a leftist movement and rejecting right-wing

---

82 Hayek, F. (1944). *The Road to Serfdom*. Chicago : University of Chicago Press. p. 33-34

values such as the individual, liberty, and limited government end up being seen as right-wing? The explanation is complex.

Right or Left?

Part of the problem is that few actually know the political philosophy and reasoning behind the origins of Fascism. Few even know what Fascism is beyond the Nazis and death camps. Nor do they know what makes the political spectrum. Some of this stems from the fact that as fascism emerged, the fascists and communists competed for support from the same people. This put them in direct competition with each other as their supporters came from the same groups of people and from each other. As Hayek summarized it, they "reserved for each other the hatred of the heretic."[83] This gave them the appearance of being on opposite sides.

A significant part of the answer lies in the changes to traditional socialism the Fascists made by embracing nationalism instead of class and cooperation instead of conflict. Traditional socialism had a universal, not national, focus. This led to the false conclusion that nationalism was right-wing.

Nationalism emerged in the eighteenth and nineteenth centuries, and like the countries it describes, it comes in many different forms. For some, the nation is based on ethnic or cultural lines. For others, it is centered around a set of ideas. For still others, the nation is based on arbitrary geographical or even political lines.

Like many ideas, nationalism can have positive and negative expressions. Positively it can be expressed in terms of patriotism and love of country. Negatively it can be expressed as a sense of exclusiveness or innate superiority. In those nations where ethnicity or race plays a role in national identity, this can result in discrimination or racism. This latter form of ethnic nationalism was a key part of Hitler's National Socialism, but not so much in Mussolini's Fascism.

---

83 Hayek, F. (1944). *The Road to Serfdom*. Chicago : University of Chicago Press. p. 34

Neither left nor right-wing, nationalism is found on both sides of the political spectrum. Just as there are right-wing nationalists, there are left-wing nationalists. The latter are now usually referred to as social nationalists to distinguish them from national socialists or fascists. Just as there are supporters of nationalism on both sides, there are also those opposed to nationalism on both sides, particularly at the extremes. The far-left rejects nationalism in favor of universalism. At the far right of the spectrum, rather than increasing nationalism, you have a growing mistrust of government. For example, the Oklahoma City bombers were right-wing extremists opposed to the government.

Nationalism, if anything, is found in the middle of the political spectrum. It weakens as you move to either of the extremes. Viewed from the far left, this gives nationalism a right-wing appearance. Considered from the far right, nationalism would appear to be left-wing. What made Nazis unique was not nationalism per se but a strongly ethnic form of nationalism combined with the normal left-wing value of centralized state power, which made it particularly toxic.

Mussolini's other major change was to focus more on cooperation among the classes rather than conflict. Because of this, he did not attack corporate and monied interests like traditional socialists. This was not because he supported capitalism. He and other fascists didn't, far from it. Rather than any sort of free market, they wanted a market completely controlled by the state. As Mussolini put it, "Everything in the State, nothing outside the State, nothing against the State." This is a line of thinking that comes from the Left with its roots going back to Rousseau. Thus neither of Mussolini's changes put Fascism on the right.

Others point to Hitler's purging of left-wing parties once taking power as a sign that he was right-wing. While plausible at one level, the problem is that Hitler eliminated all political parties and leaders, not just those on the Left. The more his power grew, the more he eliminated any potential opposition.

Once Hitler had eliminated threats outside the party, he proceeded to eliminate any possible threat within his party. In July 1934, in what has come to be called the Night of the Long Knives, he had a thousand potential threats from within his party arrested; many were murdered. The left-wing movements were hardly unique in Hitler's purging of opponents.

Some of it stems from a simplistic view of WWII. While Communists and Fascists started the war on the same side, Hitler eventually broke with and invaded the Soviet Union. Thus, by the end of the war, Fascism and Communism were on opposite sides. Since they were on opposite sides of the war, why not put them on opposite sides of the political spectrum.

There was also a sense of balance in the conventional view, with problems at both extremes. Some of it comes from the Left's horror at the Concentration camps and the understandable desire to see Nazism, and thus Fascism, as something on the other side.

It should be noted that when it comes to Hitler and the Nazi party, there is a problem with seeing them as part of the political spectrum at all. While Mussolini's Fascism can be understood as a political movement, Hitler and the Nazis might be better seen as a criminal enterprise. One that used Fascism to gain power during the suffering caused by the Great Depression, driven more by hatred and ambition than any well-thought-out political ideology. Whatever the reasons, now conventional wisdom holds that Fascism is a right-wing movement.

Problems

This view, of course, leads to all sorts of problems. As mentioned above, if you start in the center with the right-wing values of liberty, individualism, and limited government and start moving right, these values become more pronounced. This makes sense as you move from those considered moderates to various forms of conservatism and then to the various forms of libertarianism. The more to the right you go, the more you get liberty, increased individualism, and even smaller government.

This progression makes sense, and there are certainly people who fit all the various locations along the spectrum. It also helps answer questions such as; what is the difference between a conservative and a Libertarian? But where is the room for Fascism?

At what point as you go right, do you start moving towards Fascism? Put another way, at what point as you move towards smaller and smaller government do you approach totalitarianism? The simple answer is you don't, and therein lies the problem with the conventional view. It is nonsensical.

While nonsensical, it is also widely accepted. One attempt to fix the problem sees the spectrum as a horseshoe with the two ends close to each other. But that is a description, not an explanation. Why and how does it curve? Others try redefining 'right-wing' to be more in line with fascism instead of the values of liberty, individualism, and smaller government. One can certainly do that, but this just creates a different set of problems.

Where do people who embrace liberty, individualism, and smaller government to various degrees fit on the spectrum? The problem becomes, why are they called right-wing? Others, realizing the similarities, distinguish between the collectivist right (Fascism) and the collectivist left (Communism). Again the problem becomes what to do with the non-collectivists, i.e., the various forms of individualism, particularly its extreme forms. How do they fit?

One obvious option is to correct the conventional understanding and place Fascism on the Left where it belongs, perhaps as an aberration. The spectrum would then become coherent with various forms of anarchist individualism on the far-Right and various forms of totalitarianism on the far-Left. In the middle, you end up with the various democracies seeking ways to balance liberty and equality, struggling over the government's proper size.

If only it were that easy. Conventional wisdom is not easy to change at any time. It is even harder when there are people invested in the status quo. Far too many people on the Left are emotionally invested in Fascism being "on the other side." They have lived their lives seeing Fascism as a danger from the right to change so easily.

Of course, conventional wisdom leads to its own absurdity, not the least of which is Antifa. The name comes from Anti-Fascist. They are a left-wing group believing they are opposing Fascism by attacking those on the Right. Yet their tactics and methods are eerily similar to the Fascists of the 1930s. Of course, as members of the Left, they don't think they have to worry about that; after all, they are just using the Fascist's own tactics against them. However, if they ever realize that Fascism was, in reality, a left-wing movement, they might see that they had themselves become what they were attacking.

Finally, there is the problem of where to put what have traditionally been considered Right-wing dictatorships. Where do they fit? The simple answer is, again, they don't. There is no natural extension of liberty as a political idea leading to a Right-Wing dictatorship; there is no place along the Left-Right spectrum where they would fit.

One possible solution to both the problem of right-wing dictatorships and the problem of Nazism is to see them as aberrations not fitting on the Left-Right spectrum at all. As mentioned above, while Italian Fascism fits on the left, Nazism is better seen as a criminal enterprise than a political philosophy. Likewise, dictators are not driven by well-thought-out political theories but by a desire to gain and hold power. Rather than an extension of political ideas, they are more a corruption of them.

They would be best seen as existing on a spectrum separate from the normal Left-Right spectrum that is centered around liberty and equality. Instead of Liberty and equality, a spectrum for dictators would be based on the degree of control. One end would have the authoritarian dictators whose main concern is their immediate power and wealth. In such regimes, as long as you do not challenge that, dictators are unconcerned. It also means they don't care, and as such, those under their control are often left to suffer in poverty.

At the other end of the spectrum are totalitarian dictators. They believe they must control most aspects of life to preserve their power. Under a totalitarian dictator, you have more opportunities to come into conflict with those in power. Still, you are also more likely to have things like healthcare and education than under authoritarian dictators.

Instead of one political spectrum, there are two. Democracies tend to operate in the Left-Right spectrum. In contrast, dictatorships are better understood as operating on a spectrum based on the degree of control from authoritarian to totalitarian. With any given government, you first determine if it is a democracy or dictatorship to determine the spectrum to use, and then determine where it fits on that particular spectrum.

One potential source of confusion is there is some overlap between the Left-Right spectrum and the Authoritarian-Totalitarian spectrum. As you move from right to left on the Left-Right spectrum, you move from a smaller government to a larger and more powerful one. At the extreme Right, you have anarchy, while at the far Left, you have Left-Wing totalitarian government. The Left-Wing totalitarian government fits on both spectrums and can be seen as an intersection between them. However, many on the left would claim an actual dictatorship is a corruption of the political ideas of the Left.

This intersection is undoubtedly behind the authoritarian being seen as Right-wing. If you have only a single spectrum, where else would you place them? Yet if you view dictatorships as fundamentally different from democracies, it becomes clear they do not fit on a spectrum used to describe the differences between various democracies.

These two spectrums give us a way to understand and talk about differences between political groups and governments. It would certainly make more sense, giving us a way of understanding political battles without demonizing the other side. While there are people at various positions, the numbers of people advocating for either extreme are exceedingly small. They thus can be ignored, particularly in democracies such as the United States.

As such, labels such as Communist, Fascist, and Anarchist are almost always wrong. That someone wants a larger, more centralized government does not mean they want a totalitarian dictatorship.

That someone wants a smaller, more limited government does not mean they want anarchy. Such labels detract from the real issues dividing people and only get in the way of discussions. They should be avoided.

Three Lessons

There are three lessons in the preceding examples. The first is two people can have significant disagreements over important issues without being deficient in some fashion. For example, suppose someone uses one meaning for "tax burden" while others use a different one. In that case, disagreements can, and probably will, occur. Likewise, differences will occur if one person values equality more than liberty, while another values liberty over equality. Many such areas can lead to disagreements without either side being either wrong or bad in some way.

Second, these also show life is complex. Our views are an amalgam of facts, opinions, distortions, and even errors. Errors can be so ingrained into our thinking they are very hard to correct. While it might be tempting to see these problems as only existing with 'others,' the simple fact is no one is perfect.

Finally, many disagreements are multi-layered. Many people will defend positions without understanding the foundational beliefs upon which they are based. In fact, they may even reject the foundational beliefs, which would render their position incoherent. Yet they defend their position anyway.

The solution for all of these problems is an honest, open discussion. A discussion clarifying definitions and exploring the underlying foundation for various beliefs. Sadly, it is becoming increasingly difficult. As our technology has made communication easier, our attitudes have made it more difficult. Still, it is possible to seek truth while trying to avoid error. We may not always settle every disagreement, but we can at least come to a better understanding of why the disagreements exist.

Chapter 7

Disagreeing Agreeably

Truth does not become more true by virtue of the fact that the entire world agrees with it, nor less so even if the whole world disagrees with it. – Maimonides

He who cannot put his thoughts on ice should not enter into the heat of dispute. – Nietzsche

The last chapter ended by arguing that discussions are vital and important for anyone who sincerely seeks truth. The most important aspect of a discussion is the ability to disagree agreeably. It may also be the most difficult. Not only does it ask a lot from you, but it also depends on others, something not completely under your control.

Any real discussion of any substance whose goal is truth will inevitably involve disagreement. Granted, not all discussions need to be substantial, nor do they need to seek truth. There are any number of valid reasons for discussions not falling into this category. For example, much of the discussion taking place among friends need not be placed into this category. Nor is this type of discussion relevant when there is a vast difference in expertise, such as seeking legal advice from a lawyer or medical advice from a doctor. After all, if you do not trust the advice the expert is giving you, why are you there seeking it?

While you can discuss any number of topics for many different reasons, your views are not being tested unless there is disagreement. Talking with those who agree tends to reinforce your views, not test them, regardless of whether they are correct. It is the process of testing one's ideas that is important. Prior to the enlightenment, many people had a range of ideas about how the world worked.

Many were wrong. The scientific method brought the concept of testing those ideas to see if they were true.

The more the disagreement, the greater the test. Perhaps there is no disagreement because what you believe is true, and everyone knows it. Perhaps there is no disagreement because everyone is wrong. As discussed in chapter one, the Ptolemaic system was accepted and taught for over a thousand years. Of course it was true that the sun, moon, and stars circled the earth. One just had to look that the sky to see that. You can see that they appear on one horizon, travel across the sky, and set on the other. They moved at different speeds. Still, there was some strange behavior. Sometimes, a planet would stop and move backward in relation to the stars for a short period of time before resuming its normal direction.

All this was known to be true long before it began to be studied systematically. The earliest traces of what could be called the science of astronomy are found in the First Babylonian Dynasty, nearly 2000 years before the time of Christ. The early Greeks further developed and refined this model. Still, the masterwork on the subject was *The Almagest*, written by Claudius Ptolemy sometime after 150 AD in Egypt. The Ptolemaic system explained all this and allowed people to predict where the celestial bodies would be at any given time. It was accepted and worked for over a thousand years.

A Change in Perspective

Then came Nicolas Copernicus to challenge what everyone could see with their own eyes in his book *On the Revolutions of the Heavenly Spheres* in 1543. Copernicus was not the first to question the generally accepted view. As observational tools and techniques had improved, some issues began to arise with the Ptolemaic system. Still, Copernicus was the first to lay out a complete and detailed alternative, a heliocentric view, rather than the Ptolemaic geocentric view.

Copernicus's theory soon found a number of supporters, the most notable being Galileo. But, likewise, the older and more established Ptolemaic system had its supporters as well. Conventional history portrays this as a clash between science and religion, but things were hardly that neat and tidy. Galileo did clash with the Catholic church, which attempted to suppress the new theory, something the Catholic Church would later regret.

Still, by the time of Galileo, the Reformation was about a hundred years old, and many Protestant theologians supported the new view. On the other hand, Galileo also faced opposition from the Aristotelean professors at the local university and had some supporters within the Catholic Church. In short, there were the religiously and scientifically minded on both sides of the question.

Nor was the case for the heliocentric system as straightforward as it appears now. Defenders of the Ptolemaic system asked if the earth is spinning, why we don't notice it? Why is it when you drop an object, it goes straight down? Why doesn't it land to one side as the earth spins underneath it?

Galileo responded that everything is spinning, even the objects you drop, so it only appears to go straight down because it rotates as it drops along with the earth. While a reasonable and, even better, a correct explanation, it also argues we cannot tell we are moving.

This lack of evidence of spin was a problem, for it argued for something that could not be detected. Galileo did point to one piece of evidence for the earth's rotation, the rising and falling tides in the ocean. Of course, now we know Galileo was wrong about the tides. They are the result of the moon's gravitation, not the spinning of the earth, and the moon is one object that does rotate around the earth.

As a result, Galileo argued we should abandon a system that had worked for a thousand years for a new theory. Unfortunately, one of his key pieces of evidence for making this change was wrong. It would not be until 1851 that Leon Foucault devised an experiment showing the earth was both round and spins on its axis. Foucault suspended a 62 lb. ball on a cable, swinging it back and forth. As it swung back and forth, the endpoint of each swing seemed to move. However, it was not the endpoint moving, but rather the earth spinning beneath it.

Still, it did not take until 1851 for the geocentric system to be replaced by the heliocentric. Copernicus's system was much simpler than Ptolemy's. Over time the evidence grew and convinced more people until it became the accepted norm, replacing the Ptolemaic system. Later scientific discoveries would show the whole system was much more complex than envisioned by Copernicus, while Einstein showed that the choice of a coordinate system was somewhat arbitrary. It did not really matter if you picked a geocentric or heliocentric system. Both systems could be made to work.

LESSONS

The preceding example has many lessons when it comes to disagreement and truth. The first and perhaps most important is we should be cautious about what we think we know. Neither side was completely right nor completely wrong. The earth is not the center of the universe, and the Copernican system is much better. Still, Galileo's pointing to ocean tides to demonstrate the earth's movement was wrong. Ultimately, the truth was more complex than anyone at the time knew.

Second, a lot depends on what you mean by true, if your goal is pragmatic, to have a system that can predict where the celestial bodies will be at a given time, the Ptolemaic system did that well. Sure, problems were beginning to appear, but there were problems with the Copernican system as well. Ultimately both systems are conceptual models. Einstein would eventually show that accurate predictions could be made in either system.

To see this, consider the question, what time is sunrise tomorrow morning? Both systems can provide the same answer to this question, so in what sense is one system true when it says sunrise will be at 6:46 AM, and the other is false when it says the sun will rise at 6:46 AM? One can certainly argue the Copernican system more accurately models what the celestial bodies do. Still, in some respects, this takes us back to the first point. The Copernican system also had its problems, so perhaps it would be better to say it has fewer errors than the Ptolemaic.

THE PROBLEMS OF SUPPRESSION

The real lesson in this incident is that suppression rarely works and is often counterproductive when it comes to questions of truth. Atheists often point to Galileo as a victim of religion and the Copernican system's eventual adoption as the triumph of science over religion, but that is hardly an accurate analysis. As mentioned earlier, there were religiously and scientifically minded people on both sides of the controversy.

Rather than a conflict between science and religion, this is better understood as a conflict between an established view and a challenger. Sadly, history is full of examples of established views seeking to build barriers against or even suppressing alternatives. In some respects, the story of Galileo's challenge to the establishment parallels that of Alfred Lothar Wegener and his theory of Continental Drift mentioned in chapter one or Ohm and Ohm's Law mentioned in chapter four. While Wegener was not imprisoned, he was effectively driven from the field of Geology. He had to leave his country to find a university that would hire him, and then only in meteorology.

Nor is this just a problem with well-entrenched views backed by a power structure. Small fringe groups can also resort to suppression among their members lest they be "corrupted." We all do it to some extent. For some, this takes the form of trying to ignore alternative points of view. For those with power, this can be a formal ban. They can have the opposition arrested, if they have police power. For those with less power, it may just be getting people to avoid those with whom they disagree.

Down through history, the desire to suppress opposing points of view seems to be the norm. The emergence of notions of freedom of speech and freedom of religion in Western cultures was long, difficult, and rarely complete. Even in the United States, where freedom of speech and religion are spelled out in the Constitution, historical examples of suppression are sadly all too common. Evelyn Beatrice Hall summed up the pinnacle of free speech in a biography of Voltaire. She described his attitude as, "I disapprove of what you say, but I will defend to the death your right to say it."[84]

In recent years, we have begun to move away from Voltaire's standard. The tendency to suppress has become common with bans on so-called hate speech and the emergence of Cancel Culture. In one sense, this is different. Rather than the government suppressing speech, now it is large corporations and groups. Yet, in many ways, it is still the same. Those who have the power to suppress opposing points of view do so because they can.

Whatever the means, this sort of suppression is extremely harmful to any open discussion and thus any search for truth. It creates an atmosphere of intimidation where people are afraid to express what they believe. Suppression is not an argument. It is a tactic, and without the ability to discuss our differences, we will never understand why some people disagree. Rather than moderating our differences as we seek a common understanding, we exacerbate them. As a result, our differences become more extreme, and the search for common ground and understanding even harder.

Conflict

An example of this in America was the issue of slavery. Slavery was the norm throughout most of human history. However, with the enlightenment's views on liberty and individualism, slavery was starting to be questioned in the 18th century. This change coincided with the American Revolution, as typified by the life of Benjamin Franklin. Earlier in his life, Franklin had owned a slave. By the end

---

[84] Sylvester, B. (2019, September 17). *FACT CHECK: DID VOLTAIRE SAY, 'I MAY DISAPPROVE OF WHAT YOU SAY, BUT I WILL DEFEND TO THE DEATH YOUR RIGHT TO SAY IT'?* Retrieved from CheckYourFact: https://checkyourfact.com/2019/09/17/fact-check-voltaire-disapprove-defend-death-right-freedom-speech/

of his life, he condemned slavery. At the time of the Constitutional Convention, he was president of an abolitionist society working both to free slaves and to improve the lives of former slaves.

As differences of opinion occur, either one side wins, or some compromise must be achieved. At the time of the Constitutional Convention, neither side was strong enough to prevail on the issue of slavery. The result was the three-fifths compromise for determining representation and taxes. With the changing attitudes at the time of the convention, many expected slavery to disappear over the coming decades. Some in the south saw slavery as a regrettable part of the human condition or even a necessary evil. Some slaveholders even struggled with how to eliminate it. That did not happen and instead attitudes concerning slavery changed with time.

Early in the nineteenth century, a new view arose. This new view saw slavery not as a necessary evil and regrettable but as a positive good. Like John C. Calhoun, some explicitly rejected the Declaration's claim that "all men are created equal." Calhoun called this claim a "great error." He argued that it lay dormant in the Declaration of Independence but had "began to germinate, and produce its poisonous fruits."

As a result, slavery came to dominate the nation's politics. While there was a lot of discussion within the camps, there was not much between them. Given the inherent conflict between the principles upon which the country was founded and the existence of slavery, only two resolutions were possible; change the principles or eliminate slavery.

This issue came to the forefront whenever the country grew. Would the new states or territories be slave or free? This outcome would determine if the country would be on a path to eliminate or embrace slavery. Instead of a national resolution, compromises were struck, such as the Missouri Compromise (1820-21), allowing the nation to grow half slave half free.

This disagreement between the pro-slavery movement and the abolitionist movement continued. Such disputes can only be settled by discussion or conflict, words or force. It is also pretty clear which side avoided discussion and wanted force.

Elijah Lovejoy was a Presbyterian pastor, abolitionist, and editor of the St. Louis Observer who used his paper as a platform to condemn slavery. Pro-slavery forces did not want a conversation. They wanted slavery and sought to suppress the abolitionists. As a result, his presses were destroyed three times. However, Lovejoy did not stop and continued to condemn slavery. On November 7, 1837, another mob sought to destroy his presses for the fourth time. In the process, Lovejoy was killed.

The Compromise of 1850 was followed by the Kansas-Nebraska Act (1854), yet another attempt at compromise that was less successful. It resulted in a series of violent confrontations referred to as Bleeding Kansas. As the discussion became more difficult or at least less effective, violence grew.

The Supreme Court's ruling in the Dred Scott case (1857) made the discussion even more difficult. In its ruling, the court held that Scott could not be a citizen, and as a slave, was mere property. As a Supreme Court ruling, the issue was removed from the realm of political debate and placed with the courts. Thus as we saw in the Lincoln-Douglas debate, Douglas would not discuss it. As a ruling by the Supreme Court, he considered the matter settled.

According to the ruling, written by Chief Justice Roger Taney, Congress had no power to restrict slavery. Taney tried to settle the slavery issue that had plagued the country since its founding and used his power on the Supreme Court to force the resolution he wanted. Instead of settling the issue, he only exacerbated matters.

This conflict led Abraham Lincoln, then the Republican candidate for Senate, to give his House Divided speech. In the speech, Lincoln predicted the conflict over slavery would continue.

> In my opinion, it will not cease, until a crisis shall have been reached, and passed. "A house divided against itself cannot stand." I believe this government cannot endure, permanently half slave and half free. I do not expect the Union to be dissolved -- I do not expect the House to fall -- but I do expect it

Seeking Truth

will cease to be divided. It will become all one thing or all the other. Either the opponents of slavery, will arrest the further spread of it, and place it where the public mind shall rest in the belief that it is in the course of ultimate extinction; or its advocates will push it forward, till it shall become alike lawful in all the States, old as well as new -- North as well as South.

When Lincoln was elected President, the southern states did not wait for him to take office and began to secede. On April 12, 1861, a South Carolina militia began the attack on Fort Sumter, which started the Civil War. When the war was over four years later, 620,000 were dead in America's deadliest conflict. Along with all the other costs, this death toll was a very high price for failing to discuss our differences and reach an agreement.

HOW TO DISAGREE AGREEABLY

As to our differences, we can ignore them, discuss them, or have conflict over them. Given these options, discussion is the best. Yet, it is currently getting harder. A 2020 survey by the Cato Institute found most Americans, 62 percent, are afraid to share at least some of their political views.[85] This is up significantly from 2017. Is it any wonder the country is so polarized? If we do not talk with people who disagree, they cease to be people in many respects. They cease to be our friends, neighbors, co-workers, nice people who happen to hold differing opinions but instead become labels. Republicans, Democrats, Conservatives, Liberals, Socialists, Capitalists, or whatever divides us. From there, it is so much easier to demonize them, as a label is easier to demonize than a person you know.

A common reaction to this polarization is to blame the other side. However true the charge might be, in the long run, it is not helpful. Besides, there is plenty of blame to go around. The only

---

85 Ekins, E. (2020, July 22). *Poll: 62% of Americans Say They ahve Political Views They're Afraid to Share*. Retrieved from Cato Insitute: https://www.cato.org/survey-reports/poll-62-americans-say-they-have-political-views-theyre-afraid-share

real solution will be for both sides to begin talking again. A few already do this; still, the number needs to be much larger.

Ideally, open and honest discussion should be the norm, particularly in a democracy, rather than an exception if we are going to get past the labels and barriers we have created and understand people. We must understand the reasons they hold the views they do. This effort is not easy, and it will take both sides. The first step is to become someone who can disagree agreeably. You should avoid five things and do nine. All of these are just common sense. Still, it is amazing how quickly they are forgotten when one gets caught up in a discussion.

Avoid a Loud Voice

The first one is fairly obvious; avoid raising your voice. Sadly, some people respond to disagreement by increasing the volume of their voice rather than the cogency of their argument. This makes any discussion virtually impossible and thus is to be avoided. Sometimes the line between appropriate passion and inappropriate emotion is not so clear. Nietzsche's warning cited at the beginning of this chapter is sound advice. "He who cannot put his thoughts on ice should not enter into the heat of dispute."[86] If a subject is too emotional for you, find other things to discuss.

Avoid Negative Personal Statements

The second is to avoid negative statements about people. Nothing will cause a discussion to deteriorate faster than personally criticizing the other person. Not only does it make discussions difficult, but it also risks falling into the logical fallacy of ad hominem attack and therefore being irrational. You may seem to win a tactical victory by using them. Yet, such irrational arguments hardly form a solid foundation upon which to build a position.

---

86 Nietzsche, F. (1878). *Human, All too Human: A book for Free Spirits*.

Avoiding personal criticism can be somewhat tricky. You may be criticizing a public figure personally for supporting a policy, not the person with whom you are talking. Yet, if the person you are talking with also supports that policy, you have just attacked them personally as well, whether you intended to or not. Instead of attacking the person, just say why the policy is bad. In short, it is the policy that matters, not the person. This is why ad hominem attacks fall into the broader category of fallacies of irrelevance.

Avoid Unwarranted Labels

The third thing to avoid is labeling those with whom you are talking. Nothing is more absurd than when I have been in discussions with someone, and they are trying to explain what I really believe as if they knew better than I did. This inevitably stems from labels, where what I believe does not align with what they think I am supposed to believe because of a label. The misuse of labels has resulted in some trying to reject all labels. This is impossible. All words are labels. Get rid of all labels, and you get rid of all communication.

We use Republican, Democrat, rich, poor, etc., to refer to various groups, and properly so. Still, when in a discussion, it is important to realize you are talking with an individual person, not a group label. Lots of people are Democrats; lots are Republicans; many are something else. No individual is perfectly a Republican or Democrat. In fact, not all Democrats agree, neither do all Republicans. You must allow them to be who they are, when talking to someone, and not try to force them into a position because that is what the label says they should believe.

Avoid Conflation

Fourth, avoid conflating issues. Most issues are complex and made up of many considerations needing to be broken down and considered. If this was not hard enough, people will sometimes combine seemingly related issues to strengthen their case. For example, the issues of abortion in general and partial-birth abortion are related but separate. While some people oppose all abortion or support all abortions, others support abortion in general but oppose partial-birth abortion. These are separate issues and should be considered separately.

Yet, in discussions, these two issues are often conflated by both sides. Those who are Pro-choice conflate them because it is easier to defend abortion in general than partial-birth abortion. Those who are Pro-life conflate them because it is easier to criticize partial-birth abortion than abortion in general. The result is that, at times, both sides are not actually discussing the same thing despite appearances. Both sides are talking about abortion, but the pro-choice side is defending abortion in general, while the pro-life side is attacking partial-birth abortion. Neither side is really talking to the other. They are talking past each other, like two trains traveling on different tracks.

Avoid Reactive Thinking

Finally, reactive thinking is when you react to phrases or words, often emotionally, rather than the argument's substance. At times, it seems like you are not in a discussion as getting a list of pre-programmed responses. Mention something in an argument, and it triggers a given response. Mentioning something else triggers a different response. When this happens, the discussion becomes a disjointed series of reactions rather than a coherent series of arguments and responses.

For example, you could be discussing any number of topics when you mention a controversial person. This sparks a reaction in the person you are talking to as they go into how they like/don't like that person. For example, I am sure that some readers reacted negatively to the discussion on Context in chapter five because the example mentioned Trump and Biden. You know you have reactive thinking if their comments don't actually deal with the substance of your argument. There is a difference between reacting to an argument and responding to it. Our goal should always be to respond.

Realize Your Fallibility

As for the things you should do, the first and perhaps most important thing is the realization, strangely enough, you do not know everything. I say 'strangely enough' because this is a proposition with which virtually everyone will agree, at least in the abstract. Yet, this proposition is often quickly forgotten when there is a disagreement, then it becomes, 'I am right; you are wrong.'

As we have seen, rarely are things that simple. Issues are too complex; the data available is too varied. If someone makes an argument challenging your position, don't automatically reject it. Ask for a source rather than saying it is wrong, when they cite a statistic conflicting with your perspective. You can always check it out later, but tentatively accept and ask yourself how that would impact your belief as a default. Is this a fact for which you need to account? A nuance you need to consider?

Be a Listener

The second thing is to be a listener. We have almost certainly all seen, or even been a part of, discussions where both sides were trying so hard to make their points that neither side was listening to the other. As a result, the discussion goes nowhere. Such disputes often generate a lot of heat but rarely any light.

By listening, you can better understand why someone could hold a position you see as unsupportable. Perhaps, it only seems unsupportable because there are things you are not considering. Being a listener not only makes discussions more enjoyable, it can also be a very effective means of persuasion. By carefully listening to the concerns, arguments, and data on the other side, you can better see the weaknesses in their position. A good question based on careful listening can often be far more effective at changing someone's views than a good argument in favor of what you believe.

Be a Learner

Third, be a learner. Approach discussions with the realistic prospect that you will not change any minds. Still, you will probably learn something. Do this, and things will be better off all around. I have had many discussions with people over the years. Some of these discussions were with people with whom I generally agreed. Some were with people with whom I had major disagreements.

While I may have influenced people a bit one way or the other, rarely have I ever knowingly changed someone's mind. Yet, I have normally learned something. I learned data and perspectives that I did not know. I then incorporated these into my views, giving them more nuance. For example, say I support a particular bill before Congress. When talking with someone who opposes the bill, I may not change my mind, but I may think the law should be more carefully written to account for the factors I had not considered.

Seek Clarity over Agreement

The fourth comes from talk show host Dennis Prager. One of the guiding principles of his show is clarity over agreement. Issues are complex. Often there are many things to consider and enough ambiguity in a disagreement that neither side completely understands what the other actually believes. In many, if not most, in-depth discussions I have had, the discussion has ended up uncovering a lot more agreement than disagreement. On a few occasions, the disagreement disappeared completely. After all the factors and nuances were understood, we actually agreed. The initial disagreement centered more on the different ways we had summarized our position than on anything substantive.

Seeking Truth

Despite this, most discussions end in disagreement. At the end of the discussion, we have not changed each other's minds; we still vote for different candidates or take opposite positions on a particular issue. Yet, we understand each other better. Too often, we see those who disagree as strawman versions of what they believe. We fill in our ignorance with caricatures of their actual beliefs that we can easily reject. Seeking clarity dismantles such false images. Strangely enough, a better understanding of what someone believes can make the position easier to reject and refute. At other times it requires us to modify our position to account for information we had not considered. It is always beneficial, if the goal is truth.

Assume the best

Often in a discussion, multiple explanations can be given for people's views and actions. Some will be good; some will be not so good. Someone might support a particular policy because they generally believe it is the best policy that will do the most good. Or perhaps they oppose a new program because they generally believe it will do more harm than good. On the other hand, they may hold the positions they do because of selfish reasons.

Assume the best intentions for those who disagree with you, when in doubt. Never assume that just because someone disagrees with you, they must have negative motives. Even when there is a clear problem you should assume the lease worse possibility. As one saying puts it, never attribute to mendaciousness what can be attributed to incompetence. You may reach that as a conclusion, but only if there is clear evidence. Mere disagreement is not enough.

Keep a Realistic Perspective

Six, keep a realistic perspective. Unless you are in a very special situation, your discussion will not change the world. While the subject may be significant, your discussion probably is not. There is no need for the argument to get heated. Your discussion will not determine the outcome of world peace. It will probably not even change any minds. Granted, you are not in complete control of this. It is best to change the subject to something less contentious, when a discussion does begin to get heated, or if that is not possible, to politely retreat.

Allow the Other Person to be Wrong

Seventh, let the other person be wrong. If the expectation going in is that you probably will not change someone's mind, it is much easier to agree to disagree. At some point, the discussion will likely reach an impasse. It can legitimately happen for many reasons. Perhaps there is a disagreement on data, and further research is needed to determine who is correct. Perhaps there is a difference of values, as discussed in the last chapter. Perhaps one person tilts towards liberty, the other equality. One person might see the outcome as more important, another the process. Whatever the reasons, impasses will occur. You may still think they are wrong, but it is best to agree to disagree when there is no clear path to proceed. After all, there is always the possibility it is you who are wrong.

Reflect

Much of the above comes under the broader heading of humility. We will all admit we are not perfect and make mistakes. Still, we do not always talk like that, particularly in contentious discussions. Keeping a sense of humility is very important and can help with the eighth thing to do, reflect on discussions. What did you learn? What do you need to learn? How do you need to change? What could you do better? Asking such questions is very difficult to do in the middle of a discussion, but far easier afterward. What points did they make for which you did not have a good answer? If you did not, why not? What points did you make that were not very effective? If not, why not.

While you can ask these questions to become a better debater, it is far better to ask them to seek true answers. For example, suppose you never find anything needing correction, nothing you need to account for in your position. In that case, this is either a sign that you are perfect or that you are not really listening to what others are saying. This leads to the ninth and final point.

Admit Errors

Be willing to admit error, at least to yourself. It is better, all around, if in the middle of a discussion you can admit you were wrong on a point, or correspondingly that a point made by someone you disagree with was a good one. Nothing encourages real discussion better than the sense that both sides listen to each other and seek truth over winning. Of course, in and of themselves, such concessions do not guarantee the discussion will arrive at the truth. Still, there is a far better chance of doing so than when both sides are locked solidly to their position, neither willing to give on even the smallest point. Thus, not only is admitting error important, error itself has an important role to play in truth, which is the subject of the next chapter.

Chapter 8

The Importance of Error

The margin of error of the human condition is often our greatest area of excellence and discovery. – Stewart Stafford

In all science, error precedes the truth, and it is better it should go first than last. – Horace Walpole

We all make mistakes. Sometimes we are in error. It is both a simple and a profound fact of life. It is simple in that virtually everyone will acknowledge this to be true. It is profound because it demonstrates there is such a thing as truth. While, in theory, truth could exist without error, error cannot exist without truth. Truth is what is. Truth is reality. Error is a lack of truth; it is, as Aristotle put it, to say something is, when it is not, or is not when it is. So, while truth is defined in terms of reality, error is defined in terms of truth. Therefore, for there to be error, there must be truth.

That we all make mistakes is a given. It is universal. While we may lament such a condition, it is hardly that significant. What is significant is not that we make mistakes. Rather, it is what we do next. Do we steadfastly hold on to them or try to correct them? If the latter, how do we go about it? These are closely tied to perspective, and you can see this in the different types of businesses. In my career, I have over the years worked for many different businesses and organizations. When it comes to error, there are two main types, though some are a mixture. On the one hand, you have a blame-oriented organization. If you make a mistake, you are punished; potentially, you could get fired.

The worse business meeting I ever had the pleasure of being a part of attempted to create a project plan. The manager leading the meeting clearly had a blame-oriented mentality. An unstated but controlling assumption of the meeting was that the project was going to fail. There simply was not enough time or resources to complete it in the time allotted.

For an hour, the manager attempted to break down the project into clear, definable tasks tied to particular people. This goal was not, in and of itself, a problem. The problem was he wanted to do this so that one person could be held responsible when the project ultimately failed. Still, there were too many variables, too many people involved, and too many interrelations among all the tasks. As a result, no such clear lines of blame could be drawn.

Making matters worse, at least for the manager, many of the people who could potentially end up responsible were in the meeting. No one wanted to be the one left with the blame. As such, they were very clear about all the contingencies with the tasks assigned to them. As the meeting progressed, the manager became more and more frustrated. Finally, the meeting ended in failure. Creating the schedule of blame was not completed, to the great relief of most in the meeting.

The other type of organization is success-oriented. In these organizations, the existence of mistakes is seen as a given to be minimized. When a problem occurs, blame is not a major consideration unless it is needlessly repeated. Rather than focusing on placing blame, the focus is on developing a solution. If the problem is likely to reoccur, there is also consideration given to reducing them in the future. Such organizations use problems, not as an opportunity to assess blame, but to seek continual improvement. In doing so, they normally run better than blame-oriented organizations. They can do this because they see errors as normal and opportunities to learn and improve.

An additional advantage is success-oriented organizations are very likely to identify problems much earlier. Since they are identified earlier, they can be dealt with while they are smaller and more easily handled. On the other hand, blame-oriented organizations foster an atmosphere where problems are more likely to be hidden.

Seeking Truth 147

Perhaps, no one will notice, is often the hopeful attitude. When problems are finally noticed, they tend to be bigger and costlier.

Steps Towards Truth

There are other reasons why errors are important in the search for truth. When you start, all you have are possibilities. You can stop there and say, 'I don't know.' Or you can develop theories about what is going on. There is a very high probability your first attempts will be wrong. You will be in error. Still, if you or someone else shows your claim is mistaken, the possibilities are narrowed. Your mistakes become the first steps towards the truth.

On July 19, 1595, Johannes Kepler was teaching mathematics when he thought he had an amazing insight that geometrical shapes might relate to the orbits of the planets. Eventually, he settled on the Platonic solids. Platonic solids are 3-dimensional objects where all the sides are identical, and since at least the time of the ancient Greeks, it was known that there are only five. As far as Kepler knew, there were only six planets. Between the six planets, there would be five spaces. Kepler's insight was, what if these five spaces were related to the five platonic solids?

Of course, Kepler was mistaken. We could blame him for not knowing what we know now. If for nothing else, there are more than six planets. Still, the seventh, Uranus, would not be discovered for another 186 years. So, from Kepler's point of view, this was as good an explanation as any, especially given the new Copernican theory published just 52 years earlier and still being debated, that the planets revolve around the sun, not the earth. Kepler's book laying out his new theory, the *Mysterium Cosmograhicum*, was also the first published defense of Copernicus and improved the theory. Galileo's conflict with the Catholic church was still several decades in the future.

If Kepler had stopped there, he probably would have remained little more than a footnote in history. But he didn't. Instead, Kepler tried to confirm his theory. He started by comparing where his theory said the planets should be with the observed position of the planets. It was close but not close enough for confirmation. Still, measuring the position of the planets in the night sky was itself imprecise. So was the error in Kepler's theory or the poor measurements available to him? To settle the issue, he sought out the astronomer who had the best available data, Tycho Brahe. Kepler went to work for him, and when Brahe died in October 1601, Kepler was appointed his successor.

Now with data accurate enough to demonstrate his theory, Kepler set to work. Yet try as he might, the predictions of his model did not line up with Brahe's observations. They were close. Very close, but not close enough. Eventually, he concluded the problem had to be with his theory, not the data. Okay, if platonic solids were not the answer, what was? This new search led Kepler to discover the three laws of planetary motion; today called Kepler's laws.

Kepler's laws came as a result of a wrong theory. It was not the mistake that ended in the laws but how Kepler attempted to test his theory and, more importantly, would not settle for a partial confirmation or close enough. He sought the truth, and when it became clear his theory was wrong, he set it aside and tried something else. Compare Kepler's willingness to go where the evidence took him, with the reaction of the President of the American Philosophical Society, to Wegener's theory which is now accepted as Plate Tectonics discussed in chapter one, "If we are to believe this hypothesis, we must forget everything we learned in the last seventy years and start all over again."[87]

ERRORS THAT CONTRIBUTE

A reluctance to change your position is not necessarily bad. Changing your position too often can be equally problematic. As with mistakes themselves, it is far more important why you change your position. Your position on issues should be determined by the evidence, not the last person to whom you talked. When you dis-

---

87 Winchester, S. (2003). *Krakatoa, The Day the World Exploded August 27, 1883.* New York: HarperCollins . p. 74

agree, what is key is how you disagree, discussed in the last chapter. You can be wrong and still make a significant contribution to the truth. A great example of being wrong, but in an important way, is Albert Einstein and his rejection of Quantum Mechanics.

Quantum Mechanics is flat-out weird. It describes a subatomic universe where what we understand as the normal way things work breaks down. For example, in the normal everyday world, you can affect someone in another country. You could send them a package, email them, or call them on the phone. However you do it, something has to travel from where you are, to where they are, be it a package in the mail or electrons on a wire. Break the link, such as your cell phone losing its signal, and your ability to affect the other person is gone.

Say you had a counterpart in another country. You are both streaming podcasts. Every time you change to a new podcast, you would call your counterpart, and they would also change. Your calls would keep both of you in sync. This is the world of Newton and Einstein, and it is not a problem. It is how we expect things to work.

Einstein noticed something that troubled him in the quantum version of the universe; things seem to have a link where there was no link. It would be like the scenario above, but without phones or any other means of communication. You would still change podcasts, and your counterpart in another country would likewise change to the same podcasts but without being told. They would just change. You could randomly pick a new podcast, and at the same time, your counterpart would "randomly" pick the same podcast. Einstein called this "spooky."[88] How can this possibly be correct? This sounds more like magic than science.

Einstein rejected this. Instead, he argued, there must be some sort of programming allowing them to react the way they do. In this case, both you and your counterpart had something about the two of you leading you to change to particular podcasts at given times.

---

88 Greene, B. (2004). *The Fabric of hte Cosmos*. New York: Vintage Books. p. 80

Your counterpart was not actually responding to your choices but only appeared to do so. The problem for Einstein's view was that there was no known mechanism by which this "programming" could happen. This was not a huge problem. After all, he was postulating an unknown mechanism, so of course, it was unknown.

Who was right? At the time Einstein raised this objection, there was no means to test either theory. Thus, it was the equations of Quantum mechanics that explained a lot but also seemed to defy our common-sense view of reality versus Einstein's unknown mechanism, but one that would match everyday experience. It would not be until the 1980s that the issue could be settled. When it was, it was settled in favor of Quantum Mechanics. Einstein was wrong.

More recent theories attempt to remove some of the spookiness by fundamentally re-envisioning the concept of space-time. The established view is that space-time is the existing area and time where everything occurs. It is like the canvas upon which reality is painted. The modular space-time theory sees space-time as something emerging from the quantum world. This could significantly change the concept of what it means to be close, if true. Objects could be close in a quantum sense, even when they are very far apart in space-time. Still, this new theory is only being developed and remains to be confirmed.

Definite vs. Probable

This was not the only objection Einstein had. Probably more fundamental was Quantum Mechanics moving from the definitive answers given by physics until that point to probability-based answers. In Newtonian physics, there is a clear reason that things happen. In the Quantum universe, probability is the best you can do. Given an amount of radioactive material, Quantum Mechanics can say what the probability is that it will undergo decay. For a lump of Carbon-14, half of it will decay in about 5730 years. But Quantum Mechanics cannot tell you in advance when an individual Carbon-14 atom will decay or why it did decay after it did.

Seeking Truth 151

Because of this, Einstein believed that what we call Quantum Mechanics was only a poor model. There had to be some deeper yet-to-be-discovered theory allowing future physicists to dispense with probability and return to definitive answers once again.

In 1935 he set out to demonstrate this. A central component of the uncertainty principle is that certain properties cannot be determined beyond a given level without losing the ability to know something else. This is known as the measurement problem. For example, you cannot know both the position and momentum of a particle precisely. You lose the ability to know its position, if you determine the momentum exactly. Not only did you lose the ability to know, but Quantum Mechanics also seems to be showing that the particle lost its position.

Working with Boris Podolsky and Nathan Rosen, Einstein wrote a paper demonstrating this flaw that came to be known as the EPR paradox. Conceptually the approach was simple. Their starting premise was, "In a complete theory there is an element corresponding to each element of reality."[89] For a theory to be complete, it must be able to account for everything. If something happened the theory cannot account for, the theory could not be complete.

They wanted to show that every particle has a precise momentum and a precise position at all times. If this was correct, because of the uncertainty principle and its claim that you cannot know both, Quantum Mechanics could not be a complete theory. It would be a weakness in the theory, as there was a part of reality that the theory could not account for, i.e., the ability to know both the position and the momentum simultaneously.

The amount of uncertainty is far too small to affect even the smallest things we can see. Yet, it is significant in the subatomic realm. Still, to understand what troubled Einstein about Quantum Mechanics and how he, Podolsky, and Rosen hoped to show there

---

89 Einstein, Albert; Podolsky, Boris; Rosen, Nathan. (1935). Can Quantum-Mechanical Description of Physical Reality Be Considered Complete ? *Physical Review*, 777-780.

was a problem, let's assume the world of cars acted like objects in the subatomic world.

In the normal everyday world, this would be equivalent to saying that you can know the location of a car or how fast it is going, but only to a certain level. Attempting to know precisely how fast a car is going, you lose the ability to know where it is. The car could be anywhere, not just in the United States but in the universe. Again, this did not seem right to Einstein. A particle had to be someplace; it had to have a definite location, even if we could not measure it. This must be a flaw in Quantum Mechanics.

An early explanation for the uncertainty principle was that when you measure a particle, that act of measuring disturbs it. "The usual conclusion from this in quantum mechanics is that *when the momentum of a particle is known, its coordinate has no physical reality.*"[90] Einstein, Podolsky, and Rosen postulated two entangled particles moving away from a common point with the same momentum except in opposite directions.

Entangled particles show the "spookiness" of reacting the same that troubled Einstein in the last problem. Say you have two particles, A and B. Since both particles have the same motion but in the opposite directions, measuring the momentum of particle A would allow you to know the momentum of both. You could then measure the position of particle B, which would again allow you to determine the position of both. You would then know both values for each particle.

Returning to our car analogy, we will use the related property of speed to keep things simple rather than momentum. In this example, mass and direction will be constant. Assume for a moment there were two perfectly straight and level roads leaving St. Louis, one going due east, the other due west. You have two identical cars that simultaneously leave from the same point in the city, one going east, the other west. While their speeds may change, they always

---

[90] Einstein, Albert; Podolsky, Boris; Rosen, Nathan. (1935). Can Quantum-Mechanical Description of Physical Reality Be Considered Complete'? *Physical Review*, 777-780.

Seeking Truth

change in the same way. At any given time, you do not know how far they are from the city or how fast they are going, but they are going at the same speed and will be the same distance from St. Louis.

This example is trying to mirror the Quantum Universe, so you cannot measure the speed of one car without disturbing it and thus losing the ability to know its position. Granted, a police officer using a radar gun to get the speed of a vehicle will not affect its position in any meaningful way. Still, in the sub-atomic world, the idea was that any attempt to measure momentum would disturb the object. So, the idea was that using the sub-atomic equivalent to a radar gun would disturb the sub-atomic particle measured. Still, while it may disturb the measured particle, it will not disturb the corresponding entangled particle.

In our car analogy, an officer using a radar gun to get the speed of the car going east may affect that car, but it cannot affect the car going west. Since you know the car's speed going east, say 68.7532 mph, you also know the other car will be going 68.7532 mph without disturbing it. Since you have not disturbed it, you can then measure its position, say 23.7845 miles from St. Louis. You would then know the position and speed of both cars, something Quantum Mechanics says you should not be able to know. Quantum Mechanics would be incomplete.

Again, in 1935, the technology to do the actual experiment at the sub-atomic level did not exist. For many decades this remained a thought experiment only. When the experiment was finally conducted, it was not with position and momentum but a different pair of complementary properties involving the spin of a particle. The actual test is complex. Still, the results were clear. Einstein, Podolsky, and Rosen were wrong in their reasoning. You can know one or the other, but not both. Measure a property of one particle, and you lose the ability to measure the related property on both, regardless of the distance between them. Measure the momentum of one, and both particles lose their position. Quantum Mechanics may be spooky, but it also seems to be correct.

Wrong But Valuable

When it came to Quantum Mechanics, Einstein was wrong and repeatedly so. Still, his contributions were, nevertheless, valuable. His attempts to find flaws in Quantum Mechanics caused the supporters of Quantum Mechanics to consider aspects and implications of the theory, which led to new insights. His theories on how Quantum Mechanics could be shown to have flaws led to experiments that confirmed some of its stranger aspects.

The key was that Einstein did not just reject and denounce Quantum Mechanics. He did not try to suppress it or have it banned. Instead, he engaged with the theory's supporters and developed ways the theory could be tested. While Einstein was often wrong, his objections helped advance our understanding of Quantum Mechanics.

After all, it is still possible he was right. Whether there is some deeper underlying theory currently unknown to us but one that would eliminate the uncertainty and "spookiness" of Quantum Mechanics remains unknown. The search continues, and many questions remain to be answered. Science has undergone considerable change during the twentieth century. It may do so again in the twenty-first. Yet doing so requires open and honest discussion seeking truth, not denunciations attempting to suppress alternative theories and views.

Suppression and Censorship

Throughout history, those in power have frequently responded to those they perceive to be in error with attempts at suppression. Sometimes they succeeded; most of the time, they did not, at least in the long run. The use of force to settle what are fundamentally intellectual questions is never a good solution. This lesson was difficult for Europe to learn and resulted in many religious wars and persecutions that followed the Protestant Reformation. One of the few good things to come from these conflicts was a growing push for intellectual freedom and tolerance.

The futility and danger of such conflicts were major reasons for placing freedom of religion and speech in the Bill of Rights, yet it was a tenuous realization. Censorship of ideas has repeatedly emerged at various times and in various places. Those calling for suppression always claim the moral high ground. They are just trying to protect people from bad information or dangerous ideas.

In recent times this goes under labels such as hate speech, offensive language, or fake news. To be clear, there is nothing wrong with these labels, in and of themselves. Some speech is hateful, and some offensive. Some news is fake. The problem comes when we try to suppress such speech instead of countering it.

There are two different problems here. The first is what is hateful and offensive is often very subjective. For example, some people would find the movie *Blazing Saddles* offensive for its racial language and stereotypes. Others would find it incredibly funny and see in its ridiculing racist attitudes a strong repudiation of racism. Still others, would not care for the movie as it is just not a type of humor they like. Thus, different people will have vastly different reactions.

More problematic, often what is hateful and offensive is defined, not by the speaker but by the listener. As a result, it does not matter what a person actually said, intended to say, or even whether what they said was true. The only thing that matters is whether someone took it as hateful or offensive. For some, merely expressing disagreement with a particular position is considered hateful and offensive. Giving specific reasons and evidence against the position is even worse.

Given this, it should be concerning that the current trend is towards more suppression of speech instead of more discussion and debate. A 2015 poll asked if the government should be able to prevent people from saying things some found offensive. The younger the age group, the more respondents said yes. Only 12 percent of those 70 and above thought it was a good idea to ban such speech. This number steadily increased to 40 percent for Millennials, those between 18 and 34 at the time.[91] The same poll found that people in Europe were even more willing to suppress speech. Support for government censorship ranged from 38 percent to as high as 70 percent, depending on the country. A poll conducted in 2019 found that 48% of Americans were concerned their freedom of speech was at risk.[92]

The other problem concerns limits on things like "fake news." Of course, the immediate question becomes who gets to decide what is fake? A related question is who decides who decides? There is also the question about how they are going to decide. At first, fact-checkers seemed like a good idea, and in many areas, they are. They normally can be fairly accurate on simple facts and things that fall into the category of urban legends. However, the closer they come to contentious issues, the more suspect they become. All the issues of context and language discussed in earlier chapters come into play. This is particularly true as issues become more complex.

As we have seen, claims are often complex and difficult to assess. Some fact-checkers account for this with a scale including some sort of partial truth. Still, this does not really address a situation where there are many judgments made to reach a conclusion. Such issues do not lend themselves to the binary nature of how they check.

For many, unless a claim is verified as correct, it is labeled false. There is no room for disputes or unknowns. Life is often messy. We often do not have all the information we would like. As a result, many disputes do not easily resolve into a clear true-false paradigm. There are disputed areas and ambiguities. Then there is the whole issue of who is reliable. I have even seen claims questioning the

---

91 Poushter, J. (2015, November 20). *40% of Millennials OK with limiting speech offensive to minorities*. Retrieved from Pew Research: https://www.pewresearch.org/fact-tank/2015/11/20/40-of-millennials-ok-with-limiting-speech-offensive-to-minorities/

92 Bote, J. (2019, December 16). *92% of Americans think their basic rights are being threatened, new poll shows*. Retrieved from USA Today: https://www.usatoday.com/story/news/nation/2019/12/16/most-americans-think-their-basic-rights-threatened-new-poll-shows/4385967002/

truthfulness of an official account fact-checked as false because they differed from the very statements they were questioning.

This type of true-false scale can be particularly problematic where a claim rests on personal testimony. Normally in such he-said/she-said situations, the truth cannot be determined with any confidence. Yet, I have seen such cases also fact-checked false due to lack of supporting evidence.

One justification for this type of scale is that a person is presumed innocent until proven guilty in a court of law. A good standard for a courtroom, but courtrooms only determine legal status, not reality. There have been many cases where there was a miscarriage of justice; an innocent person was found guilty, or a guilty person was set free.

For significant disputes, fact-checking becomes virtually impossible. A major reason is the larger the dispute, the more likely experts and authorities will be on all sides. When this happens, the fact-check will depend solely on which experts are deemed authoritative. Yet, on what basis are they authoritative? Consider two experts, equal in every relevant measure and well regarded by their peers during their careers. After graduating from college, one decided on a career in government, the other in university research.

Then a controversy develops in their field of expertise. They happen to end up on opposite sides of the issue. Which should be deemed "authoritative?" There would be no rational basis to make this decision. Yet to fact-check this issue, the fact-checker must choose one expert or the other. This leaves the decision in the hand of a non-expert, i.e., the fact-checker. Did they have a bias towards government authorities? Did they prefer university researchers over government authorities? Why do they get to make the decision?

The fact-checkers would likewise be reversed, if these experts had made opposite career choices upon graduating. This would lead to the absurd situation where truth was determined, not by knowledge in the field but by the career choices of college graduates. Yet this is the basis for many fact-checks in areas of major disputes.

This is not much of a problem if the fact-checkers merely give their opinion about which side they think is correct. Increasingly, however, social media companies are using fact-checkers to suppress stories they consider false. If such a mechanism had existed at Galileo's time, the fact-checkers very likely would have labeled Galileo's claims fake news. They certainly would suppress Wegner's theories of Continental Drift as false. After all, the scientific consensus was clearly against him. Of course, now we know the scientific consensus was also clearly wrong.

Benefits of Error

An important benefit of an error is it allows a discussion to continue. It forces people to reexamine and question what they believe. Is what they believe true, or is it just conventional wisdom passed down to them. Most of the time, this is a beneficial process, even for things that are false. Take, for example, the idea of a flat earth.

Conventional wisdom is that before Columbus, people thought the world was flat. Columbus refuted that, though there are still a few holdouts. Could the holdouts be correct? How do you know the earth is round? Is it just because that is what you were taught? That would not necessarily be a bad thing. After all, no one has the time to research everything.

If you remember the discussion on Galileo in the last chapter, you may also remember the Foucault experiment not only showed the earth was spinning, the same experiment also showed the earth is a sphere. At the equator, the pendulum's swinging is fixed and does not change relative to the earth. At the pole, the earth spins under the pendulum in a circle. The pendulum's swing changes exactly as expected if the earth is a sphere between the pole and the equator.

Why bother with the flat-earth supporters, if this is true? Frankly, most of the time, they can be ignored. The point I am making is they should not be suppressed. Put another way, what harm do they do? What do I care if someone is posting articles and doing podcasts supporting a flat earth? If they are misleading people, a greater concern would be how? Is there not enough good information to counter their claims? Of course, there is, but often it is not presented.

Notice I did not just denounce the flat earth theory; I gave evidence to support that the earth is a sphere. Flat earth supporters have a response, and there is a response to their response, which is the nature of a debate. I am content with the evidence and satisfied with how the debate will end, at least for the vast majority who are curious enough to pursue it. As for a small minority who would be convinced the earth is flat, I will argue my case should I ever encounter one.

As a side note, it does turn out there is a problem with conventional wisdom. At the time of Columbus, people, at least educated people, did not think the world was flat. For example, about two hundred years before Columbus, Dante wrote one of the greatest literary works of the Middle Ages, if not all times, *The Divine Comedy*.

In that work, Dante the pilgrim is taken on a journey through Hell, Purgatory, and Heaven. The journey into Hell is one that takes him down to the center of the earth, at which point he and his guide Virgil have to turn around and begin climbing. Eventually, they come out at Mount Purgatory, which is described as being on the opposite side of the earth from Mount Jerusalem. For Dante and most others, the world was a sphere.

As for the myth that everyone thought it was flat, that was invented by Washington Irving.[93] Even when conventional wisdom is basically right, there can still be errors to be corrected. Yet if challenges to conventional wisdom are suppressed, this can never happen.

One might argue we should only suppress the clear stuff, like the flat earth and wild conspiracy theories. Yet, that brings us back

---

93 Russell, J. B. (1991). *Inventing the Flat Earth: Columbus and the Modern Historians*. Westport, Connecticut: Praeger.

to the issue of who decides what is clearly false? One of the current trends in discussion is to label any theories one does not like as conspiracy theories, as if that were some sort of refutation in and of itself.

I do not believe in conspiracy theories, beyond things like a few people conspiring to rob a bank. Whether it be the JFK assassination, the moon landing, the various 911 conspiracies, UFOs, or any of the many others I have looked at, I reject them all. Yet, I do not reject them because they are conspiracy theories. I reject them because I have looked at the evidence and do not think the evidence supports them.

Problems with Suppression

Another problem with suppression is that supporters of the claim being suppressed argue they have secret information that those in power do not want you to see. What is it they are trying to hide? Of course, suppression only confirms these arguments. Unfortunately, they are effective. I have seen people use such arguments even without any suppression. 'Watch this video before we are forced to take it down!'

If there is no argument, there will be no rebuttal. As a result, suppression of arguments bolsters them even further for those that still encounter them. When people hear such arguments, they normally only hear one side. Without a rebuttal, these arguments are more believable and thus more likely to be accepted.

There have been times when I hear claims that at least seem plausible or at least worth considering. Yet when I try to check them out, they are simply labeled conspiracy theories without any evidence. As such, I am left wondering why? This is frustrating even if I am sure the claim is wrong; a label is a description, not a reason. When people refuse to discuss something because it is a conspiracy theory, I get only the assessment, not their reasons for that assessment. This approach may be safeguarding information,

Seeking Truth

but it does not encourage critical thinking; it discourages it. It is saying don't think for yourself, just trust us.

Such an approach is fine if you can 1) guarantee total accuracy and 2) ensure complete suppression. Of course, neither of these is possible. Thus you will end up suppressing the truth at some point. In addition, some will still hear the claims being suppressed. When heard, these claims will, for the most part, be unchallenged. People will hear the pro for the claim, but suppressing the pro also suppresses the con. As such, the claim will seem more supported than it really is.

OPEN DEBATE

The best antidote for bad information is good information. The best response to a bad argument is a better argument. The best response to bad speech is more speech that refutes it. Suppression is very difficult to do and can preserve error instead of protecting the truth.

On the other hand, free and open debate can keep us honest. It encourages critical thinking and challenges us to avoid conventional wisdom looking instead to the evidence for our position. It keeps us from becoming locked into positions not supported by the evidence as we continually update and tweak our beliefs as we move closer to the truth. As for the risks of error winning, that was perhaps best summed up by Dudley Malone, a defense team member in the Scopes Trial. In the trial, he argued,

> There is never a duel with the truth. The truth always wins and we are not afraid of it. The truth is no coward. The truth does not need the law. The truth does not need the forces of government… The truth is imperishable, eternal, and immortal and needs no human agency to support it. [94]

---

94 Malone, D. (2020, June 15). *Malone's Trial Speech (Full Text)*. Retrieved from Historical Thinking Matters: http://historicalthinkingmatters.org/scopestrial/1/sources/44/fulltext/

It is error that needs protection. It is error that cannot stand examination. It is error that requires competing views be suppressed. The truth need not fear. We should celebrate the correction when we are shown to be wrong.

Effective learning requires risking being wrong. Often you must risk being wrong in order to learn to become right. As a software developer and someone who has taught software development, you can copy all the examples in the book exactly and have them run perfectly, but that does not mean you know how to program.

You learn programming, not by the programs that work, but the ones that don't. When you write a program, and it does not compile or work as expected, you learn. You have to go over it line by line and see what it is doing to understand what went wrong. You have to understand it to know what your error was. Only when you can do this do you know how to program.

Just as we must allow for errors in ourselves, we should allow for errors in others. At the end of the day, we may not agree. We may need to leave them in their error. Or is it them, leaving us in ours? Still, in the end, we can at least have the confidence that as important as error is, the truth will win. If we believe that, suppression is not needed.

Part III
Seeking Truth

CHAPTER 9

KNOW THYSELF

The most difficult thing in life is to know yourself.
– Thales of Miletus

The last section stressed the importance of discussion as a means of testing and therefore determining the truth. What is it that you believe, and why do you believe it? Before you can discuss what you believe, you must know what you believe. As such, our first debate opponent should be ourselves. Debating yourself is also a great way to develop a critical attitude and thinking skills. It can also make your initial discussions much easier and more productive.

You have a range of beliefs you accept and many that you reject. Why? Why those beliefs? At first glance, those may seem like easy questions. Still, unless you have spent considerable time thinking through your beliefs, they are probably a chaotic, even contradictory, mixture of facts, opinions, and theories; some true, others false.

Moreover, these beliefs will come from various sources of varying reliability; many of these you will be unaware of. For example, we get a lot of information from friends and acquaintances but often do not know where they get their information. So while you may know what you believe, you probably are not fully aware of why.

Take something clear cut for many people, such as which political candidate they support. You may vote for a candidate because you like what they intend to do. Or perhaps you will vote for them because you think they are better than the other candidate. Pretty clear cut. Or is it? Let say it is because you like the platform on which they are running, though the same line of reasoning could just as well be applied to the other possible reasons. Why do you like their platform? Political platforms are made up of many subjects or planks. Do you like them all equally? Probably not, and if so, which are the most important to you and why?

Each plank will consist of a range of policies and programs. Do you even know what they are? Few people actually read the platforms, which is little wonder as these are often only campaign documents that are at best loosely followed once in office, if at all. Often, voters decide based on party affiliations or the candidate's position on a few important issues. Sometimes, the candidate is irrelevant. For a single-issue voter, the only question is, are they on the right side of the issue?

Still, we come back to the question of why? Why are those issues more important than the others? Why do you prefer your candidates' positions over their opponents? For example, say one of the issues that is important to you is Foreign Policy. Why is it important? Why do you hold the position on Foreign Policy that you do?

Why Not?

Another important way to ask this question is why not? Why don't you accept an opposing view? As you begin to work through the reasons, are they valid intellectual reasons? Do they fall into some of the problems discussed in earlier chapters, such as disparaging such views' supporters? If you have not done such a mental exercise in the past, it will probably be a mixture of good and bad reasons. Once you toss out the bad, what is left?

As you work through these reasons, you end up with a better idea of why you reject a particular view. Put another way, this would be a list of what it would take to convince you. At this point, you should ask yourself, would this do it? Would this really be enough to convince?

Putting together such a list is not easy. It is rather difficult because we normally spend a good deal of effort to protect and reinforce our beliefs, not question them. Some may even find the exercise unsettling, but it is a good way to understand why you hold your beliefs.

It can also help you understand your real issues. Some of the beliefs we hold are in and of themselves inconsequential. Still, we resist any change. When this happens, it may be that this belief is protecting another, and what is for us, a more important belief. An acquaintance thinks they may have seen your spouse the other day. That they may or may not have seen your spouse is inconsequential. Yet, suppose the implications were that your spouse was deceiving you. In that case, that could be a very troubling implication and thus could be much more difficult to accept.

One area where this is common is with core beliefs. These are the beliefs that tend to define our self-conceptions. The core beliefs for one person may be irrelevant to another. It could be a particular political belief for one person, whereas someone else has no interest in politics. We tend to protect our core beliefs behind a barrier of other secondary beliefs. These secondary beliefs we defend more doggedly than we might otherwise because they are protecting our core. For example, we may believe something bad or be reluctant to accept something good about those we disagree with, making it easier to reject their beliefs.

LIMITING PRINCIPLES.

In logic, there is a slippery slope fallacy where one refuses to agree to or accept A because it might lead to B. Allow people to be a couple of minutes late for meetings, the next thing you know, they will not show up at all. On the other hand, sometimes, there is a degree of truth to these arguments. While not quite as extreme, I have worked in business cultures where it was ok to be late and in those where it was not. Those organizations where being late was not acceptable, meetings tended to start on time. Those where it was okay to be late rarely started on time. At times, it took ten or even fifteen minutes for everyone to arrive.

The difference between the two arguments is a lack of hyperbole or exaggeration and a limiting principle. Allowing people to be late does not automatically lead to people not coming at all. However, it does lead to more people coming later. In fact, at some companies, people planned to be late because they knew the meeting would not start on time.

The other difference is a limiting principle. what is the limiting principle, if A is not going to lead to B? The lessening of standards does not mean the abandonment of standards. On the other hand, if you lower standards in one area, why not others? What is the limiting principle that says you should lower them for A but not for B? Basically, this comes down to where you draw the line, and why do you draw it where you do? Is this arbitrary? Do you have a reason, and if so, what is it?

Ambiguity

As you work your way down through this chain, normally, it will not be long before you come to vague statements. With taxes, for example, some of the vague language includes lower, higher, fair, rich, poor, and middle class. Does the politician you support want lower or higher taxes? How much and on whom? What do these words mean?

Even a seemingly clear term like 'corporation' refers to a large range of businesses. When hearing the word 'corporation,' many people tend to think of large multi-national corporations. Still, there are vastly more corporations that only have a small number of employees. Some only have one. In addition, different types of corporations are taxed in different ways, or not at all when it comes to charities.

Often decisions are made on directions (cut or increase) rather than amounts. What is someone's fair share? Virtually everyone would agree that all should pay their fair share. At least, I have never seen anyone publicly advocate that someone should pay an unfair share. Yet, I have rarely seen anyone define what amount is fair. Should the "rich" pay 30 percent? 40? 50? 60? 70? More? How much is fair?

You could also ask how much is rich? Most would agree that anyone who has a nice house and cars, can travel around the world whenever they want, and does not have to work to afford all this is rich. What about the same circumstances, except the person has loans on the house and cars and must work to afford all this? Then again, what is a "nice house and cars?"

Taxes are just one issue. Add to this all the other issues, and just understanding what you believe is very complex. A key point here is that most issues are far more complex than our opinions about them. As a result, we normally have a lot of room to learn, develop, and even change our position.

There is also the whole issue of why you believe the things you do. It is easy to say the rich should pay their fair share. It is much harder to say why someone, for example, making a particular dollar figure should pay a particular level of taxes; why someone making $120,000 a year at a job should pay 40% of this in taxes.

There are, of course, selfish reasons. For example, if you make less than $120,000, you might want the government spending money in a certain area, but want someone else to pay for it, someone who makes more than you do. Still, not everyone decides for selfish reasons.

Pros and Cons

When we look at the possible reasons, they are many and varied. Again, we come back to the question of why you find the particular reasons persuasive. It is a truism in life that there are pros and cons to everything, even when the decision is fairly clear. For example, smoking cigarettes has certain pros, such as pleasure, weight loss, and increased mental concentration. While pros, they hardly outweigh the many health risks which are on the con side. Thus, most people find the decision an easy one.

A key question is whether your position was an informed choice or something you just drifted into without knowing why? Ideally, all our decisions would be informed ones made only after fully understanding an issue. Still, understanding an issue to make an informed choice requires understanding all the pros and cons of that issue. This type of understanding runs counter to what we normally do, which is one-sided thinking. We consider only the Pros or the Cons, depending on the outcome we desire. Often this type of thinking is more like a mirror, where we consider the pros of our side and the cons of the other. For example, I am sure some people were troubled by the very mention above that smoking had pros. If you only look at the pros, anything can be accepted. If you only look at the cons, anything can be rejected.

As you begin to look at the pros and cons of various issues, you will quickly see that they are not all created equal. Some things will be secondary issues, while others are more fundamental. To see this let us briefly look at the issue of the death penalty, which, while current, has not been the hot-button issue it once was, so hopefully, this will allow us to explore the concepts without getting too involved in the overall debate.

There are lots of arguments circulating pro and con. For example, while both sides will make cost arguments, some death penalty supporters argue it is cheaper than life in prison. Meanwhile, opponents of the death penalty point to the potential for mistakes. Both issues, while valid and important, are often secondary. For the cost argument made by supporters of the death penalty, all justice costs something. Trials cost money, but supporters do not argue we should do away with that cost. While an important consideration, it does not go to the core of the issue.

As for the argument about potential mistakes, while certainly a concern in some cases, it is not always the case. In some cases, there is no chance of a mistake. What about the death penalty in those cases? Thus, this argument also does not go to the core issue. The core issue is should the state ever have a death penalty?

One way to avoid side issues is to frame the question to eliminate them. For example, suppose an organization raised the money to pay the cost of life in prison for murderers. Would that mean those who made the cost argument would agree to abandon the death penalty? If not, then cost is secondary to the core issue.

As for mistakes, say you had a particularly heinous murder of a young child filmed by the murderer. The film is lawfully discovered when the police catch the murderer, showing their guilt without question. In addition, there is a signed confession with no issues of coercion. The murderer is completely unrepentant. Would it be acceptable for the state to execute such a murderer?

All the other issues do not matter, if someone says no. Only after the core issue is settled do the secondary issues come into play. For example, discussions about costs or mistakes don't matter when discussing with someone with a core opposition to the death penalty. They would not support the death penalty regardless of how those issues are resolved.

A factor that makes such discussions difficult is it requires a judgment between two values. As mentioned earlier, justice and mercy conflict. On the one hand, is justice; on the other is mercy. Most people want both to be important factors in our justice system. Still, they are mutually exclusive. You cannot have 100 percent of both at the same time. Getting one, you must give up some of the other. So, where is the proper balance?

Distinctions

Breaking down issues often involves finding the right balance between distinctions and conflation. Distinctions fundamentally involved separating things into meaningful categories. A difficult issue here is that these can change from issue to issue. Thus, if the question being considered is the overall tax burden, the type of tax will not be all that important. However, if the issue is tax fairness, there is a significant difference between various taxes.

The impact of income taxes is by definition linked to income. As a result, the ability to pay is not as much a concern as with a poll tax. With a poll tax, people are taxed a fixed amount regardless of income. On the other hand, sales taxes tend to impact those with lower incomes, who spend a larger percentage of their income on taxable goods. Property taxes are somewhat in between; they are closely tied to the ability to pay at the time of purchase. Still, people's incomes can change over the years, as can the value of their property. As a result, people can be taxed out of their homes if they are on a fixed or declining income while the property values increase.

Conflation

Just as the failure to make proper distinctions can lead to a range of problems, the conflation of things that are not the same can likewise lead to errors. This is particularly true when dealing with complex issues. For example, at the fourth Lincoln-Douglas debate, held in Charleston, Illinois, Lincoln went first and started his opening speech saying,

> While I was at the hotel to-day, an elderly gentleman called upon me to know whether I was really in favor of producing a perfect equality between the negroes and white people. [Great Laughter.] While I had not proposed to myself on this occasion to say much on that subject, yet as the question was asked me I thought I would occupy perhaps five minutes in saying something in regard to it. I will say then that I am not, nor ever have been, in favor of bringing about in any way the social and political equality of the white and black races, [applause]-that I am not nor ever have been in favor of making voters or jurors of negroes, nor of qualifying them to hold office, nor to intermarry with white people; and I will say in addition to this that there is a physical difference between the white and black races which I believe will forever forbid the two races living together on terms of social and political equality. And inasmuch as they cannot so live, while they do

remain together there must be the position of superior and inferior, and I as much as any other man am in favor of having the superior position assigned to the white race.[95]

These comments have led some, including some historians, to label Lincoln a white supremacist. While there is certainly some justification for such a charge in this comment, this leads to many problems. Are Lincoln's views on supremacy really the same as those of a KKK member? If not, is it correct to use the same term for both? If he was a white supremacist, why did his election as President cause the southern states to secede? What about the rest of Lincoln's statements? In the first debate, Lincoln stated that,

> There is a physical difference between the two, which, in my judgment, will probably forever forbid their living together upon the footing of perfect equality, and inasmuch as it becomes a necessity that there must be a difference, I, as well as Judge Douglas, am in favor of the race to which I belong having the superior position. I have never said anything to the contrary, but I hold that, notwithstanding all this, there is no reason in the world why the negro is not entitled to all the natural rights enumerated in the Declaration of Independence, the right to life, liberty, and the pursuit of happiness. [Loud cheers.] I hold that he is as much entitled to these as the white man.[96]

At the seventh and last debate in Alton, Lincoln made his strongest argument.

> At Galesburgh, the other day, I said in answer to Judge Douglas, that three years ago there never had been a man, so far as I knew or believed, in the whole world, who had said that the Declaration of Independence did not include negroes

---

95 Lincoln, A. (1858, September 18). *Fourth Debate: Charleston, Illinois*. Retrieved from Lincoln Home: https://www.nps.gov/liho/learn/historyculture/debate4.htm

96 Lincoln, A. (1858, August 21). *First Debate: Ottawa, Illinois*. Retrieved from Lincoln Home: https://www.nps.gov/liho/learn/historyculture/debate1.htm

in the term "all men." I reassert it to-day. I assert that Judge Douglas and all his friends may search the whole records of the country, and it will be a matter of great astonishment to me if they shall be able to find that one human being three years ago had ever uttered the astounding sentiment that the term "all men" in the Declaration did not include the negro. Do not let me be misunderstood. I know that more than three years ago there were men who, finding this assertion constantly in the way of their schemes to bring about the ascendency and perpetuation of slavery, *denied the truth of it.* I know that Mr. Calhoun and all the politicians of his school denied the truth of the Declaration…

And when this new principle—this new proposition that no human being ever thought of three years ago—is brought forward, *I combat it* as having an evil tendency, if not an evil design. I combat it as having a tendency to dehumanize the negro, to take away from him the right of ever striving to be a man. I combat it as being one of the thousand things constantly done in these days to prepare the public mind to make property, and nothing but property, of the *negro in all the States of this Union.*[97]

Four years later, Lincoln was President in the mists of the Civil war. Earlier in the year, he had written Proclamation 95, otherwise known as the Emancipation Proclamation. He did not issue it immediately, lest it be seen as an act of desperation. After the battle of Antietam, fought on September 17, 1862, was perceived to be a victory for the union, Lincoln issued the proclamation on September 22.

That on the first day of January in the year of our Lord, one thousand eight hundred and sixty-three, all persons held as slaves within any State, or designated part of a State, the people whereof shall then be in rebellion against the United States

---

97 Lincoln, A. (1858, October 15). *Seventh Debate: Alton, Illinois.* Retrieved from Lincoln Home: https://www.nps.gov/liho/learn/historyculture/debate7.htm

shall be then, thenceforward, and forever free; and the executive government of the United States, including the military and naval authority thereof, will recognize and maintain the freedom of such persons, and will do no act or acts to repress such persons, or any of them, in any efforts they may make for their actual freedom.

A year later, as part of the ceremony to dedicate the Soldiers National Cemetery in Gettysburg on Nov 16, 1863, Lincoln gave perhaps the most famous speech in American history. The Gettysburg address begins, "Four score and seven years ago our fathers brought forth upon this continent, a new nation, conceived in Liberty, and dedicated to the proposition that all men are created equal."

The Civil War started when the southern states seceded over the issue of slavery and then fired on Fort Sumter. Initially, Lincoln's main aim was to preserve the union. Still, as the war progressed, the issue of slavery could not be ignored. Finally, with the Emancipation Proclamation and the Gettysburg Address, the issue of equal rights came to dominate the conflict. Following the war, the Constitution was amended to ensure that Blacks would have equal rights. However, following the election of 1876 and the resulting compromise of 1877, much of this would be ignored for over 80 years.

Where does this leave Lincoln and the charge that he was a white supremacist? Lincoln was like all of us, a man of his time. What is important is not the ways in which he reflected the views common to his day, but rather the ways he went beyond those views and improved society. Lincoln was opposed to slavery. He also believed in the Declaration of Independence. He called the Declaration the golden apple and the Constitution the silver frame that surrounded it. Just as the frame is not more important than what it holds, the Constitution is not as important as the Declaration of Independence. For Lincoln, the key statement is that "all men are created equal."

The issue that dominated Lincoln's day was slavery. While important, racial equality was not the main focus, though it was important in the slavery debate. The defenders of slavery used it as a threat should slavery be abolished. Thus, it is not surprising that Lincoln, as a candidate for Senate, would attempt to downplay this issue in favor of his main objective: abolishing slavery. In addition, Charleston, Illinois, the site of the fourth debate, was a stronghold of pro-slavery sentiment. Thus, while Lincoln was a statesman, he was also a politician and attempted to craft a message countering Douglas's charges against him.

Of course, it might be possible to argue that Lincoln's statements on equality were politically driven instead of those on supremacy. Still, his statements of equality were more common but also more central to his message. Additionally, Lincoln grounded his argument on the belief that Blacks were "entitled to all the natural rights enumerated in the Declaration of Independence, the right to life, liberty, and the pursuit of happiness." He had other options. He could have argued slavery was wrong without arguing that Blacks, in terms of enjoying the fruits of their own labor, were "my equal and the equal of Judge Douglas, and the equal of every living man. [Great applause.]"[98]

Lincoln believed he was constrained by law. The Emancipation Proclamation did not free all the slaves because Lincoln did not believe he had the power to do so. Still, he did have the power in "any State, or designated part of a State, [where] the people whereof shall then be in rebellion against the United States." Lincoln freed those slaves. His actions when given a chance to act, were more in line with equality than supremacy.

This is especially true with his actions to pass the 13th amendment which, not only freed the remaining slaves but outlawed slavery. Following the Emancipation Proclamation, there remained some concern it might be overturned in the courts. There were also

---

98   Lincoln, A. (1858, October 13). *Sixth Debate: Quincy, Illinois.* Retrieved from Lincoln Home: https://www.nps.gov/liho/learn/historyculture/debate6.htm

the slaves in the states that had not rebelled. The only way to secure the freedom of the slaves was to change the Constitution. While the amendment passed the Senate on April 8, 1864, it floundered in the House. In December 1864 and January 1865, Lincoln took a very active role persuading representatives and securing the votes needed for passage, which it barely did on January 31, 1865. It was ratified by the necessary three-fourths of the state and became law after Lincoln's death.

On April 11, 1865, Lincoln gave his last public address from the White House balcony. He said he supported giving the vote to blacks who were "very intelligent, and on those who serve our cause as soldiers." Not quite a modern view, but very much a step in the right direction from no vote at all.

One of those in the crowd that heard Lincoln that night was John Wilkes Booth. Booth's reaction was clear. Allowing Blacks to vote was too much, and he told his friend, "Now, by God, I'll put him through. That is the last speech he will ever make."[99] Three days later, on Good Friday, April 14, Booth shot Lincoln while watching a play. He died early the next morning.

Lincoln did not hold modern views of complete racial equality. Still, his views were much closer to racial equality than others in the first half of the nineteenth century; those who were white supremacists, such as John C. Calhoun, mentioned in chapter seven. Thus, to label Lincoln a white supremacist clouds rather than clarifies the issue. If Lincoln, who was called the great emancipator, worked hard to secure passage of the amendment banning slavery, and was assassinated in part for wanting to give some blacks the vote, was a white supremacist, then how do we classify Calhoun?

Earlier in the chapter, I said most issues are far more complex than our opinions about them. That will remain true, even when we spend a good deal of time thinking about them. The more you summarize a view, the more distorted it will become. For example,

---

99 *Booth's Reason for Assassination.* (n.d.). Retrieved from Teaching History.org: https://www.teachinghistory.org/history-content/ask-a-historian/24242

saying Lincoln was the greatest president (chapter five) and Lincoln was not a white supremacist might very well be true. Still, these statements hide a whole range of complexity and detail. This is fine, as long as we realize this.

ISSUES OF TIME

To some extent, this is an issue of time, i.e., views of white supremacy and blacks during the time Lincoln lived vs. today. However, there are other considerations of time. When considering the ramifications of a choice or policy, these do not happen at the same time. Choosing to eat a gallon of your favorite ice cream might taste very good while eating it, but you may pay the price for that later on.

You work hard for several years, to earn a college degree or a skilled trade, the con. Only afterward do you hopefully get a better paying job; the pro. Obtaining a new credit card, the pro might be the better lifestyle you will have until you reach your credit limit; the con would be the lower standard of living you will have while you pay it off. Those periods will not only be offset, but they will often not be the same length. Normally it takes much longer to get out of debt than to get into it. Driving a brand-new car brings enjoyment for weeks, maybe even a few months. Driving a used car that is paid off brings joy as long as it runs well, which can be many years. Which is better?

The same can be said of many governmental programs. There may be a short-term positive benefit, followed by a long-term negative benefit, or short-term negative benefits followed by long-term positive benefits. One problem with a lot of political debates is that each side is usually talking about different things. The side supporting a measure will focus on the positives, the opposition the negatives. Often these will occur in different timeframes, making following the discussion very difficult.

When considering your beliefs, do you know the pro and cons? Do you really have a good understanding of each? Have you considered both the short-term and long-term effects? Have you broken it down to the core issues, avoiding any conflations that would cloud the issue? These deal with the things you know. When seeking truth, an important and more difficult consideration is what you don't know?

UNKNOWNS

One consideration is what you don't know but would like to. Perhaps there is data or statistics that would help settle a dispute but you don't have it. Unfortunately, this is common enough to be a norm. When a decision must be made, rarely do you have all the information you would want. For example, the battle of Gettysburg was the turning point of the Civil War. The battle itself was unplanned. The Confederate troops had invaded the North but were left blind by their cavalry under the command of J.E.B. Stuart. As a result, the Confederate army stumbled upon Union troops in Gettysburg without intending to do so. They wanted to know where the Union troops were but didn't.

Even more difficult than that are, in a phrase made famous by Donald Rumsfield, the unknown unknowns; things you do not know that you do not know. These are the most difficult to deal with for obvious reasons. At least when you know you do not know, you can seek to learn, or at least estimate. How can you seek answers to questions you did not even know were questions?

During the middle of the 14th century, the bubonic plague swept from Asia into Europe. Estimates for the death toll range as high as 25 million in Europe and ten times that in the rest of the world. The percentage estimates range from a third to a half of the population of Europe died. People of the time literally had no idea of what was happening.

The cause was bacteria, but that knowledge required the invention of the microscope that was still two hundred years into the future. Even then, it would be an additional 300 years before Louis Pasteur put enough pieces together and came up with the germ theory of disease. At the time of the Black Death, this was truly an unknown unknown. The knowledge they would need was 500 years in the future.

As a result, they made sense of it the best they could, which was not very well. Very large numbers of people were dying for no apparent reason. Entire families were being wiped out, in some cases even towns. The idea that someone could go to bed healthy and die before morning had to be extremely frightening. Some blamed a conjunction of the planets, others bad air, the miasma theory that would exist up to the acceptance of the germ theory of disease. For others, it was sent by God either to bring people into heaven or punish them for their wickedness. Take your choice. All were wrong.

While we may look down on the people of the 14th century for their ignorance, it should be remembered we do not know everything today. In a few hundred years, people will be able to look back at us and wonder about our ignorance. Given the rapid pace of the growth in knowledge, it may not even take a few hundred years.

The key point here is that there are unknown unknowns in most of what we think we know. What are they, and how would they affect your position? This is an area where discussion with those who disagree can be most helpful. As you explore ideas and particularly their objections, you can discover aspects you had not considered; you can uncover at least some of the unknown unknowns.

As you think through an issue, considering the various position's pros and cons, you will better understand your position and the alternatives. As you listen to proponents of alternative views describe your position, you will often find such descriptions inaccurate and distorted. While common, an important consideration is that your descriptions of their positions are probably not any better. This is because we are careful with our views, understanding all the nuance. We are not as careful when it comes to views we disagree with. As a general rule, we are better at the pros of the position we agree with and the cons of those with which we disagree.

DOCTRINE OF THE MEAN

In his Nicomachean Ethics, Aristotle discussed a Doctrine of the Mean or middle. He argued that virtues are not binary but a spectrum. Take the example of courage. It is not courage vs. cowardice. Rather you have two extremes, recklessness at one end and cowardice at the other. The desired virtue, in this case, courage, is in the middle. Virtue is not either/or but a balance between two extremes.

He also argued an individual would be variously pre-disposed. Some tended towards recklessness, while others tended towards cowardice. As we seek the mean like courage, we should be aware of our predisposition and counter it. If we know we tend to be rash, we should strive to be more hesitant to rush in. If we know we are too timid; we should strive to be bolder. In this way, we are more likely to arrive closer to the desired virtue.

The same approach applies to seeking truth. Given our tendency to look at the pros of positions we accept and cons of those we reject, we should counter with the opposite. Take any issue where someone disagrees with you. Can you name a pro for their side? A con of yours? If you cannot, that is a sign that you have not thought through the issue completely.

Consider a politician you do not like; can you name something they have done that you can support? If you have a politician you support, can you name something they did that you did not support? The more you can do this, and the more central the issues, the more likely it is you have a good understanding of the situation.

The idea of understanding pros and cons is important in a range of areas. My approach is the same, whether in business decisions (should we launch a new product) or in life decisions (should I change jobs). I try to layout and consider all the pros and cons before making a decision. I do this even with decisions where I do not have a vested interest. For example, when people have asked for advice, I normally ask a series of questions about the pros and cons. When I have done this, it is very common to get some pushback. If they wanted a yes, I am suddenly too negative with all my questions about the cons. If they wanted a no, I suddenly am biased in favor of the yes position.

The beginning of chapter six asked, considering a person just like you, just as smart, just as well informed, just as concerned, just as compassionate. You are equal in whatever positive adjective you wish to specify. There is only one difference. They disagree with you on a particular issue. Why is that? What is it that leads you to different views? What are the pros of their position and the cons of yours that lead them to reach different views? They must exist; if you cannot state them, why do you believe they are wrong?

Questions

Having a good understanding of the pros and cons of both sides, you will be able to assess why you believe what you believe. In addition, you will have a better understanding of the core differences causing people to reach different conclusions. This will almost certainly leave you with several questions. Some of these questions will help clarify the differences. For example, you may see in the other position some apparent contradictions. Are those real contradictions, or rather a lack of understanding on your part? Is there some aspect to their view that would reconcile the seeming contradiction?

You will also see conflicts with your views. What are the key strengths and weaknesses? There may be data or reasoning you see as important that seem to support your side. How do those who disagree deal with it? Are they unaware, or do they have a good response? Doing the things suggested in this chapter, you will better understand your position. In addition, you will have the basis for a good discussion. After all, discussions proceed much better when you ask questions about their position, rather than just telling them why they are wrong. In addition, asking questions is far more likely to change minds. It is also far more likely that you will learn something, at least if you are open-minded.

Chapter 10

Open to Open-Mindedness

If someone is able to show me that what I think or do is not right, I will happily change, for I seek the truth, by which no one was ever truly harmed. It is the person who continues in his self-deception and ignorance who is harmed. — Marcus Aurelius, Meditations

The measure of intelligence is the ability to change. — Albert Einstein

Every plane crash brings us closer to safety, improves the system, and makes the next flight safer. – Nassim Nicholas Taleb

The evidence seemed both clear and definitive. In his test, mortality rates dropped from 18 percent to one percent, a 94 percent reduction. It was convincing enough for Ignaz Semmelweis, yet not for the vast majority of doctors. At the Vienna Hospital where Semmelweis worked, there were two maternity clinics. Both clinics were for teaching, the first for doctors, the second for midwives. The only other difference was the mortality rate for the midwife clinic was less than half that of the doctors, the women dying from puerperal fever.

This difference in mortality rate was common knowledge among the public. Thus not too surprisingly, women did not want to go to the first Clinic. On those days when Clinic One was the only option, many would give birth outside the hospital, so-called street births. Semmelweis noted these women rarely contracted puerperal fever. This data was the opposite of what he would have expected. Doctors should give the best care and thus have the lowest mortality rate, followed by midwives. Street births should have had the highest mortality rate. Perplexed, Semmelweis began looking for an answer.

Perhaps there was something in the way the mothers were being treated. To test this, Semmelweis had both clinics switch their procedures. The only effect this had was getting the first clinic's director so upset he had Semmelweis demoted for questioning how he ran things.

Then a friend of his died after accidentally being cut by a knife used in an autopsy; more importantly, he seemed to have died of puerperal fever. Perhaps the knife had transferred something from the corpse to his friend, causing the disease; perhaps there was something in the body.

This explanation was at least plausible. After all, the medical student often spent time in the morgue dissecting cadavers as part of their studies before going to the clinic. The midwife students never worked in the morgue. Armed with a theory, Semmelweis decided to try something new; he had doctors wash their hands following autopsies and in between examining patients.

Not only did the mortality rate for the clinic drop, but it also dropped below that of Clinic Two, the midwife clinic. It was a major breakthrough. Yet other doctors resisted. When political turmoil caused Semmelweis to leave Vienna, he became head physician at a hospital in Pest Hungary. Originally a separate city, in 1849, Pest was connected to the city of Buda by a bridge across the Danube, and in 1873, along with Óbuda the three became Budapest. Like the clinic in Vienna, the hospital in Pest also had trouble with puerperal fever. After becoming head physician, the rates again dropped drastically.

While the evidence was clear and definitive, it was also ignored. Semmelweis' work was done before the Germ Theory of disease. The Miasma theory dominated. Illness was caused by bad air or an imbalance of humors, not something transferred from one body to another. Washing your hands was a waste of time; it could not possibly help, so women continued to die.

MAPPING THE PROBLEM

At about the same time in London, John Snow had a very similar experience. Snow had been investigating the causes of cholera. At the time, cholera was a mystery. It seemed to strike without rhyme or reason. All in one household would get the disease while no one in the house next door would. During a cholera outbreak in 1854, Snow could finally explain why some got sick while others did not. He did this using very careful mapping of the victims and where they got their water.

He showed that the outbreak's source in one area could be traced to a single pump on Broad Street. Why people would choose one pump over another was complex. Perhaps it was the closest. Perhaps it was closer to something else they wanted. Perhaps it was not as crowded or easier to operate. Perhaps they just liked the water better. Whatever the reason, people in the same area often got their water from different pumps.

Everyone who got sick in the area Snow investigated used one particular pump, the Broad Street pump. Those who lived in the same neighborhood but for whatever reason used other pumps, but not the Broad Street pump, did not get sick. John Snow did not know exactly why that pump was causing the problem, but he knew it was causing it.

While he was able to get the pump handle removed, his theory was rejected by the medical authorities of his day. Several more outbreaks would occur, and many more would die before the medical authorities realized Snow was correct. Even then, they were reluctant to give him credit. Later investigations showed that the well had been dug close to an old cesspit, a cesspit which not only contained the bacterium causing Cholera, but it had also begun leaking into the well water for the pump.

Nor were these problems just a thing of the distant past. In 2005, Frank Marshall and Robin Warren won the *Nobel Prize in Physiology or Medicine* for work that had caused them to be ridiculed twenty years earlier. At the time Marshall graduated from the

University of Australia School of Medicine, a common illness was ulcers; the cause was known: Stress.

That stress led to ulcers was not a completely unwarranted conclusion. Much of the research had been done in large cities, where businessmen in high-pressure positions were discovered to have ulcers. So the link was made between stress and ulcers. It was confirmed with studies on rats. These were induced to develop ulcers by putting them under stress. When the rats were given antacids, they would be protected from developing ulcers, which seemed to settle the issue. As is often the case, things were much more complex than first supposed.

Marshall and Warren noticed that biopsies of ulcers all showed a particular corkscrew-shaped bacterium called Helicobacter pylori. This is a very hardy bacterium that could live in stomach acid. In their research, they looked at patients who were suspected of cancer. Upon checking, they found twenty who did not have cancer but did have Helicobacter pylori. One was an 80-year-old man with severe stomach pains. He was thought to have a rare but inoperable condition. At the time, little could be done, so they gave him some antibiotics and sent him home.

Two weeks later, "He's got a spring in his step, he's practically doing somersaults into the consulting room. He's healed. Clearing out the infection had cured him."[100] At that point, they started a more formal study. Eventually, they showed that Helicobacter pylori could not only cause ulcers but cancer as well.

When they presented their findings at the annual meeting of the Royal Australasian College of Physicians, the reaction was not good. "To gastroenterologists, the concept of a germ causing ulcers was like saying that the Earth is flat." They continued to amass their evidence, wrote letters, and tried to publish papers on

---

[100] Weintraub, P. (2010, April 8). *The Doctor Who Drank Infectious Broth, Gave Himself an Ulcer, and Solved a Medical Mystery.* Retrieved from Discover Magazine: https://www.discovermagazine.com/health/the-doctor-who-drank-infectious-broth-gave-himself-an-ulcer-and-solved-a-medical-mystery

their findings. Part of the problem was that experiments on pigs, mice, and rats failed to reproduce ulcers. Yet, a key reason was the bacterium did not live in those animals, only primates.

Marshall continued to see the patient of other doctors in his hospital suffering from bleeding ulcers and having their stomachs removed surgically as a result. He said in an interview, "I knew all they needed was some antibiotics, but they weren't my patients." Finally, desperate for evidence, he took some bacteria, cultured it, mixed it into a broth, and he drank it. As expected, he got seriously ill, and gastritis developed. Once he confirmed he had the disease, he took antibiotics and cured himself.

The Medical community still would not accept his work. Yet, magazines such as *Readers Digest* and the *National Enquirer* reported on the strange doctor who experimented on himself. As a result, word of his finding was slowly getting out to the public. Ultimately, pressure grew till it reached a tipping point. Once that happened in the mid-1990's, acceptance was fairly quick. By 2005, they had won the Nobel Prize.

CLOSED TO THE TRUTH

In these and many other examples, there is the rejection of a theory that would later turn out to be correct. These rejections were not based on evidence. The evidence given by Semmelweis, Snow, Marshall, and Warren was both clear and definitive. They also had the added benefit that they were correct. We look back on it now with amazement. What else did their critics want?

Semmelweis demonstrated huge reductions in mortality if doctors would just wash their hands. Snow showed a one-to-one correlation between those who contracted cholera in that area and a particular pump. Marshall and Warren showed not only a clear link between ulcers and Helicobacter pylori but a cure. Yet, the experts of their day rejected their theories. These authorities were men of science, open to the science of their day, a science with new ideas making great progress and rapidly developing. Still, while they may have had an open mind to the new science, they were not open-minded to being wrong.

Being closed-minded about our own errors is a problem in many disputes. Making this worse is that it is often not the various sides are wrong, but they only have part of the truth. Time and time again, we have seen how reality is complex and more complex than our views of it. In taking sides, we also become invested in our choice.

There are stress-induced ulcers. Yet they are not the only ones. The early studies showing a link between stress and ulcers did not take into account all the complexities. Those doctors thought they had the truth. Dispassionate objectivity does not come easy. It usually takes a lot of concerted effort. Understanding all the complexity involved in a given issue is not easy.

The rewards are a better understanding of the situation. Only once the truth of a situation is understood can the issues of what, if anything, should be done be accurately assessed. Only then can we develop a nuanced position taking into account all the various complexity. The hardest of all can be communicating complex and nuanced positions to someone fixated on only part of the story.

Consider an accident and its causes—two cars crash at an intersection. The question of who is at fault can be very contentious at times and difficult to sort out. The similar but different question of what happened to cause the accident, while still difficult, can be far easier. It can be easier because stating what happened does not attempt to assess blame. Separating what happened from who is at fault has proven very successful when investigating airline accidents.

No Single Cause

The crash of a major airliner never has a single cause. The entire commercial aircraft network is constructed with safety such that it is rather difficult to have an accident. Because of all the safeguards, crashes are very complex events with numerous causes;

Seeking Truth

many things have to go wrong at the same time for an accident to occur.

Such was the case of the Tenerife accident on March 27, 1977, when two Boeing 747s collided on the runway, killing 583 passengers, the deadliest crash in commercial aircraft history. A clue into the complex nature of events is that neither aircraft was scheduled to be at the Tenerife airport that day. Both had been diverted to Tenerife following a terrorist bombing at the Gran Canaria Airport.

KLM flight 4805 was preparing for takeoff at the southeast end of the runway, while Pan Am flight 1736 was heading down the runway towards it. This situation was one of the many factors that led to the crash. The airport was so crowded because of all the diversions that departing aircraft needed to use the runway to taxi into position for takeoff. Both the KLM and Pan Am flights were preparing for takeoff.

The KLM flight entered the runway first at the northwest end and taxied to the southeast end, where it turned around and waited for takeoff. Meanwhile, the Pan Am flight was also directed onto the runway at the northwest end. They had been instructed to turn at the third taxiway, C3, getting off the runway and onto a parallel taxiway out of the path of KLM 4805. On the recording, the Pan Am crew can be heard counting out taxiways C1 and C2, but not C3. No signs identified the taxiways, and there was reduced visibility due to heavy fog, another factor in the accident.

Yet another factor was the instruction to turn onto the third taxiway. This instruction would have required Pan Am 1736 to follow a backward Z path (Σ). First, they would have to make a 148-degree turn to the left to get off the runway. Then another 148-degree turn to the right to get on to the taxiway parallel to the runway. Given that the taxiways were only 73.8 feet wide and that model of 747 requires a minimum of 142 feet to do a 180-degree turn, investigators determine this was "practically impossible."[101]

---

101 Roitsch, P. A., Babcock, G. L., & Edmunds, W. W. (n.d.). *Human Factors Report on the Tenerife Accident*. Retrieved from www.webcitation.org: https://www.webcitation.org/5zRT8z0Rm. p. 19

The Pan Am Crew had seen other 747s at the airport that day, including KLM 4805, so they concluded that the controllers couldn't be asking them to make an impossible turn. They believed that the taxiway after C3, which had a very easy 35-degree turn, must be C3, the one they were supposed to take. Again, no signs were marking which was which.

Meanwhile, the crew of KLM at the southeast end of the runway was anxious to take off. At this point, the tower radioed the following instructions, "KLM eight seven zero five, you are cleared to Papa beacon, Right turn after takeoff, proceed with heading zero four zero until intercepting the three two five radial from Las Palmas VOR." When the KLM Captain heard this, he said, "Yes! We go --- Check thrust."

But did the tower clear him for takeoff, or just let him know that he was already cleared to Papa beacon after takeoff? He did not ask for clarification. He did not even wait for his first officer to finish reading the clearance back to the tower. On the recording, the first officer is "noticeably hurried and less clear." He finished saying, "We are now.. eh taking off." At that point, a squeal somewhat distorted the tower's reply though it was understandable, "Okay (pause) Stand by for takeoff. I will call you."[102]

When the crew of Pan Am 1736 heard the KLM first officer report that they were taking off, they immediately reported, "we're still taxing down the runway – the Clipper one seven three six." This transmission is what caused the squeal on the KLM radio, distorting the message to "Stand by for takeoff." While the crew of KLM only heard a high pitch squeal, the tower only heard "Clipper one seven three six."[103]

At that point, the tower asked that the Pan Am crew to confirm they were clear of the runway. They responded, "okay, we'll

---

102 Roitsch, P. A., Babcock, G. L., & Edmunds, W. W. (n.d.). *Human Factors Report on the Tenerife Accident.* Retrieved from www.webcitation.org: https://www.webcitation.org/5zRT8z0Rm. Appendix 2

103 Roitsch, P. A., Babcock, G. L., & Edmunds, W. W. (n.d.). *Human Factors Report on the Tenerife Accident.* Retrieved from www.webcitation.org: https://www.webcitation.org/5zRT8z0Rm. Appendix 2

Seeking Truth

report when we're clear." At this point, the flight engineer of the KLM flight reacted by saying, "Is he not clear then?" Both the Captain and the first officer said "yes." Was that 'Yes, [he is not clear]' or 'Yes, [He is clear]'? Certainly, it was the latter as they continued their takeoff run. Four seconds later, the Pan Am crew saw the bright light of the KLM approaching them out of the fog, and the Captain said, "There he is --- look at him."

At that point, the Pan Am Captain went to full throttle to try and get out of the way. Three seconds after that, the KLM flight still had not seen the Pan Am plane when the first officer announced they had reached V1, the speed beyond which it is too late to abort the take-off. Two seconds after KLM reached V1, Pan Am's first officer is heard yelling, "Get off! Get Off! Get off!" Two seconds after that, four seconds after reaching V1, the KLM crew finally saw the Pan Am flight appear out of the fog, still blocking the runway as it turned off onto C4, the fourth taxiway.

By that point, KLM 4805 was going too fast to stop. The KLM captain tried to take off so quickly that the tail of his aircraft struck the ground and left a streak of metal 20 meters long. Two seconds after seeing the Pan Am plane, KLM 4805 had just cleared the ground when it struck the side of the Pan Am plane almost dead center. With a full load of fuel taken on for a long flight, it burst into flames, crashing back onto the runway in a massive fire. All 248 passengers and 14 crew members on the KLM flight were killed. Of the 396 aboard the Pan Am flight, 335 were killed; 61 people, including the flight crew, survived.

As expected, many factors led to this crash. Here is but a partial list.

1. The bombing at Gran Canaria Airport with the resulting diversions and congestion.
2. The reduced visibility from the fog.
3. The lack of signs marking C3.
4. The instruction to use C3 that would have required an impossible turn.
5. The Pan Am crew using C4.

6. The tower's ambiguous instruction to the KLM flight that they were "cleared to Papa beacon."
7. The KLM captain's anxiousness.
8. The KLM crews took the instructions about Papa beacon as permission to takeoff.
9. The radio distortion caused by simultaneous messages from Pan Am and the tower distorting the message, "Okay (pause) Stand by for takeoff. I will call you."
10. The failure of the KLM crew to understand that message.
11. Ambiguous use of "Okay" in messages.

Again, this is just a partial list. Changing just one of these, and there would not have been an accident. No bombing, no diversions, no accident. No fog and the Pan Am flight would have been seen on the runway, no accident. All of these things needed to happen for there to have been an accident.

Building off the knowledge that perception is theory-laden, investigators realized that any ambiguity would be taken the way the listener expected. This is particularly true when focused on other tasks that take a lot of attention, such as a pilot during takeoff. So, for example, when someone says 'Okay," that could mean "Yes" or just "I heard what you said."

The latter is what the Pan Am Co-pilot meant when he said, "okay, we'll report when we're clear." This meaning of 'Okay' is probably what the tower meant when they told the KLM crew, "Okay (pause) Stand by for takeoff. I will call you." However, the KLM crew took this as, "Okay, go ahead and take off." Because of the pause, they were already focusing on takeoff; they never heard the second part telling them to wait. That would have been unexpected, and thus they did not hear it.

Unintended Consequences

A major factor was the KLM captain's anxiousness. Even the Pan Am crew can be heard commenting on this just before the crash. As the KLM crew started its takeoff run, the Pan Am crew told the tower they would report when they were clear of the runway. On the cockpit recording, Pan Am's first officer can be heard saying, "He's anxious isn't he." Why was the KLM captain so anxious?

One factor was that the flight time to Amsterdam would put them close to the end of their duty cycle. Four months before the crash, the Dutch government changed the rules restricting how many hours a pilot could fly. According to the report, "As a direct result of this change, computation of work and rest time became rather difficult, and the captain no longer had any discretion in extending duty time."[104] These were extremely strict limits the crew were legally responsible to follow. According to the report, the KLM crew "discussed the possibility of fines, imprisonment or loss of licenses, should the time limits be exceeded."[105]

The crew had already "expressed great concern about being able to return to Amsterdam that evening while remaining within the regulations." If they did not get in the air soon, they would have to cancel the flight until the next day. In addition, there was concern the weather would deteriorate even further and close the airport.

The KLM captain was one of KLM's most experienced pilots involved in both training and management. He was even featured in KLM advertising. He knew the "chaotic conditions" this would have, not only on his passengers stuck in an already overcrowded airport but how it would ripple through the entire KLM flight schedule. In one of the ironies, when KLM officials first learned of the disaster, they tried to reach out to him to help them manage the crash, only to find out he was the pilot.

---

104 Roitsch, P. A., Babcock, G. L., & Edmunds, W. W. (n.d.). *Human Factors Report on the Tenerife Accident*. Retrieved from www.webcitation.org: https://www.webcitation.org/5zRT8z0Rm. p. 14

105 Roitsch, P. A., Babcock, G. L., & Edmunds, W. W. (n.d.). *Human Factors Report on the Tenerife Accident*. Retrieved from www.webcitation.org: https://www.webcitation.org/5zRT8z0Rm. p. 19

In one of the clearest examples of the law of unintended consequences at work, one of the factors that led to the worse crash in aviation history was a Dutch law aimed at improving airline safety. This law removed discretions from the captain.

COMPLEXITY CAUSES DISPUTES

Given all the various factors, is it any wonder that disputes can arise. All made mistakes. There are explanations and reasons for what everyone did. Still, this is only clear because a lot of effort was put into fully understanding what happened in order to improve the system. It is such detailed reports that help make airline crashes so relatively rare.

As a result of this crash, many changes were instituted. For example, in communications between the tower and aircrews, "takeoff" is only used for actual takeoff. Crews when ready for takeoff, will now say they are ready for departure. Overall, the messages between crew and tower are much more standardized to preclude misunderstanding.

Normal everyday interactions do not have this level of analysis or precision. One lesson to learn from this is that it is extremely important to separate analysis from judgment. Before you can make a judgment about something, you must first know what happened. As in the accident above, often multiple causes and factors must be considered.

As a normal dispute, one could easily envision someone arguing the KLM captain was responsible for taking off too early. On the other hand, one could argue it was the Pan Am crew's fault for missing the C3 taxiway, or the tower was at fault. One could easily see such arguments with all sides fully convinced they have the facts on their side, certain of their view of the truth.

Based on the detailed analysis of the accident, we can see there is merit in all these claims. Still, without the detailed analysis, none would have the complete picture. More importantly, rarely do we have the benefits of such analysis in normal day-to-day disputes.

We should always be open to the possibility we do not have a complete understanding. There may be factors we have yet to take into consideration.

The tendency to put judgment ahead of analysis particularly becomes a problem in any situation where there is a need or desire to assess blame. Thus, a quick internet search will discover articles calling the KLM captain a mass murderer for the accident above. It is also a problem with many political disputes. Rather than focusing on what happened, the various sides seek to either place or avoid blame.

IDEAS AS POSSIBILITIES

A good attitude is to take ideas as possibilities to play with, not uncontestable truths to be defended at all costs. There will certainly be some beliefs worth defending, but we can take an open-minded approach to their range and extent. As such, a good question to ask is, 'what if they are right?' Phrased more dangerously, 'what if I am wrong?' Many people do not like to even think about this possibility, at least not on the beliefs they hold dear.

This leads to a paradox; we know we are imperfect and not everything we believe is true. Yet we often insulate ourselves from that reality and even at times strenuously resist even the suggestion we might be wrong. Oh, we will admit we are not perfect in an abstract sense, just not in our actual beliefs.

A good test for this is the question: Have you ever changed your mind on a major belief? Hopefully, the answer is, at least to some extent, yes. As you look over the times your opinion changed, four additional questions will help explore your openness. The first is how much? Was the change a complete reversal or just a minor tweak? The greater the change, the more openness is required.

Second, how invested were you in the belief? It does not require much openness to change a view on a subject about which you care little. Take, for example, something you learned in school but have not thought about much, if at all, since. Say you learned in school that Sparta was to blame for the Peloponnesian War. You have not thought much about it but then read an article causing you to think you were wrong and Athens was to blame. While a complete change, such a change required little openness. Such a change comes, not from openness, as much as disinterest. Generally, the more invested we are in a belief, the less open we are to making the change. Consider someone who lived through the Vietnam war and had strong opinions about it. It would take considerable openness to change their mind.

A third question is why the change? Was it based on a strict consideration of the pros and cons, or something else? When it comes to political parties, many people are strongly influenced by their parents. For some, this is having similar political views as their parents. Others differ from their parents, not because they did a careful analysis, but more out of rebellion. They become the opposite of their parents. Others changed because of the strong influence of a teacher or close friends. So what caused your change?

The third question leads directly into the fourth: what were the dynamics of the groups to which you belong? These could be formal, such as a school or church, or informal, like a group of friends. We are social animals. As much as we like to think for ourselves, those around us strongly impact our views. This influence is easiest to see with historical issues.

Consider the question: Being born during the Roman Empire, would that have affected your views about slavery? While we might like to think we would still have thought slavery was wrong, it is almost certain your view of slavery would have conformed to the period, just like everyone else did at the time.

Slavery during the Roman empire was seen as a part of nature. Slaves were seen as weak. This view was a bit self-reinforcing as many slaves were those defeated by the Romans. Thus, Romans had the right to be masters because they won the wars. Those defeated deserved to become slaves because they lost. This was the norm. Slaves even accepted it. When Spartacus led a slave revolt, they enslaved the Romans they defeated and forced them to fight in gladiatorial games. It was just the way things were, and very few questioned it. Had you grown up in that era, it is what you would have been taught and what you believed.

This is what makes the charges of white supremacy against Lincoln and other reformers so baseless. The norm would have been the status quo that had lasted for thousands of years, since before the beginning of history. So it is not surprising that Lincoln did not have modern notions of racial equality. What is amazing is that he broke with historical norms to advance human rights and equality despite great cost and resistance, a view that ultimately cost him his life.

When it comes to your opinion changes, did they change against the groups you were in at the time or with it? What opposition did you face? It is always easier to go with the crowd, though some enjoy the role of a contrarian. A contrarian's views can be shaped by the crowd, just as much as a conformist, just in opposite directions.

At times, it can take more openness to keep a position than to change. For example, following the attack on Pearl Harbor that started WWII, there was considerable anti-Japanese sentiment on the west coast. Some were swept up, not due to openness to the evidence and reason; it was what the crowd was doing. At times like these, standing for what is right takes an openness to facts and evidence. It also takes courage.

TESTS FOR OPENNESS

Openness and courage go hand-in-hand when it comes to the truth. One must be both open to the truth and courageous enough to stand for it. Thus, when it comes to openness, how close do you come? Have you ever significantly changed a position that you thought was important? Did evidence and reason play a major role in this change? Did the change go against the views of those you value? The closer you get to saying yes to these questions, the more open to the truth.

Still, you could answer yes to all these questions because you joined a fringe group. While important, openness requires more. Another good indicator of openness is how often you encounter the best of the other side. It is far too easy to watch or listen to those you disagree with making bad or illogical arguments and conclude your position is justified. Still, this would be an unwarranted conclusion. All major positions have what might be called their serious advocates, their popular ones, and their fringe. While these can overlap, often, they do not.

In ancient Greek battles, troops were lined up with the best troops in the place of honor on the right and the weakest on the left. As the two armies met on the battlefield, this would have each side's best, fighting their opponents' weakest.

Early in the fourth century BC, the major city-state at the time, Sparta, invaded Thebes to reverse a recent democratic revolt. On July 6, 371 BC, the two armies met. Theban general Epaminondas was outnumbered in the coming battle. Even worse, there was doubt concerning the reliability of the allies he did have. Spartans, on the other hand, were known for their military ability. In a traditional battle, Thebes was going to lose.

Epaminondas, to give his army a chance, broke with tradition. The change was really quite simple; he reversed the traditional order of battle, putting his best troops on the left instead of the right. On top of that, he reinforced them. As a result, when Epaminondas' army rammed into the Spartans, they overwhelmed them.

While Epaminondas' army knew who they would be fighting, Spartan's best had expected to fight the weakest part of the Theban army. Yet, the soldiers they faced were much stronger than expected, and when the rest of the Spartan army saw their strongest had been defeated, they fled. Epaminondas's tactics were so successful they influenced future generals, including Phillip II of Macedon and his better-known son, Alexander the Great.

The same goes for debate. Addressing the weakest of the other side's arguments says little about the truth of the matter. Listening only to the weakest arguments is not an indication of openness.

Seeking Truth

You must be open to your own error, to be truly open to the truth. You must value the truth more than you value your own opinions and beliefs. Yet, the more central the belief, the more important we think a belief is, the harder this is to do, and the more we will resist it.

Overcoming Closeness

This tendency is at the core of why discussion with those who disagree is so important. We find it far easier to find problems with a belief we reject than with beliefs we hold dear. Thus, just as we are more likely to find errors in opinions we disagree with, those who disagree with us are more likely to find problems with our beliefs.

This tendency is one of the areas where confirmation bias is so detrimental. When we encounter evidence that agrees with our beliefs, our beliefs are strengthened and confirmed. We rest intellectually assured that we know the truth of the matter. When confronted with evidence that conflicts with our beliefs, our first instinct is to ignore it. 'That can't be correct.' When we cannot simply ignore it, we put effort into discrediting it, countering it, or showing how it can be reconciled with our belief, perhaps as an exception or special case. We will do a more detailed analysis, if we cannot ignore it. As seen earlier with the Tenerife accident, real-life events are complex enough to find a range of supportive data for a number of differing views, particularly if we stop as soon as we find what we want.

Open-mindedness requires us to work against this tendency. As with Aristotle's Doctrine of the Mean, we must realize our tendencies and counter them. We should slow down and think about things. Realizing our tendency, we should question whether it is true when we hear something that confirms what we believe. Does it confirm our beliefs in the way we think it does? Similarly, when we encounter information that conflicts with our beliefs, we should also pause. Is this really true? Does it impact my view more than I think it does?

Even doing this a little can greatly improve our search for the truth and help us become more critical thinkers. Still, being critical thinkers requires us to develop skills for detecting errors, which are all too common. That is the subject of the next chapter.

Chapter 11

Avoiding Errors

All growth depends upon activity. There is no development physically or intellectually without effort, and effort means work.
– Calvin Coolidge

Seeking truth is a process, and one that never ends. No matter how close you come to the goal, complete truth will elude you. This is to be expected. Truth is reality, and reality is more complex than we can comprehend. Yet, it is possible to be accurate, and accuracy is a more realistic goal. On the other hand, it is much easier to be wrong.

In earlier chapters, we looked at many examples of people who were wrong but whose errors were at least steps in the right direction. Another example of this was the early attempts to understand the basic construction of the universe; while different cultures had slightly different lists, in Western culture, this came from the Greeks. The basic question was, what is everything made of?

The answer was that everything we see around us is made up of parts or components. A house has walls, doors, windows, and a roof. These components were then composed of even more basic components. A door can have wood, hinges, and a lock. Eventually, however, you get down to some basic components or elements. In the middle of the 5th century BC, Empedocles listed the elements as four, Earth, Air, Fire, and Water. He also said there were two forces, one that pulls things together and another that pulls things apart. Everything in the universe was made from various combinations of these four elements and two forces.

Of course, now we know that Empedocles was wrong, but only partially. He was correct that the large amount of things we see in the universe around us are made from a relatively small number of basic elements. Rather than four, there are about a hundred. Instead of two forces, there are four. Empedocles even did a few basic experiments. For example, he took an empty bucket, turned it upside down, and submerged it underwater. The water and the air would not combine. From this, he concluded that air and water must be separate elements.

At roughly the same time, Leucippus and his student Democritus suggested a limit to how many times you can cut anything in half. For example, take an apple and cut it in half. Now you have two pieces of apple. Take a half and cut it again into two more pieces. But how many times can you do this? Leucippus and Democritus said that at some point, you could no longer cut the remaining piece in half and still have an apple. When this happens, it is uncuttable. In Greek, adding 'a' (α) negates the word. Adding this to the Greek word meaning 'to cut' 'tomos' (τόμος) result in 'atomos' or atom. They were very close to being right. So, why was their theory not accepted?

One problem was that they said atoms were so small as to be invisible. In addition, as an explanation, it did not explain much. They were also wrong on many points. For example, Leucippus and Democritus said that atoms are solid, have no internal structure, and have finite size. In many respects, while wrong, Aristotle's refinements to Empedocles did a better job of explaining the world around us. It worked better. Aristotle added the qualities of hot-cold and wet-dry. Fire was hot and dry; Water was cold and wet; Air was hot and wet; Earth, cold and dry. Aristotle's view served as a foundation for over a thousand years.

LEARNING: THE PROCESS OF REMOVING ERRORS

What we would call modern chemistry started in the 17th century. By that time, the investigations into the nature of matter had been systemized into the proto-science of alchemy, with its pursuit of the creation of gold and the search for an elixir of life. Robert Boyle began the transformation of Chemistry out of alchemy with his book *The Sceptical Chymist* in 1661. While still a book of alchemy, Boyle rejected Aristotle's view of four elements along

Seeking Truth

with others that had arisen. He thus began the process of putting chemistry on a more solid footing.

Still, there remained a key problem. If Aristotle's view was wrong, yet there were elements, what were they? Aristotle believed one of the elements was Air. By the 18th century, it was becoming clear that there were different kinds of air. Johann Beecher suggested Phlogiston, a substance supposedly released when something burns. Then, Joseph Priestley and others produced what was variously labeled dephlogisticated air, fire air, or vital air. If you covered a flame, once the air absorbed all the phlogiston it could hold, the flame would go out. Uncover the flame, and as more dephlogisticated air came in, the flame would come back.

Antoine Lavoisier cast doubt on this theory when he burned paper and dephlogisticated air and found the ashes of the paper weighed more than the original paper. Rather than releasing phlogiston into the air, it seemed the paper was gaining something from it. Eventually, he showed the air was composed of two gases, vital air and lifeless air. After more research, Lavoisier gave vital air the Greek name oxygen (acid-maker). Because of its reactions, he mistakenly thought it made acid. In 1783 Henry Cavendish, produced water by burning oxygen and 'inflammable air.' As a result, Cavendish called the 'inflammable air" Hydrogen, Greek for water-maker.

The ability to get oxygen and hydrogen from water and then recombine them by burning to get water showed water was not an element as Aristotle thought. Instead, water was made up of hydrogen and oxygen, which we now know are elements. Twenty years after Cavendish, John Dalton came up with the atomic theory giving a firm foundation for modern Chemistry.

A key point of this brief outline is how the search for truth, in this case, the field of chemistry, is a process, often a long and ongoing one. Today, it is easy for us to look back at Aristotle or the alchemists and point out how wrong they were. But if you were to somehow go back in time to talk to Aristotle, how would you convince him?

The eighteenth and nineteenth-century chemists reached their conclusions because of all the trial and error before them. As a result, they inherited a body of knowledge and improved it. In addition, it was not just the field of chemistry that developed. A large range of developments in other areas yielded the tools and techniques important to their discoveries.

Around 1700 Guillaume Amontons showed there was a relationship between pressure and temperature of a gas. However, the equipment he had to work with was not precise enough to exactly say what that relationship was. It would have to wait one hundred years when Joseph Louis Gay-Lussac, with better equipment, could formulate this into what is now known as Gay-Lussac's Law. However, it is also known as Amontons' law.

THE COST OF MISTAKES

The development of chemistry is a story of trial and error, testing, and correction. This was a process of making mistakes, realizing them, and then learning from them. Of course, it is better not to make mistakes in the first place and to avoid them as much as possible. It is important because not all mistakes are equal. Some mistakes have large, even catastrophic downsides. Nowhere is this clearer than in wrong decisions about war.

This is not to say, as we will see, that all decisions to go to war are mistakes. War, by definition, involves at least two parties. While at least two sides are needed to fight a war, only one side needs to start it. Military Historian Victor David Hansen described war as ultimately resulting from ambiguity concerning military strength. Wars are fought for many reasons. They can be fought for land, resources, food, power, religion, and ideology, to name a few. While there are many reasons, still they are normally not fought unless there is a dispute over who will win.

Consider a land dispute, for example. Such a dispute can go on indefinitely. If the side that wants the land is too weak, they will never start a war, for they know they will lose. If the side that wants the land is strong enough, the other side will surrender it rather than try to keep it in a war they know they will lose. War will only break out if the side that wants the land thinks it can succeed in taking it by force, while the other side thinks they can hold on to it. One way to avoid war is to keep aggressors weak and defenders strong. Ambiguity about military strength risks war.

Military strength is not just a measure of weapons but also includes the willingness to use them. Here mistakes can be easier to make. For example, in January 1950, then-Secretary of State Dean Acheson delivered a speech to warn the Soviets against any military actions in Asia. However, he was less clear when it came to national independence movements. It was clear the United States would oppose direct military action by the Soviets, but would it oppose national movements backed by the Soviets?

Acheson, to make matters worse, failed to mention Korea as an area the United States would defend. This ambiguity was taken to mean the United States would not interfere with an invasion by North Korea into South Korea. Six months later, on June 25, 1950, North Korean forces invaded South Korea starting the Korean War.

Ambiguity and miscalculation are dangerous. Nowhere is this clearer than with World War I. Many factors led to WWI. The initial spark was the assassination of Arch Duke Ferdinand of Austria in the city of Sarajevo, Bosnia. However, the real reasons were much deeper and long-standing and are still debated today. Yet one factor common to all the powers involved was a serious overestimation of their own strength combined with underestimating their opponents. The generally accepted belief on all sides was that the war would be quick, with most estimates being that it would last 30 days. Everyone thought they would win.

However, when the war ended, it had lasted four years and cost 20 million lives, even more, if you count the Spanish Flu spread by the troops. World War I reshaped the governments of Europe. It was a major factor in the Russian Revolution and the emergence of the Soviet Union, which was to cause many problems, rippling down to the present day.

Learning the Wrong Lessons

An easy lesson following the War to End All Wars was that you should not fight wars. Yet, it was the wrong lesson. Its acceptance by the French and English governments was a major factor in their failure to stop the rise of Hitler's Germany. In the economic problems caused by the Great Depression, Hitler's National Socialist party rose from obscurity to win the most votes in the 1932 elections. In January 1933, he was appointed Chancellor. From that point forward, Hitler steadily increased his power. He created the Gestapo, banned other political parties, and defied the Treaty of Versailles by building an army and air force. In March 1936, Hitler judged that while France and England were much stronger, they did not have the will to fight. He gambled on this by sending troops into the Rhineland.

Had France and England reacted, they would have easily stopped the Germans. Such an embarrassing miscalculation would probably have toppled Hitler from power. Yet Hitler was right; the French and English had the power, but not the will.

Rather than topple him from power, Hitler's gamble gave him even more power and standing, which he showed off at the Berlin Olympics later that year. After the Olympics, he signed agreements with Italy and Japan. Two years later, having used the time to grow stronger, Hitler used his new power to annex Austria. Again, while this was a direct violation of the Treaty, France and England did nothing.

Having annexed Austria and grown even stronger, Hitler turned his sights on Czechoslovakia. With the real prospect of a German invasion, British Prime Minister Chamberlain flew to Germany to negotiate with Hitler. The Czechoslovakian officials were not included. Along with the French, Chamberlain agreed to let Hitler have half of Czechoslovakia. Hitler promised that was the end of his ambitions. These negotiations became the Munich treaty. The Czechoslovakian officials were informed that they had lost half their country. When Chamberlain flew back to England, proclaiming "Peace in our time," the second world war was less than a year away.

The peace did not last. In March 1939, six months after the Munich treaty, Hitler took the rest of Czechoslovakia. Finally, it was becoming clear that Hitler could not be trusted; war might be unavoidable. While they did nothing about Czechoslovakia, the French and English made it clear that Hitler could go no further; they would defend Poland.

In theory, this left Hitler boxed in with France and England in the West and the Soviet Union to the East. In August, the Soviet Union and Germany signed a non-aggression pact, secretly agreeing to carve up Poland. This agreement allowed Germany to invade Poland on September 1, 1939. The Soviets invaded on September 17. Poland was gone, World War II had begun.

On September 3, Britain and France declared war on Germany. Even then, there was a reluctance actually to fight Hitler. In a phase now referred to as the phony war, little happened as Hitler prepared to invade France. When he did, it was on his terms, and France fell quickly. So did the government of Neville Chamberlain, who was replaced as Prime Minister by Winston Churchill on May 10, 1940.

Had they acted in 1936 when Hitler entered the Rhineland, France and Great Britain could have stopped him with relative ease and likely ended future threats. Four years later, when Great Britain finally had a Prime Minister who would fight, the situation looked almost hopeless. Many thought it was, and it has been called their darkest hour.

For the next year and a half, Great Britain stood alone against Hitler and the Axis powers until the United States entered the war following the attack on Pearl Harbor. In the end, casualties in World War Two far exceeded the horrific numbers of even the First World War. Estimates for combined military and civilian deaths are between 60-85 million.

No Easy Decisions

These examples show that these are not easy decisions. Key here is that these decisions were not only wrong, they did not have to be. They were not only mistakes; they were mistakes that could have been avoided. When asked what he would call the new war with Germany, Prime Minister Winston Churchill called it "The Unnecessary War." If instead of ignoring the violations, France and England had enforced the Treaty of Versailles, WWII, at least in Europe, would not have happened. It certainly would not have been as long or as deadly. Still, as with many things, the easier it is to deal with a problem, the easier it also is to ignore.

Luckily, most decisions are not this costly. More importantly, we can do things to avoid at least some errors, costly or not. One of the biggest problems is that, as mentioned before, we often drift into decisions without much consideration. At other times, we are so focused on one aspect of the situation that we fail to take into account all the considerations. For WWI, all sides were focused on an early victory. For WWII, France and England were focused on avoiding war. This is where seriously looking at the pros and cons, as discussed earlier, is so important.

There are numerous ways of approaching decision-making and many books on the subject. Here we will just outline a few general principles. Think about some recent decisions you made where, looking back now, you believe you made a mistake, or at least think you could have done better. What can you learn from them? What steps did you take to make that decision? Was it an impulsive decision, or did you give it some thought? If the former, the way to improve is pretty clear; Don't make impulse decisions; always look for pros and cons.

If the latter, think about your thought process. Was there a problem with your list of pros and cons? Why do you now see the decision as flawed? What do you know now that leads you to your conclusion that you did not know before? What could you have done to get that knowledge before you made your decision? As you look at several of these, does a pattern begin to form? This is where Aristotle's Doctrine of the Mean comes into play. What are the tendencies that you should try to counter to become a more critical thinker?

FOOLED BY REASON

Even decisions we think through can be flawed. Fundamentally, this is because critical thinking is difficult, and often, our information is incomplete. More importantly, things can seem to make sense but still be wrong. Our brains are so wired to see patterns that we will see them in places they do not exist. We will make connections that are not there. Just think of a time you looked at the clouds. It probably did not take long until you began to see some identifiable shapes, shapes that, in reality, could not possibly be there.

This very strong ability to see patterns where they do not exist leads to problems. This is particularly true in areas where evidence is limited. In the absence of evidence, we will fill in the gaps with speculation. We seem to be virtually hard-wired to see patterns, to seek complete explanations. We abhor loose ends and the unexplained.

Faced with something we do not understand, we will invent ways to make sense of them; we will speculate. In and of itself, there is no problem here, and this is the origin of many discoveries. The problem enters when we forget these are speculations and begin to treat them as fact. Before long, we have speculation built on speculation, upon speculation. Our beliefs can become a house of cards.

This tendency is the origin of many conspiracy theories. We are confronted with an event that does not make sense. That a lone gunman can so radically alter history by killing a president is hard to grasp. Such significant events should have complicated origins. Thus we fill in the gaps with speculation. At times we can even be led to conclude that the evidence we do have is not real. It must be planted.

Before long, reality ceases to shape our speculation, and instead, our speculations drive reality. With the assassination of President Kennedy, the only thing the numerous conspiracy theories seem to agree on is that Oswald was not alone if he was involved at all. As for who was, take your pick. Theories exist pointing to people and groups across the political spectrum and around the world. Once you free yourself from the evidence, anything becomes possible.

Still, this tendency to see patterns has a good side. It is the foundation of our search for truth and the origin of science. But the downside is that lacking all the evidence, which is the norm, often our speculation will be wrong. The history of science is full of scientists making seemingly logical conclusions only to be incorrect.

Aristotle thought that heavier objects would fall faster than lighter ones. It is harder to lift heavy objects, so why shouldn't it be "easier" for them to fall. There is even experimental support. Drop a hammer and a feather at the same time, and the hammer hits the ground first. Of course, now we know that air resistance affects the feather more than the hammer, resulting in the different speeds we see. Still, there is something strange in seeing Apollo 15 astronaut David Scott perform this experiment on the moon. The feather and hammer hit the moon's surface simultaneously.

Historically, the basic pattern for science is that people develop theories about what is happening that seem to make sense. Then they conduct experiments that show they were wrong. Then they come up with new explanations that fit the evidence, and the cycle repeats. The key here is that what we think are good explanations are often wrong when tested. Sometimes we discover we are not even asking the right questions.

In the latter part of the twentieth century, a major question in cosmology was whether or not there was enough mass in the universe to stop the universe's expansion. Since the Big Bang, the universe has been expanding. Gravity resulting from the mass of the universe slows that expansion. Yet, as the universe gets larger, the force of gravity would lessen. Thus the question was whether there was enough mass to stop the expansion before the universe got so big that gravity would have little effect. The question was important, for if there was not enough mass to stop the expansion, then the universe was a one-time event. If the expansion stopped, the universe would collapse back on itself. That would raise the possibility that our universe was part of an infinite series of Big Bangs, followed by collapses, resulting in new Big Bangs.

The answer to these questions depended on the total amount of mass in the universe. Early measurements showed nowhere near enough mass, but there were questions about the accuracy of such measurements, particularly in regards to dark matter. Then in 1998, two different groups of scientists discovered the expansion of the universe was accelerating, not slowing down. This finding was completely unexpected. They had been asking if the expansion would slow down enough to stop. They should have asked the more fundamental question, was it even slowing?

Science?

The major corrective factor in science is the ability to test. This ability to test is the difference between the hard sciences such as physics, chemistry, and astronomy and soft sciences, i.e., the social sciences. Given how often the seemingly reasonable theories in the hard sciences have turned out to be wrong when tested, it should give us pause when considering the "findings" of the social sciences, where the ability to test is much more limited. Even when some testing can be done, the results are far more open to interpretation and confirmation bias.

Philosopher Karl Popper argued that for a theory to be scientific, it must be falsifiable. The theory of Quantum Mechanics is scientific because it is possible to test the theory in such a way, it could fail. As we have seen, Einstein tried to do just that, but Quantum Mechanics passed the tests. When testing a theory, it is more important to try and disprove the theory than confirm it.

A problem with many studies and surveys is that they are designed to confirm beliefs. As we have seen, perception is, to some extent, theory-laden. Researchers approach issues with theories. They construct surveys based on those theories and examine the finding in light of those theories. How much of this is actual research, and how much is confirmation bias? The researcher designed a survey to get certain results, and they got the results the survey was designed to get. These surveys say very little about factors that may be more significant but were not included in the survey.

One of my professors cautioned us with the correlation between concrete and crime. There is a link. The more concrete per square mile, the greater the likelihood of crime. At first glance, this would lead to the conclusion that concrete causes crime. Of course, that would be absurd. The connection is that there is a common factor between the amount of concrete and the amount of crime: the number of people. The more people, the more concrete, and the more people, the more crime. The rule: correlation does not mean causation. Still, suppose a researcher believes that X contributes to a given problem and does a study that finds a correlation. In that case, confirmation bias will lead them to conclude they have established X as a cause.

An additional problem is that in the hard sciences, the theories are normally, to some extent, forward-looking. They make predictions that can be tested. When the tests are run, often the result is unexpected. Many theories in the softer sciences fall more into the category of explanations. They do not make clear predictions that can be tested. These problems have led some to question if it is correct even to consider the social sciences science. Whether they are or not comes down to how you define science.

The Unexpected

There is also the problem of things often being counter-intuitive or even paradoxical. This is a problem because we frequently will assume a process is much simpler than it actually is. Consider the business paradox. The purpose of any business is to make money. It is not only important, but it is also vital for the business's very existence. A business that does not make money cannot stay open very long. If the business has a monopoly or some other means of protection, this is not a problem. It is a problem in a free market.

In a free market, this creates a paradox in that the purpose of the business is to make money, but any business that makes this their primary purpose will fail. The reason for the seeming paradox is that there is another factor to consider, the customers.

Nobody likes to do business with a company whose main goal is to take their money. When constrained by monopoly or other factors, people may not have a choice. Still, they can and will go elsewhere in a free market, and the business will fail.

Thus, the main purpose of a successful business in a free market is to figure out how to provide goods or services that people want at a price they are willing to pay and still make a profit while doing so. This is more complicated than just making money, and it is why most businesses fail.

Similar considerations apply to counter-intuitive ideas. Consider the early smallpox vaccinations. Smallpox was a disease that was much more deadly than COVID-19. Where fatalities from COVID-19 were a little over one percent and largely confined to the elderly, smallpox fatality rates were around 30 percent and even higher for the young. If it did not kill you, it could leave you blind and badly scarred. So what do you do in an age before even the germ theory of disease? How can you protect yourself? Why you give yourself the disease!

If that sounds counter-intuitive, it is, but a few people noticed a mild form of the disease with a higher survival rate. More importantly, people who had the mild form did not get the more severe form. So around the fifteenth century, starting in China, people began inoculating themselves with material taken from pustules that formed on the skin of smallpox victims. It was still a risky procedure. As many as two percent died from the vaccination, which is higher than the fatality rate for COVID-19 but far lower than the death rate from the more severe form. It was literally taking a small risk to avoid a much bigger risk.

Now we know about the Germ Theory of disease and much more about how the immune system works. We know about the cause of smallpox, the variola virus, which has major and minor forms. We also have far superior vaccines that have far fewer side effects and where deaths are almost non-existent. As a result, smallpox, which killed an estimated 300 million in the twentieth century, was completely eradicated. The last naturally occurring case was in 1977. Today the only threats from smallpox are either from a lab leak or use as a bioweapon.

The immune system itself is, in some sense, counter-intuitive. One might think that the best way to protect oneself from disease is to practice strict hygienic measures to avoid getting sick. While it seems at first glance a reasonable strategy, there is a problem.

The human immune system is something that Nassim Nicholas Taleb has labeled *Antifragile*. Fragile things break under minor stresses. Robust things resist stresses, but over time wear out. Things that are antifragile grow stronger under stress. Not only do they benefit from stress, they also grow weaker without it. Your muscles are antifragile. Stress them by lifting weights, and you will grow stronger. Don't use them, and you will grow weaker.

Your immune system is antifragile. It needs to be stressed to function well. In short, you benefit from being exposed to germs from time to time. Protect yourself from all illnesses, and you weaken your immune system to the point that you become even more susceptible to any illness you might get. A disease that otherwise would only make you sick now could kill you because your immune system is not strong enough to fight it off.

Even when we have a good explanation for something that seems to fit the facts that we have, it does not mean that we are correct. Even when something does not seem right, it does not mean that it is wrong. We must always be open to the possibility that there is something that we are missing, information that we do not have. Perhaps we are just asking the wrong questions. Thinking critically involves being open to the possibility that you are wrong or do not have the full picture. It involves asking if the pattern we see is real or just a cloud in the sky.

The subject of critical thinking is large and would be a book by itself. It covers a range of topics, such as logic, fallacies, the role of emotions, perception, and how to approach problems. Luckily many books have been written, and so here, I will only discuss it briefly. Mastering critical thinking will help you think more clearly, and spot errors. For example, with even a brief knowledge of logical fallacies, you will discover that they are ubiquitous. You will encounter these errors. It is not a question of if, but how many you can spot each day.

FALLACIES

Ad Hominem Attack

The most common of these fallacies is ad hominem attack and deserves special mention because it is so common. It falls into the broader category of the Fallacies of Irrelevance. These fallacies are attempts to change the subject. Rather than discuss the core issues, they attempt to shift the focus to something that has no bearing on the argument; In this case, the person on the other side. Such arguments can take many forms, and, in fact, ad hominem attack is so common, it has at least five major sub-forms. Still, any attack on the person rather than the argument they are making is an irrational ad hominem attack, with one exception.

The exception occurs when the person is the argument, it is acceptable to question the person. For example, when a person gives eyewitness testimony, a judgment, or an expert opinion, questioning whether they might be biased would be legitimate. While this is a significant exception, it covers a small fraction of the personal attacks daily. Still, trying to determine if a personal attack is legitimate is not always straightforward.

For example, during the first debate with Lincoln, Stephen Douglas said that Lincoln "could ruin more liquor than all the boys of the town together."[106] Accusing Lincoln of being a drunk was certainly a personal attack; was it an irrational ad hominem attack?

In terms of the issue being debated, that is slavery; it certainly was an ad hominem. Whether Lincoln had a problem with alcohol was completely irrelevant to the arguments he was making. Even if the charge had been true, and there is no indication that it was, Lincoln's arguments against slavery would have been just as valid.

However, the issue of slavery, while the main subject of the debate, was not the only one under consideration. There was a broader one. The debates over slavery were part of a larger campaign for Senator. Running for office is very much like a job interview. The candidate, and their fitness to hold the office, are the issue.

Understood in this context, Douglas' raising the issue of a supposed drinking problem would not in and of itself be an ad hominem attack, particularly in light of an emerging temperance movement. So, if viewed as part of the slavery debate, it was a fallacy. If viewed as part of the larger issue of fitness for the office of Senator, it was not. The question would then be whether or not it was true. Apparently, it was not.

Slanting – Emotionally Loaded Language

This argument was not the only questionable one Douglas made in that first debate. Douglas also used Slanting, or emotionally loaded language, probably the second most common fallacy, even today. Emotionally loaded language attempts to sway opinion, not by reasoned arguments, but through labels. Labels can attempt to sway opinion in favor or against a view. Either way, they seek an emotional reaction rather than a rational one.

Douglas began his first speech with a historical review. This background was more important than it may at first seem. Not only was there the complex history of slavery, but the two major parties

---

106 Douglas, S. (1858, August 21). *First Debate: Ottawa, Illinois.* Retrieved from Lincoln Home: https://www.nps.gov/liho/learn/historyculture/debate1.htm

were still fairly new. The Democrat party was just over 30 years old, formed out of the Democratic-Republican party following the controversial election of 1824. The Republican party formed as an anti-slavery party only four years before the debate, being organized following the collapse of the Whig party over the issue of slavery. As Douglas put it,

> In 1854, Mr. Abraham Lincoln and Mr. Trumbull entered into an arrangement, one with the other, and each with his respective friends, to dissolve the old Whig party on the one hand, and to dissolve the old Democratic party on the other, and to connect the members of both into an Abolition party under the name and disguise of a Republican party.[107]

Note the use of the term disguise implies there was something deceptive or dishonest about the Republican party. It gets worse. Douglas changes the way he refers to the Republican party. For the rest of his speech, he frequently referred to "the Black Republican party." Undoubtedly, for Douglas, this was an emotionally loaded label meant to disparage the party and create negative feelings against Lincoln in the audience. As Douglas said later in the debate,

> If you desire negro citizenship, if you desire to allow them to come into the State and settle with the white man, if you desire them to vote on an equality with yourselves, and to make them eligible to office, to serve on juries, and to adjudge your rights, then support Mr. Lincoln and the Black Republican party, who are in favor of the citizenship of the negro.[108]

Emotional language can also be used to create support. One just needs to survey the names assigned to recent legislation to see a list of examples. Label something a "Jobs" act, and you force those against the bill to vote against jobs. This practice is so pervasive and

---

107 Douglas, S. (1858, August 21). *First Debate: Ottawa, Illinois*. Retrieved from Lincoln Home: https://www.nps.gov/liho/learn/historyculture/debate1.htm
108 Douglas, S. (1858, August 21). *First Debate: Ottawa, Illinois*. Retrieved from Lincoln Home: https://www.nps.gov/liho/learn/historyculture/debate1.htm

ingrained into standard practice; there is little if any hope of eliminating it any time soon. A good rule of thumb is to assume the opposite of the name as a starting point. Say there is a new "Jobs" bill, start by assuming it is not a jobs act and then ask, what does it really do? Be sure to look at sources that support and oppose the bill. Look at the actual language. Then make a decision based on your investigation, not just on the label.

BIAS

Such investigation can take a lot of time, and frankly, no one has the time to do all the research that would be required. As such, we must rely on shortcuts, normally news sources we consider reliable. While good in theory, the question quickly becomes how reliable our sources are? Bias and errors abound. A better way to phrase this question would be, are any of our sources reliable? How would we know?

Unless you have on occasion checked out your sources, you really cannot know. If you want to check out your sources, here are some considerations. The first and most important is to realize no one is truly unbiased. If nothing else, all are prone to confirmation bias. It is something that takes great care and considerable effort to work against and overcome. Even then, it is something that is never completely achieved.

Many who claim objectivity often point to criticism they receive "from both sides." The idea is that if both sides are criticizing them, they must be in the middle and thus objective. There are three flaws with this argument. The first is it assumes a single homogeneous spectrum. Yet life is composed of various issues and concerns, where no two people hold identical views on all topics. Thus, there are many intersecting spectrums. The claim that someone just happens to be at the exact center of all of them is untenable. Even if we restrict the consideration simply to United States politics, there are still many issues where even people on the same side disagree in some ways.

The second problem is this argument assumes all issues are binary with only two sides. Most issues have a wide range of different views and nuances. Wherever you are on the spectrum of a particular view, there will be people on either side of your position. However far to the right or left, there will be people who are further.

This problem can easily be seen if we imagine a numeric spectrum from 0 to 100, with 50 being the middle. A reporter who was at 75 could be criticized from both sides by those above and below. If you are criticized by people at 10 and 90, it only says you are somewhere in between, not that you are in the middle. As a result, the fact that someone says they are "criticized from both sides" says nothing about where they are on the spectrum and thus says nothing about their objectivity.

Finally, there is yet another flawed assumption with this claim: the middle represents objectivity. The middle is just another position on the spectrum. One can be biased to the middle, just like they can be biased to the left or right. Just as the two sides can reject the argument of the other because of bias, the middle can reject the arguments from both sides due to a bias of the middle.

Wherever one is on a spectrum is independent of the question of bias. Everyone has some bias. Given that, anyone who claims to be objective is not being honest with you or themselves. In fact, objectivity is something we cannot judge for ourselves. Rather than being attacked by both sides, a much better claim is being praised for objectivity from both sides. Better yet is if the praise comes from those farther away on the spectrum. On the other hand, praise from one side and criticism from the other clearly indicates a problem.

There are many types of bias. One can be biased toward the old, resistant to change. One can be biased for the new and different. Classical historian Victor David Hanson has suggested in his book, *Who Killed Homer?* that one of the problems with getting a Ph.D. in classical studies is that after 2000 years of study, there is not a lot of new ground to be covered. As such, new candidates are forced to explore irrelevant side issues or statistical studies of little interest except for other scholars, and possibly not even them, in an attempt to do the original research required to earn a doctoral degree. As a result, the classics that have been so important to Western Civilizations have become so bogged down in minutia as to be irrelevant to most students. He suggests changing the criteria to allow candidates who are good at teaching the classics to earn a doctorate.

Detecting Bias

Bias can affect a discussion in many ways. One easy way to detect bias is to look at the words chosen to represent various groups and positions. Groups and movements label themselves to be seen in the best light. They often have negative labels for their opponents. Does your source consistently use self- designations for all sides? If an information source uses the positive self-designations for one side but negative labels for the other, they are biased.

Another consideration is the adjectives chosen to represent the various sides. If one side tends to get a lot of positive adjectives, while the other gets negative adjectives, you probably have bias. Sometimes the bias is in the decision of when to label. If groups on one side are identified with just their name, while those on the other are normally qualified as being part of the political spectrum, this is bias.

Consider two groups introduced as "the XYZ institute and the ABC institute, a partisan think tank." This description makes XYZ seem more objective and ABC more partisan and thus unreliable. In reality, the only difference is in how they are labeled. If you watch for such things, you will see them, and they are signs of bias.

A more difficult area to judge is that bias often appears in the selection of information. At least in theory, you can have a completely accurate source but one that is also very biased. This is because bias often involves what is not said, more than what is said; what is left out, rather than what is put in. A source can be highly reliable when presenting the pros of their side and the cons of the other. Still, you do not get the full picture.

Again, there are pros and cons to everything. For example, candidates for an office have strengths and weaknesses; they have things they do well, and they make mistakes. If the information sources you are considering give you only the pros of one candidate and the cons of the other, they have bias.

A key consideration is that stories can be positive, negative, or neutral. For news sources, how the story comes out is mostly under the reporter's control and influenced by the editor. While some stories will be positive or negative by their very nature, most can be neutral.

Take most stories; you can report just the facts. You can report the facts with some comments from supporters balanced with comments from opponents. These would be neutral. The coverage will be positive if you include mostly the story's positive aspects and comments from supporters. Likewise, a preponderance of problems and criticism would result in a negative story. The reporter controls the mix. Any imbalance between the ratios of positive-negative-neutral stories between groups is an indication of bias.

A contributing factor here is headlines and the order of a story. It is a simple fact that we read far more headlines than stories. As a result, bias can be in the headlines. Objectivity here is particularly difficult because headlines are meant to get attention. It is also true that we start more stories than we read completely. A story could be neutral, presenting both sides, but structured such that the side favored by the reporter comes first and so is read by most people. As a side note, many online sources track what articles and podcasts people click on and how many minutes or how many paragraphs are viewed. As such, bias can appear when the leading parts of stories, the parts most people read, trend one way or the other.

The ubiquitous use of the Internet and Social Media provide other avenues of not only bias but manipulation. One of the main profit models on the Internet is to offer people services in exchange for their data. This data is then used to target advertising. Yet, the models did not stop there but are increasingly aimed at manipulation. Manipulation comes on several levels. One is to get you and keep you using the services to collect more and more data. The other is to get you to respond to the advertising. This same ability to manipulate can be applied to politics and toothpaste, and many studies have shown such manipulation is occurring. It is also very difficult to detect without detailed analysis.

One sign of bias that is easy to detect is an inability to discuss a problem on one side without mentioning how the other side is worse. Suppose a politician from one party is caught in a scandal. In that case, it is not news that some opposing party members have been caught in similar scandals in the past. This is certainly biased if such a "historical perspective" is missing when the parties are reversed. For those in the middle, this tendency is often modified to the claim both sides do it, lest they appear to be on one side or the other.

Bias can also appear in the amount of coverage a story gets. A news source can claim to be objective in that they report all the stories, pros, and cons from both sides. Yet, they can still be biased because they give far more coverage to the stories favorable to their side. A story that puts their side in a negative light may get only one brief mention. Yet, stories that put their opponents in a negative light can get a lot of coverage for days.

The final indicator of bias we will look at deals with the benefit of the doubt. As we have seen, reality is complex, and our knowledge of it is often limited. Many disputes and controversies have gray areas where the truth of the matter cannot be determined. When these occur, you either live with the ambiguity or give one side the benefit of the doubt. A source that normally gives the benefit of the doubt to only one side but not the other is biased.

This bias is often apparent in charges of wrong-doing. If it is someone they like, they will point out that the charges have not been proven and express a desire to withhold judgment until all the facts are known. These claims are fine as long as the same consideration is given to those they do not like. If it is not, you have bias.

As we have seen, bias can come in a lot of different forms. To avoid all of them is difficult and takes a lot of effort. Even then, given the difficulty of seeing our own problems, complete success is impossible. The first step is to acknowledge the problem, and so you should be most skeptical of those who deny there is any bias. If someone cannot admit they are biased, they cannot deal with it.

Dealing With Bias

That a source is biased is not necessarily a reason to reject it. It just means you need to adjust for it. It also means that you need to look elsewhere for the things they are not telling you. Thus, the best remedy for bias is to seek out good views from all the various sides of an issue. In politics, this would mean seeking out good sources from the Left, Middle, and Right. When considering a source of information, check out a few stories to see how accurately they are portrayed. Aristotle's doctrine of the mean is helpful here. Of course, you should have a healthy skepticism for all. Still, to guard against your own bias, you should be a little more skeptical of views from your side.

Another good way to test sources is to look at older stories or read recent history occasionally. There is an adage that first reports are usually wrong. Unfortunately, this applies to the news. It is not necessarily that people lie, though that is a problem. Rather it is a mixture of lack of information, perspective, and confirmation bias.

When we first encounter something, we, by definition, do not know the full story. As a result, we fit the information we are given into our existing framework of beliefs the best we can. Later, when we get more information, details emerge that can change our view. The real problem occurs when we fail to adapt to changing information. Too often, we hold on to our beliefs longer than we should.

A classic example of this was the D-Day invasion. The allies executed a brilliant deception. Creating a mock army, they convinced Hitler and most of the German High Command that the invasion of Europe would be led by General Patton and occur at Calais. Field Marshal Erwin Rommel was not convinced. But Hitler was. When the D-Day landing occurred, not at Calais but Normandy,

Hitler held on to his previous belief. What about the invasion in Normandy? He convinced himself it was only a diversionary tactic. By the time Hitler realized his mistake, it was too late. Any chance to stop the invasion was lost.

One strategy for checking bias is to read books about recent events. Reading such books may seem a waste of time. After all, you lived through it, so you already know what happened. Yet when I read such books, they quickly demonstrate two things. First reports are often wrong, and reality is far more complex than our understanding of it. Even when you come away with your overall view remaining unchanged, you will gain a wealth of understanding of the complexity of recent events. Such an understanding can then be used to realize that today's news headlines are only the first reports. They will be incomplete and may be wrong.

Problems with Information

Anecdotal

Even when you have a range of good sources of information, there are still problems. Our knowledge of events and policies comes in two basic forms: anecdotal and statistical. Neither tells the complete story; both can be misleading.

Anecdotes are small individual stories, stories that can be comprehended and understood. They can be very powerful such as a mother being tragically killed in a car crash. We can feel for the family and their loss. Does this represent some problem that should be addressed, or is this just a tragic accident about which little can be done? That would depend on the broader context.

If it were simply a random accident with no apparent cause, perhaps nothing could be done. On the other hand, if this were just the latest in a series of accidents on a stretch of road known to be dangerous, perhaps that would indicate that the road should be improved. The key for anecdotes is how representative they are of a problem. As the saying goes, by itself, anecdotal evidence is evidence of anecdotes.

Statistics

This is where statistics come in. Whereas anecdotes can give us a better understanding of something's impact, statistics can give us a better understanding of its extent. Yet, as the common saying goes, there are lies, dammed lies, and statistics. The problems with statistics are well known, but they continue to confound and plague virtually every discussion. Joel Best summed up these problems in his wonderful book *Damned Lies and Statistics: Untangling Numbers from the Media, Politicians, and Activists.*

While part of the problem is dishonest actors, a large part is simply a strong dose of confirmation bias on the part of those using the statistics. This bias is then combined with the fact that, unlike computers, the human brain does not handle numbers very well.

You can see this in Best's lead example. In a proposal for a doctoral dissertation, there was a citation for a claim that the number of American children killed by gun violence doubled "every year since 1950."[109] Even when Best wrote his book at the turn of the century, this statistic was already absurd.

If you do not see the problem, simply assume one child died from gun violence in 1950. That would mean two died in 1951, four in 1952, eight in 1953, sixteen in 1954, and so on. By 1960 you would have over a thousand children dying each year by gun violence. By 1970 the number would be over a million. By 1980, over a billion and a trillion by 1990. If that trend had continued, by 2020, the number of children killed by gun violence each year would have been about 150 billion times the entire world population. Clearly, there was a problem.

The graduate student did cite the statistic correctly from an article in a respected journal. The author of the article got the statistic

---

[109] Best, J. (2001, 2012). *Damned Lies and Statistics.* Berkeley: Univesity of California Press. p. 1

from an advocacy group. Yet while close, the author of the article did not accurately quote the group's statistics. The advocacy group reported that the number of children killed each year has doubled *since* 1950, not that it has doubled each year.

This sort of simple error happens all the time. Most people do not remember numbers that well. As a result, they can easily grow, especially as the statistic is passed from person to person. Magnitude and time frames can change. Something that happens tens of times a year as it is passed around can easily become hundreds of times a month. Such errors are often missed because of confirmation bias.

Again, this is where Aristotle can help. When citing statistics, be aware of this difficulty. If you are not completely sure of a statistic, say so. When citing statistics, err on the side that least supports your case. Frankly, it will probably have the same impact at the moment. If checked out, the actual value will only emphasize your point.

For example, say a certain problem affects 120,000 people per year. You are unsure of the number and round up saying that it affects 150,000 people per year. Someone who checks will rightly conclude you were exaggerating the problem. On the other hand, you round down and say the problem affected "about 100,000" people per year," anyone checking will find the problem is worse than you said.

Surveys and Polls

There are other problems with numbers, particularly surveys and polls. When was it taken? How many people were involved? What questions were asked? In what order were they asked? All these factors are important and can influence the final result.

Even good pollsters working hard to get the correct results can be wrong. Nor is this just a problem of recent polls. In 1948 the polls predicted that Thomas E. Dewey would defeat Harry S. Truman in that year's presidential election. The editors of the Chicago Daily Tribune were facing time pressures, and based on the polls, were certain Dewey would win. So, they printed the headline "Dewey Defeats Truman" as the banner headline for the next day's paper, to their great embarrassment.

The four most important questions with a poll are first who was involved. Is this a random sample or a self-selecting sample, such as an internet poll? Self-selecting samples have several problems. If nothing else, polls measure only those who responded. It says nothing about those not asked or who chose not to participate because of disinterest, lack of time, or other reasons. All polls have a built-in assumption that the respondents accurately reflect the views of the non-respondents. For a self-selecting poll or survey, this assumption is dubious at best.

Lately, such problems have been entering into even the respected polls. Pollsters have reported it is increasingly difficult to find people who will respond to their questions. As the number refusing to participate grows, so does the likelihood that these non-respondents differ from those who respond. In this case, the poll only accurately reflects the views of those who responded.

The second question is how many people participated in the poll. The more, the better, but an important consideration is that the sub-group numbers can be quite small even with a decent number of respondents. A thousand people may be a good number for a random survey. Still, the more you break down the overall number into different subgroups, the fewer the number in each group.

The third question is when the poll was taken. At best polls are snapshots of opinion at a given time. Polls for an election done early in a campaign can tell you what public opinion is at that moment. They tell you little about who will win. Polls taken just before a major positive or negative event tell you nothing about the event's impact. Polls taken just before a major scandal cannot tell you anything about the impact of the scandal.

Finally, what were the questions asked? An inherent problem of polls is that by their very nature, they artificially collapse extremely complex issues into what are little better than binary choices, approve/disprove, agree/disagree. This would be a problem even for a careful, objective pollster.

This inherent problem is also one of the main reasons groups can request polls to get the desired results by carefully framing the questions. Both Pro-Choice and Pro-Life groups frequently claim they represent the majority of the public and do so by pointing to polls that back up their claim. What the polls do show is that a large majority are somewhere in the middle. So how the questions are phrased and the order in which they are asked is extremely important.

Even for careful pollsters, this is a difficult problem. Consider poll questions about presidential approval in light of the discussion in chapter five about who was the best President. We saw in chapter five that this was an extremely difficult and complex question. Even if restricted to a more specific question such as do you support the President budget? Without any context, this would be an extremely difficult question to answer.

A major problem is the psychological issue of anchoring. Suppose you ask a number of people to judge the value of two similar items, such as shirts. You don't care about one of these, shirt A, while the other, shirt B, you do. You can strongly influence the outcome based on the choice of shirt A and by showing it first.

When you do this, it becomes the anchor that influences the evaluation of shirt B. As a result, you can get a positive or negative evaluation of shirt B, whichever one you want, simply by carefully selecting shirt A. Then you can accurately report the results you wanted to get, without ever mentioning shirt A.

The thing about anchoring is that the anchor need not even be related. Ask someone the last two digits of their Social Security number before asking them to guess the price of an item. When you do this, the last two digits of their Social Security number will affect their guess. Those with high values for the last two digits will, on average, guess higher prices than those with lower numbers for their last two digits.

Seeking Truth

While there are many suggested reasons why we are affected by anchoring, it is clear that we are, and it is difficult to avoid. It also happens in a lot of areas. Even seemingly unrelated issues can be affected by anchoring. When it comes to surveys and polls, because of anchoring, the results of the questions reported can be influenced by earlier questions that were not reported.

When it comes to truth, there is another consideration with polls. The best poll cannot determine the truth. It can only determine what people are thinking at a particular moment. The majority may be right, or they may be wrong. People's opinions are based on what they know.

For example, proportionally, very few people actually know any political figure or do the research needed to understand a proposed law. They base their opinions on their sources of information, which can be biased. The difference between the truth and people's opinion is often a measure of the bias in their sources.

If all you hear about some leaders is how wonderful they are and how they are doing such a good job, you will probably have a good opinion of them. Likewise, suppose all you hear about someone is how bad they are and the problems they are causing. In that case, you probably have a negative opinion of them.

In short, polls are more a measure of our information sources than of reality. They only reflect reality to the extent that our information sources are accurate and unbiased. This is another reason looking back at recent history is so important.

Consider the publics' view of presidents while in office and the views of later historians. These are often quite different. Again, Truman had low ratings in polls when he left office but is now viewed favorably by historians. Part of this difference results from additional information; research is done, books written, and papers released. But much of it comes from the bias in information sources.

Then there is the fallacy of false choice. Most issues have many complexities and options. Say you see a poll that says a clear majority oppose a President's budget. Is it because it has too much spending? Too little? Is it because of the distribution of the spending?

Reducing complex issues into poll questions can give misleading answers. I have seen cases where a poll said a majority disagreed with a position I held. Yet when I looked at the actual question, I discovered I would have answered the poll question the same way as the majority. The problem was a badly worded question that led to misleading results. Alternatively, the poll was biased to get a particular answer.

By definition, polls and surveys cannot report the results for the questions not asked. When Polls ask for the preference concerning one or two options, it says nothing about the other possible options not included in the poll. When polls ask about preferences between two extremes, it says nothing about other compromise options that were not included.

In and of itself, these problems would be bad enough. Yet polls do not just report results; they also influence outcomes. They, in effect, become new anchor points for the future. With elections, many studies have found that polls influence the outcomes. Whether it is because people want to support the winner, avoid the loser, or just seek the majority view, studies have found that polls can shape an election's outcome by several percentage points. Polls can shape public opinion as much as they report it.

A Fifth Question?

Some people think there should be another consideration: Who conducted the poll? This issue is difficult. As in any field, there will be good and bad pollsters. Given all the inherent problems, all polls should be viewed with some skepticism; this is particularly true given the growing problems. Many elections recently had demonstrated serious problems with polling when there ended up being a significant difference between the polls and the election results. Probably more important than the actual numbers are the

Seeking Truth

trend from one poll to the next; what is the change. A trend in a particular direction across several polls probably is real.

A related question concerns studies and reports; should they be rejected based on their source? I say no and believe the question is irrelevant and often fallacious. A common example cited to justify this question are the studies conducted by the American Tobacco Institute on smoking. The claim is that they should be rejected because the source was biased; they cannot be trusted. But if that is the criteria, what organization is not biased? Using this reasoning, few studies could be trusted; most should be rejected.

The real problem with this claim is that ultimately, this translates into organizations on one side are fine; their studies should be accepted. Organizations on the other side are biased; their studies are to be rejected. It should not be hard to see that this is just a form of ad hominem attack, an appeal to bias. Unfortunately, such reasoning quickly becomes an insulator from possible correction.

This concept of rejecting based on bias is so ingrained that I am sure some will be troubled by this view, particularly when it comes to the Tobacco Institute. To be clear, I am not suggesting that their information be accepted, only that it not be rejected on the grounds of bias. Of course, they can be rejected for many reasons. Still, to be rational, these must be rooted in valid criticisms of their studies.

For example, in their 1979 report, *Smoking and Health, 1964-1979 The Continuing Controversy*, the report bases much of its conclusions on,

> Despite claims to the contrary, no one – in government or industry – can explain the reported association of smoking with lung cancer, heart disease, emphysema, low infant birth weight, and yes even cancer of the pancreas... Scientists have not proven that cigarette smoke or any of the thousands of its constituents as found in cigarette smoke cause human disease.[110]

---

110 Tobacco Institute. (1979, January 10). *SMOKING AND HEALTH 1964 - 1979 THE CONTINUING CONTROVERSY*. Retrieved from

Note that the Tobacco Institute does not challenge these associations. They only claimed that it had not been proven that smoking was the cause. They are correct that correlation does not automatically mean causation. Still, one can easily conclude that the evidence linking them was still very strong and has only gotten stronger since.

Rather than deny the obvious correlations, they instead claimed there was no proof smoking was the cause. As discussed in chapter three, demands for proof as a means to reject evidence are suspect. One can always reject a claim by demanding more evidence than is available. The real question is whether it is reasonable to take action based on the evidence that is available.

In some respects, the Tobacco Institute's argument is similar to the criticism faced by John Snow and his claim that the Broad Street pump was responsible for Cholera in that area. To his critics, Snow had not "proven" the Broad Street pump was the source. He had shown a one-to-one correlation between those who got Cholera and those who used the pump. But this was not seen as "proof," and it would be several decades till the Germ theory of disease could explain Snow's findings

Just as correlation does not automatically lead to causation, lack of clear demonstration does not automatically mean there is no link. For both the Broad Street pump and Cholera and the health risks from smoking, the correlation was strong and clear.

Once you understand the problems with these reports, you can then ask why they would make such a defense despite the evidence to the contrary. At that point, bias would become a valid consideration. But to skip these steps and go straight to bias is an error.

There is one final consideration when it comes to polls: the growing trend of people to lie to pollsters. Sometimes this is done simply to mislead the pollster. In controversial areas, the person may not want to admit their true position. Lying to pollsters is

---

UCSF Library: https://www.industrydocuments.ucsf.edu/tobacco/docs/#id=llpf0145

Seeking Truth

one explanation for the polls being wrong in the 1982 California Governor's race between Tom Bradley and George Deukmejian.

Polls showed that Bradley, who is Black, had a significant lead over Deukmejian, of Armenian descent. Deukmejian won. The reason suggested for why the polls were wrong is that voters did not want to be seen as racist for not voting for Bradley. Some dispute this explanation, but other elections showed similar trends.

PERSPECTIVE AND SCALE

One other problem with numbers that we will consider is the issue of perspective. The world is a very large place, and with a population approaching eight billion people, that is a lot of people. The world population is expected to peak in the next few decades and begin to decline, but it is still a lot of people. Even in the United States, with just 332.9 million, that is an unimaginably large number.

For example, consider all the letters that make up the words in this book. If the population of the United States were represented by the individual letters in this book, each letter would represent about 787 people. The letters on this page alone would represent over 1.4 million people. Thus when we hear numbers about the effects of something, it is really hard to grasp what that means. This difficulty is especially true given that these statistics are often presented in terms of the number per 1000, 10,000, or 100,000. But what do those mean?

We know, for example, that people die every day. If you are like most people, you occasionally see funerals and have unfortunately had to attend some. But few have any grasp of the actual numbers. How could they unless they have a reason to know? Most people only see what is around them in their family and community, and maybe what appears in the obituaries. According to the CDC, 2,854,838 people died in the United States in 2019. On average, that was 237,903 people each month; 54,900 each week; 7821 each day. We would have trouble comprehending even the daily figure, much less the annual.

Then there is the issue of scale. Often people with an agenda try to present information in a way that grabs attention. Say you have a problem, crime, poverty, disease, or whatever. Call it X. A headline could say instances of X doubled. By itself, this means very little. To make sense of this, you would have to know the numbers and the timeframe. Double since when? There would be a huge difference between doubling in the last few months versus the last few years, or as in the study above, since 1950.

There is the issue of how it doubled. Is it the absolute number or percentage that doubled? This question can be significant in a situation where there are large changes in the population. There is also the problem of small numbers. When dealing with small numbers, large percentage changes can be very misleading.

To see this consider two similar communities with the same size population, Happyville and Pleasanton. The only difference is that last year, Happyville had two murders, and Pleasanton had 100. This year Happyville had four murders, and Pleasanton had 98. Most would consider Happyville the safer place to live. Still, this could be described as Happyville saw murders double while they declined in Pleasanton. Yet both only changed by two.

This issue of perspective becomes more important when comparing events across time. It is quite natural to see things in terms of what we know, and what we know best is our life, particularly the present. For example, we hear of, or remember, when gas costs a fraction of a dollar and marvel at how cheap it was. In 1970 gas was around $0.35/gallon. Cheap compared to today. Yet if you adjust this price for inflation, in 2021, just before the recent jump in inflation and thus at a time when inflations we easier to calculate, that would be the same as $2.43/gallon. At that time this, that was a little more expensive than some places in the United States, particularly in the South, less expensive than in other places. So in that sense, not much has changed. The lower price is an illusion.

Seeking Truth

Adjusting for year can help you get perspective in other areas. For example, consider some of the wars involving the United States. A fairly easy question is which war had the most military deaths. That was the Civil War that resulted in 620,000 deaths. The revolutionary war had an estimated 25,000 killed, while World War I had 116,516, World War II had 405,399, Korea had 36,516, 58,209 for Vietnam, 249 for the Gulf War, 4492 for Iraq and 2325 for Afghanistan. The more difficult question is, in which war were you more likely to be affected by a death. How do these numbers compare to today, with our larger population?

Adjusting for our current population of 332.9 million compared to the population during the last year of the war the comparable casualties would have been over 2.6 million in the Revolutionary War, 5.9 million in the Civil War, 374,000 in WWI, 960,000 in WWII, 76,000 in Korea, 91,000 for Vietnam, 329 for the Gulf War, and 4800 for Iraq. Afghanistan is still 2325 as it has just ended at the time I am writing. These adjusted numbers give us a better understanding of the impact of these wars on the society of their day and the chance your life would have been affected by someone killed.

Both time and location are important when it comes to economics. Poverty in the United States is a serious problem. Yet to be poor in the United States in the twenty-first century is not the same as being poor in a third-world country. Nor is it the same as being poor in the United States 100 years ago. Where perspective is really a problem is when it leads to people meaning different things due to their different perspectives. Again, discussion and definition of terms can greatly reduce a lot of these problems.

Believing Your Own Rhetoric

The final problem we will discuss here particularly affects groups, especially political groups: Believing your own rhetoric. In chapter five, we discussed how hyperbole and exaggeration were legitimate ways of making a point. They are fine as long as you remember what they are. In the heat of a political campaign, politicians tend to summarize their opponent's position in unflattering ways. They often exaggerate the danger should voters choose their opponent. Perhaps politicians would be completely accurate and honest in a perfect world, but that is not our world.

Such statements become a problem when people forget these are hyperbole used to emphasize a point and start thinking they are literal. This particularly becomes a problem as this new sense of reality spreads in the group and becomes self-reinforcing. If it survives until the next election, it will go through another round of exaggeration, becoming even worse.

This problem happens to some extent with all sides in politics. Normally, it disappears shortly after the elections are over. Still, it has become more of a problem with the recently increased polarization in politics and the never-ending campaigns. Unless the cycle is broken, the group can become completely detached from reality—having a view of reality built upon exaggeration, built upon exaggeration, built upon exaggeration.

There are some pretty clear indications of when this is happening. Godwin's law that the longer a discussion lasts, the greater the chance of evoking Hitler is a good indication. The use of apocalyptic language and comparisons to Hitler or Nazis are rarely, if ever, legitimate. The more common they are used among a group about their opponents, the more likely they are believing their own rhetoric. The comparisons do not need to be to Hitler. Any overblown comparisons are suspect.

Another bad sign is the scope of the claim. Making a hyperbolic claim against a particular individual is one thing. When the charge is made against an entire group, it is far worse and less likely to be true. When a charge is made, you should ask if the charge is real or hyperbolic? Are any examples given? If they are, are they specific or vague? Justifying a hyperbolic claim by labeling a piece of proposed legislation in a hyperbolic fashion is not a legitimate justification. It only compounds the initial problem.

Here a sanity check can be very helpful. Do the claims match the people you know on the other side? For large groups, if you don't know any, that is in and of itself a concern. If the claims are restricted to an individual or small group, ask yourself why the larger group would support them if they were so bad? What do those on the other side say to counter such charges? Remember, you do not have to agree with their reasons to understand them. All you have to do is determine if their reasons make more sense than the charges being leveled against them. You can think another group is wrong without comparing them to Nazis.

All these questions may have good answers, and perhaps the claims are not hyperbolic. After all, no nation in history has lasted forever. Hitler and other dictators have seized power. It could happen again. Still, it is far more likely that such claims are hyperbolic.

Overall, avoiding errors takes a lot of work. This is particularly true when starting. Luckily it gets easier over time. You will find reliable sources for information and get an understanding of their strength and weakness. You will develop the habits of thinking critically, showing appropriate levels of skepticism, and testing information. You will, in short, be ready to make informed decisions.

Chapter 12

Evaluating Claims, Reaching Decisions

Those who direct their desires and actions by reason will gain much profit from the knowledge of these matters – Aristotle, Nicomachean Ethics

A king is history's slave – Leo Tolstoy, War and Peace

Choice, the ability to make a decision. It is that quintessentially human characteristic. In his Nicomachean Ethics, Aristotle spoke of people having a rational element. The ability to reason is meaningless without the ability to reach a conclusion. He also spoke of an irrational element and the instinct that we share with animals, along with the life we share with both plants and animals. Still, it is the ability to think, reason, and decide that sets us apart.[111]

Granted, it is an ability that is often neglected. We all live most of our lives simply reacting to the numerous and varied things that happen to us each day. We are often like pieces of wood floating on a river. Most of the time, we just go where the river leads us. Sometimes the river splits, and we deliberately go down one path, though often we are too busy or unaware. The river decides for us.

Leo Tolstoy explored this concept in his masterpiece *War and Peace*. Having reviewed the numerous causes for Napoleon's invasion of Russia, he ends up rejecting them all.

> We are forced to fall back on fatalism as an explanation of irrational events (that is to say, events the reasonableness of which we do not understand). The more we try to explain

---

111 Aristotle. (n.d.). *Nicomachean Ethics*. p. 1.13

such events in history reasonably, the more unreasonable and incomprehensible do they become to us.

Each man lives for himself, using his freedom to attain his personal aims, and feels with his whole being that he can now do or abstain from doing this or that action; but as soon as he has done it, that action performed at a certain moment in time becomes irrevocable and belongs to history, in which it has not a free but a predestined significance.

There are two sides to the life of every man, his individual life, which is the more free the more abstract its interests, and his elemental hive life in which he inevitably obeys laws laid down for him.

Man lives consciously for himself, but is an unconscious instrument in the attainment of the historic, universal, aims of humanity. A deed done is irrevocable, and its result coinciding in time with the actions of millions of other men assumes an historic significance. The higher a man stands on the social ladder, the more people he is connected with and the more power he has over others, the more evident is the predestination and inevitability of his every action.

"The king's heart is in the hands of the Lord."

A king is history's slave.[112]

Tolstoy's view is basically that Napoleon's invasion was not a choice but an outgrowth of all the historical forces that had proceeded the invasion. Napoleon chose to invade because he was the type of person who would invade Russia. This was the type of person the turmoil of the French Revolution produced. Had Napoleon never existed, the theory goes, the times would have produced another like him. It is an age-old question. Does history make the individual, or do individuals make history?

---

112 Tolstoy, L. (1869). *War and Peace.* Book IX Chapter 1

Seeking Truth

The answer is both. As in so many cases, this is not a binary situation of either/or but a mixture of both/and. We both shape and are shaped by history. To return to the analogy of a river, most people do drift. Still, some choose to swim across or even against the flow deliberately. These people impact history, some for great good such as Lincoln and Churchill, others for great evil such as Stalin and Hitler.

Lincoln and the other abolitionists pushed back against the notions of slavery that had existed from the dawn of recorded history. It certainly would have been easier to let the convention of millennium stand, not to rock the boat. Still, they chose to take a stand, denounce slavery, and work to abolish it at great cost. In doing so, they changed the course of history, and we benefit from that change today. They changed the course of the river, such that those who are just drifting drift in a recognition that slavery is evil.

But not all choices are good. Hitler also swam against the flow. One can fairly easily argue that the conditions in Germany leading up to 1933 would produce a reformer. The depression of that era was worldwide. In the United States, it resulted in Franklin Roosevelt, who was very much a reformer. But that conditions in Germany would produce a reformer did not automatically mean the reformer would be as evil as Hitler.

Historical forces are the total of all the people's choices up to that point. True, there are random natural events, storms, droughts, volcanoes, and earthquakes. Still, even here, there is a huge amount of choice, such as choosing to prepare or not and how we react to these when they happen. In *The Lord of the Rings*, when Frodo wished the turmoil that had befallen him and his friends had not happened, Gandalf told him, "So do all who live to see such times, but that is not for them to decide. All we have to decide is what to do with the time that is given to us."

We did not have a say about the times into which we were born. In terms of human history, they are perhaps the best times so far to have lived. Herodotus has a word of caution. In his work *The Histories*, the first of its kind, he recounts the meeting between

King Croesus, a ruler known for his great wealth, and Solon, a ruler known for his wisdom. The dates when these two rulers lived don't quite line up, so the story is probably mythical, but the point remains valid.

When Solon visited him, Croesus wanted Solon to tell him that he was the happiest because of his wealth. Not wanting to be too blunt about it, he simply asked Solon who was the happiest. Solon replied Tellus of Athens, a man who lived a wonderful life, blessed by many children and grandchildren all who grew up, which was unusual for the time. Then Tellus died defending Athens.

Not satisfied, Croesus tried again, but this time Solon told him of two brothers dedicated to their mother. They died getting their mother to a temple for a festival. Again, Croesus was disappointed. Ultimately, Solon's point was that no one could be considered the happiest until the end of their life was known. As it turned out, Croesus' life was about to take a turn for the worse. A short time later, he would lose all his riches and find himself tied to a stake about to be burned, pleading for his life.

While it now appears to be the best time to live, the same could have been said, on the morning of June 28, 1914, the day that Archduke Ferdinand was assassinated, which led to WWI. On September 30, 1938, it could have been said when Neville Chamberlain proclaimed peace in our time. Except for Winston Churchill, few could foresee the horrors about to be unleashed on the world. Whether we truly live in the best time in human history or are on the precipice of some new disaster is largely up to us, to be determined by the decisions we make.

But how do we make decisions? Ideally, one would gather all the relevant data and considerations, evaluate the various pros and cons, and reach a conclusion. While there are numerous books on decision-making strategies, this sort of detailed evaluation is not always practical. If, for no other reason, there is not enough time to do such a detailed evaluation for all the numerous disputes. Then some disputes involve special expertise. Even if one happens to have special expertise in some areas, one cannot have expertise in all areas.

There will be times when even after gathering all the information available, looking at the pros and cons the best you can, there will still be unknowns, not to mention unknown unknowns. Yet, decisions must be made. At those times, you can only do your best.

A common problem is the phenomenon of the Monday Morning Quarterback. It is a truism that decisions can only be made based on the information available at the time. For more difficult decisions, there will always be unknowns and uncertainty. Of course, after the fact, many of these will be resolved, though often not all. For example, in a football game, the outcome of any given play is unknown in advance. Is it better to run or pass on a key play?

It will be a brilliant call if the play chosen results in a touchdown that wins the game. On the other hand, if it results in a fumble or interception that causes you to lose, many will say your decision was a disaster. How could you have made such a bad call? The evidence they have will be the knowledge of the outcome of the play, something you did not have. However, they still do not have access to the results of the play not called.

There can even be times when you make the proper decision based on the information at hand, only to discover later that you were missing key pieces of information or that the information was incorrect. This new information showed that another course of action was, in fact, a better choice. As discouraging and troubling as such cases are, little can be done except possibly get more information next time. While a terrific goal, it is not always possible.

At other times you will need to make a choice based on the expertise and research of others, or you will need to choose between two advocates, such as two political candidates. It is common today to bemoan the state of political debate, and with good reason. Virtually everyone complains about all the negative advertising. But if no one likes it, why do politicians do it? The answer is quite simple: It works. Politicians have one goal in an election; to get elected. They may have goals, lofty or otherwise, for what they will do once in office, but none of that can happen if they lose. So they will do what is needed to win. Currently, negative ads work, so they are used.

The public is not only the ultimate source of political power in a democracy; they also have an ultimate say in how campaigns are run. We get the politicians, for which the majority vote. So the people are the ones who control the political debate; the politicians will do whatever is most effective to get their vote.

People voting more rationally would not be the end of negative ads. Again there are pros and cons to everything. A rational presentation of the evidence will contain both pros and cons. For an incumbent, criticizing their record is legitimate. The same is true for the proposed policies of a challenger. Still, these cons are a long way from the personal attacks that make up many negative ads today.

Assume you are listening to a debate about a topic you are interested in, but one that is out of your expertise. If you already have an opinion on the matter, you should attempt to be open-minded. This will mean factoring in your own confirmation bias as you evaluate what each side says. To reach a decision, you will need to avoid insulators, blockers and evaluate the arguments made by both sides. Much of this has already been mentioned or discussed at various spots earlier in the book and is summarized here.

Insulators

Insulators are the things we do to keep ourselves from having to deal with opposing points of view. The very fact that you are listening to the discussion in the first place is a good sign. One insulator would be to avoid such discussions altogether. Automatically assuming some problem or bias with the opposing side would be another. 'I do not need to hear them; I already know they are wrong' would be one form. Another would be listening mainly to see where they are wrong instead of looking for where they might be right. Censorship, be it by government, corporations, or schools,

Seeking Truth

is an insulator. It is just an insulator imposed on you rather than a personal choice.

A common insulator for most people will be their general worldview. While an insulator, it is not necessarily bad. Most have a worldview that embraces order in some fashion and thus are insulated against calls for chaos. But we should be careful about those parts of our outlook where there are significant groups that disagree. Is the disagreement because there are good reasons to think they are wrong, or is it just your worldview that conflicts?

What makes ad hominem attacks so problematic is that they also serve as an insulator. The person is bad, so you can ignore what they say. If what they are saying is wrong, then there is no problem. But what about where they are correct? You will never know because you have insulated yourself from a possible correction.

Blockers

Blockers are defense mechanisms used to deflect arguments without having to deal with them. Blockers come into play when an insulator fails, and the argument has gotten through. Still, the argument needs to be dealt with lest it is allowed to affect your thinking. Blockers take many forms. Some are simply insulators applied more directly. The claim, I do not need to listen to them because they are biased would be an insulator. To claim, I can reject that argument because they are biased would be a blocker.

Blockers come in other forms. Countering one argument with another can be a blocker. If a particular argument points to a conclusion you reject, merely pointing to a different argument that supports you does not automatically refute the first argument. You would just have two conflicting arguments. The truth would have to reconcile both. Whether they are accepted or refuted, arguments must be dealt with if truth is the goal.

Often the dividing line between insulators and blockers on the one hand, and having a healthy skepticism is a thin one. This is particularly true given the dynamic nature of most discussions. Did the person just switch to another argument as a blocking mechanism, or did they switch because they thought the new topic was interesting or important? This can be nearly impossible to tell for a single switch, though patterns can emerge over time.

Evaluating Claims

Once you are confident that you have the right mix of open-mindedness and skepticism, you still have to evaluate the arguments made by both sides. Such evaluation can be difficult if the subject is one with which you are not familiar. Still, even in these areas, there is a lot you can do, particularly given the current state of things. Perhaps at some point in the future, the norm for discussion and debate will be so elevated that evidence and reason are the norms, and fallacies are the rare exception. That is not the state of things today; if anything, it is the reverse.

Today the lawyer's adage seems to be the guide. If the facts are on your side, argue the facts. If the law is on your side, argue the law. If neither is on your side, yell a lot. Today fallacies and bad arguments are so common, misinformation and emotion so widespread, that often the best arguments are the ones that make the least errors.

The following guidelines are based on the assumption of Enlightenment principles grounded in reason and evidence as a means for discovering truth. With the growing influence of Postmodernist thought and its rejection of Enlightenment views of truth, reason, and evidence, that is no longer a given. Attempts to point out contradictions and irrational arguments might be rejected, not because they are erroneous, rather because they are seen as mere power plays aimed at suppression. Reason and rational arguments are not effective for those who reject reason. Reason does not work on those who embrace irrationality.

Even with Enlightenment principles as common ground, picking sides on such a basis will not always give you the correct answer. Still, it is generally a safe assumption that both sides want to have their ideas prevail. Hopefully, if a side consistently loses because of bad arguments, they will seek to develop better ones. As a result, the level of discussion will improve. As in the past, we will make mistakes, but if handled correctly, over time, we will improve.

How can we make a choice? The following is a partial list of some things to watch for in a discussion. The dynamic nature of discussions precludes a complete list. While they are presented here as distinct categories, these are normally found in combination. Rarely does someone make a single error in reasoning. Normally bad arguments are a series of errors jumbled together to make them seem reasonable. Still, as you begin to pull apart the bigger, easier-to-spot errors, the other more subtle errors become visible.

Ad Hominem

As mentioned earlier, ad hominem attack is the most common problem you will encounter. While it may not be found in some more formal structured debates, it is common to many discussions on controversial issues. It is problematic in that it is legitimate to question the credibility or judgment of a person in some cases, but these are few and far between. If a person is presenting evidence, then it is the evidence that matters, not the person. Attempting to avoid the evidence by attacking the person is always fallacious and thus irrational.

Strawman

Perhaps the second most common tactic is the strawman. Again, a strawman is where you create a fictitious version of your opponent's views and then attack your creation rather than deal with what your opponent actually believes. Often, this is blended with ad hominem to provide false motives and reasonings. It is also used to make an opponent's position seem irrational or conflicted in some way.

In all these cases, the test is to ask if that is what the other side is arguing. Does anyone actually make the claims being criticized? Be very careful with vague qualifiers such as implied, seemed to say, etc. These are often the means for building a strawman.

A good example of a strawman argument was made by Steven Douglas during a debate with Lincoln, held on October 13, 1858, in Quincy, Illinois. This debate was the sixth of seven, and both debaters were becoming more direct in their arguments. When Lincoln had been nominated as the Republican candidate for Senate, he gave his famous House Divided speech in which he said,

> "A house divided against itself cannot stand." I believe this government cannot endure, permanently half slave and half free. I do not expect the Union to be dissolved -- I do not expect the house to fall -- but I do expect it will cease to be divided. It will become all one thing or all the other. Either the opponents of slavery, will arrest the further spread of it, and place it where the public mind shall rest in the belief that it is in the course of ultimate extinction; or its advocates will push it forward, till it shall become alike lawful in all the States, old as well as new -- North as well as South.

At the Quincy debate, Douglas went second, and during his portion, Douglas referred to Lincoln's House Divided speech.

> Mr. Lincoln there told his Abolition friends that this Government could not endure permanently, divided into free and slave States as our fathers made it, and that it must become all free or all slave, otherwise, that the Government could not exist. How then does Lincoln propose to save the Union, unless by compelling all the States to become free, so that the house shall not be divided against itself? He intends making them all free; he will preserve the Union in that way, and yet, he is not going to interfere with slavery any where it now exists. How is he going to bring it about? Why, he will agitate, he will induce the North to agitate until the South shall be worried out, and forced to abolish slavery.

Let us examine the policy by which that is to be done. He first tells you that he would prohibit slavery every where in the Territories. He would thus confine slavery within its present limits. When he thus gets it confined, and surrounded, so that it cannot spread, the natural laws of increase will go on until the negroes will be so plenty that they cannot live on the soil. He will hem them in until starvation seizes them, and by starving them to death, he will put slavery in the course of ultimate extinction. If he is not going to interfere with slavery in the States, but intends to interfere and prohibit it in the Territories, and thus smother slavery out, it naturally follows, that he can extinguish it only by extinguishing the negro race, for his policy would drive them to starvation. This is the humane and Christian remedy that be proposes for the great crime of slavery.[113]

Of course, the idea that the plan to eliminate slavery was to starve the negro race into extinction is not one that Lincoln argued for or ever would. It was a creation by Douglas to be something he could attack and ridicule. It was a strawman.

Still, not all arguments are as clearly spotted as Douglas'. At times this can be tricky to judge whether an argument is or is not a strawman. If you are watching a debate between two candidates, this can often involve all the issues of context discussed earlier. One thing to watch for is how clearly any denial is phrased. Do they merely deny they made the claims as stated, or do they specifically reject that claim? Suppose there is a dispute over support for a particular policy. Does the person only claim their comments were taken out of context, or do they make specific claims of support or rejection of the policy in question?

With politicians, there is also the consideration of honesty. There are many examples of politicians supporting a policy or course of action. Yet because of its unpopularity, denying that they supported it during an election. Then, once safely in office, they

---

113 Douglas, S. (1858, October 13). *Sixth Debate: Quincy, Illinois*. Retrieved from Lincoln Home: https://www.nps.gov/liho/learn/historyculture/debate6.htm

change once again and implement the policy. There are also many examples of the reverse, saying they would do something and then not doing it once elected.

When it comes to strawmen, there is an additional complication. For larger groups, significant positions have large numbers of people who accept that view. Is the particular view being criticized one that is generally held, or is it held only by a fringe? For example, consider the millions of people in both political parties. In any such group, there will be subgroups and fringe elements.

When questioning the policies of a political opponent, a key question is whether the views being questioned are mainstream views or fringe? It is normally very easy to attack a fringe. Still attacking fringe or extreme views leave the majority view untouched. If someone is refuting a fringe view assuming it refutes the majority, that is a strawman.

When dealing with a political party, are the claims and policies ones that elected officials and party leaders advocate? Are they the claims of a small minority within the party but who have no power? Here quotes and citations are important. It is always easy to make one side look better by comparing the best of one side with a fringe element of the other.

Rejecting vs. Refuting

When responding to an argument, are they merely rejecting it or attempting to refute it? Rejections can sound authoritative and convincing, but when you break it down, they merely say, "I disagree." This is an area where labels can be most effective. To label a policy as dangerous or reckless might sound convincing. Still, without evidence or reasons to back up the label, it is merely a rejection. To refute an argument, you need to consider its claims seriously and give specific reasons why it is not convincing. Until an argument is refuted, it stands as a valid reason.

Canned Answers and Talking Points

Closely related to rejecting is the issue of canned answers and talking points, as these are often used. In and of themselves, there is nothing wrong with either of these. They can be quite effective in delivering a message, and good communicators can use them effectively. They become a problem, however, when they are used as blockers to avoid answering questions. Their use as blockers becomes particularly clear when repeated as responses to issues and concerns that would put them in a bad light.

Consider a politician trying to build support for a particular policy proposal. They probably have talking points, and canned answers developed to put the policy in the best light possible. Suppose they are asked about problems with the proposal; addressing the problem and then returning to the talking points would be fine. After all, they are there to sell their policy proposal. They do not want to spend the entire time on problems. Still, ignoring the problems and repeating or rephrasing the canned answer would indicate a problem.

Authority vs. Evidence

A common problem is the misuse of authority. Chapter two described the transition from the Middle Ages to the Enlightenment as a change in frameworks. The Middle Ages' top-down framework based on authority became a bottom-up approach based on evidence. Yet, the Middle Ages approach never completely went away. Some in positions of power still want to exercise that power based on authority. When listening to authorities, are they presenting clear reasons for what they want to do, or are they grounding their claims in authority?

When listening to explanations, are they clear and convincing, or do they only confuse and obfuscate? As most IT professionals know, they can quickly silence most objections from non-IT professionals with a string of jargon and acronyms. Still, while most non-IT business professionals may not understand the details and jargon, they can understand the key issues if presented clearly. As a general rule, the more someone obfuscates, the more they are trying to hide.

This is particularly true when it comes to public policy. A good expert in whatever field should present the key issues and considerations in a fashion that the general public can understand, even if the public does not know all the underlying details. When listening to such claims from two conflicting sides, are the two sides presenting clear information with clear rationales backed up by specific evidence, such as particular studies? Or are they presenting conclusions based on authority or burying arguments in a string of jargon? The more the reasoning reduces down to "Because I said so," the more you are leaving enlightenment thinking and going back to the Middle Ages.

Demanding Acceptance

Similar to the previous topic, another common tactic for stifling debate is to demand the acceptance of experts. As pointed out repeatedly in this book, appeals to authority, while not illegitimate, are fraught with problems. Even with a fairly objective subject such as science, one thing that is clear is that science is never final. Scientific theories are always provisional, subject to revision should further evidence, or better explanations appear.

Then there is the problem of scope. That someone is an expert in a given field of science does not mean they are experts in the ramification or the required policy changes. They frequently can inform a discussion, but they have no more special insight into the policies that should be adopted than anyone else.

In short, experts are, at best, a shortcut, as they can allow us to skip the detailed investigation involved. However, experts often disagree. When they do, the shortcut does not work. When an appeal is made to experts to shut down discussion, particularly if it is done to ignore contrary evidence from other experts, that is a red flag

Vague Terms

Another very common problem is the use, or better yet, the misuse of language. The fundamental purpose of language is to communicate ideas to others. But as we have already seen, language is not without its problems. The careful use of language can be used to clarify issues and distinctions. However, it can also be used to muddy the water and make the discussion more difficult.

One example of this was Proposition 71, a constitutional amendment in California that passed in 2004. In the campaign, a major issue was cloning. Supporters claimed the proposition banned cloning; opponents disagreed. It did ban cloning to create babies but also made somatic cell nuclear transfer a constitutional right in California. A more common name for somatic cell nuclear transfer is therapeutic cloning.

Such confusions are not always deliberate. On many occasions, I have discussed a disagreement I had with someone. Once we had clarified the issue and distinctions, we discovered that there was very little if any disagreement left. As Aristotle put it, "How many a dispute could have been deflated into a single paragraph if the disputants had dared to define their terms." When listening to a discussion, listen for the terms that are used. Are they broad, vague, or ambiguous? Are they slanted?

A key point is whether or not any specific examples are given. Though here, it is possible to hide one ambiguity with another. I might claim my opponent's policies are bad and cite a bill they want to pass as an example. While I have given an example, I actually only replaced one ambiguity with another. For an actual example, I would need to state what is bad about the bill. Any claim that does not have a clear example is effectively meaningless.

As such, an important consideration is which side is seeking clarity and which side is obfuscating? A really bad sign is any reluctance to define terms or give clear examples. I once observed lawmakers discussing a proposed measure before voting. While there were several issues, a key dispute was over the meaning of a particular term. I thought an easy solution was simply to define the term, and sure enough, that proposal was made a short time later.

Strangely, however, supporters of the measure were very resistant to defining the term. They wanted to leave it vague. This reluctance was a huge red flag. The country's first law is called the dictionary act for a reason. It was enacted into law on the assumption that if you expect people to follow the law, it should be clear what you expect. As such, the dictionary act gives the legal definitions for a lot of common terms.

For example, there was criticism with the Supreme Court's ruling in Citizens United for understanding the term person as including corporations. Yet, that is really not up to the courts. 1 U.S. Code § 1 defines many words. For person, it says, "the words 'person' and 'whoever' include corporations, companies, associations, firms, partnerships, societies, and joint stock companies, as well as individuals." These and all the other definitions in this section are matters for the legislature, not the courts. When the law says that person includes corporations, it is any wonder that the court's ruling follows the law?

The main point is that when someone deliberately uses vague language and refuses to clarify what they mean, their claims should be rejected. Vague claims can, at best lead to vague conclusions. To ask that you reach a specific conclusion based on vague claims is, at best, irrational. Unfortunately, these currently dominate much of political discourse.

Argument by Adjectives

Very closely related to vague language is Argument by Adjective, which occurs when a speaker's argument rests, not on sound reasoning and evidence but rather, on the skillful use of adjectives. Positions are labeled with good adjectives or bad ones, depending on which side the speaker is on. Arguments likewise get labels such as brilliant or silly based on whether or not they support or counter the speaker's position.

Seeking Truth

To be clear, it is not the use of adjectives themselves that is the problem. Adjectives are a valid part of the language, and there is nothing wrong with using them. It only becomes a problem when they effectively become the argument. If you strip away all the adjectives, is there anything left? A valid argument will contain evidence and reasons. These should then justify the use of the adjectives.

Without a good rationale for using the adjective, all the speaker has done is state their position. Vote for me because I want to win. Oppose that bill because I do not like it. In such cases, you should wonder, if there are good reasons for the speaker's positions, why are they not giving them? Why only the characterizations?

Perfect vs. Good

Another common strategy to be suspicious of is comparisons with perfection. Nothing is perfect, particularly when it comes to humanity. Any policy, existing or proposed, will have problems. The mere fact that a policy or proposal has problems is not necessarily a reason to reject that policy. The real question is, can a policy be improved? Will this proposal improve things?

Too often, people fall into what the economist Thomas Sowell calls One Stage Thinking. Issues are addressed in a binary fashion. You have a problem → here is a solution. Done. A much better approach would be to ask a series of questions.

- What are the current problems and their causes?
- How can these be addressed? This question should always have at least two options, a proposed change and do nothing. Often it will have several more. Attempts to artificially restrict available options down to the one you want is the fallacy of false choice.
- What are the pros and cons of all the various options? Here it is important to consider the negative consequences of any proposed change. For example, one side effect of campaign reform laws in the 1970s was greatly increasing political

action committees' power and importance. The law of unintended consequences applies.
- Which option appears to be the best? Again, this may be to do nothing. Not all problems can be solved.

Any informed choice must include a rational analysis of both the pros and cons for both the current situation and the proposed change.

Confusing Goals with Means

Another expression of Stage One Thinking is the confusion of the goals with means. This type of argument is most apparent in discussions when one side focuses strictly on the desired objective without any real consideration of the means proposed to achieve it. If the goal is positive, the proposed policy will be defended by pointing out how desirable it would be to achieve the goal. If the goal is to eliminate some negative, the policy will be defended by pointing out how bad the problem is.

Confusing the goals with the means results in a discussion that is difficult to follow. Say there is a policy that is meant to eliminate some problem such as crime. Opponents of the policy might argue that the policy will not be effective. In response, a supporter might defend the policy by pointing out how bad crime was. Crime may be bad, but that does not mean that the proposed policy is the best solution or that it will even help the problem. If all the complexities of a situation are not well understood, not only will there be unintended consequences, the proposed solutions might worsen the situation.

One example of this was discovered at an Israeli daycare center. The problem they faced was that parents were picking up their children late. The daycare center began to impose a fine on parents to reduce the problem. Problem: Late parents. Solution: Impose a fine. While it seemed logical, it had the opposite effect.

Before the fine, late parents imposed on the staff, the staff that looked after their child. Picking up your child on time was, in effect, a social contract between the parents and staff. To break it was a matter of guilt, and "In Israel, guilt seems to be an effective way to get compliance."[114]

When the fine was imposed, that changed the nature of the relationship from social to transactional. The parents soon saw the fine as little more than a fee and one they were willing to pay. Paying a fee for service does not involve guilt. The problem actually became worse. Within a few weeks, the Daycare center tried to reverse their policy, sadly with little effect. As researchers know, "when a social norm collides with a market norm, the social norm goes away for a long time."[115]

Thus, when considering a means of achieving a goal, focusing only on the goal itself is a cause for concern—seeing the proposed means as the only possible means, where any criticism is taken as a rejection of the goal is a red flag to be avoided.

Criticism Without Alternative

Another common problem is criticizing without ever stating an alternative. This problem can be a bit tricky, as there is almost always an implied alternative. Often it will be, or at least should be, do nothing. For elections, it is the other candidate. Is one side arguing against a proposal, falling into this problem, or are they really arguing for doing nothing? It is not always easy to tell, though it is a bit easier when a binary choice must be made, as in an election, or where doing nothing is not an option.

Say you have lost the lease on your building, and your business must move to a new location. If an advocate for location A only has negative things to say about location B, that would indicate a problem. If there is a dispute between the locations, both must have pros and cons. If the proponents only talk about the cons of the other site, that would be a red flag.

114 Ariely, D. (2009). *Predictably Irrational: Revised and Expanded Edition.* New York: HarperCollins. p. 84
115 Ariely, D. (2009). *Predictably Irrational: Revised and Expanded Edition.* New York: HarperCollins. p. 85

Focus on the Weakest

Most arguments are complex, having many parts and often with several lines of reasoning. Focusing only on the weakest arguments is a strategy that ignores the stronger arguments. Say a position had five arguments that supported it. Most are fairly strong; one is somewhat questionable. If an opponent only wants to talk about the weakest argument, that would be a problem.

While all the arguments should be refuted to refute a position effectively, the strongest arguments are the most important. Refute the strongest arguments, and you have raised serious questions about the claim. However, if you only refute the weakest argument, you have very little effect on the overall position. Thus, it is a bad sign when someone doggedly avoids the stronger arguments focusing only on the weakest ones.

Inconsistency and Contradictions

Another bad sign is the use of inconsistent and even contradictory claims to support a position. This is not always easy to see during the flow of an argument. Still, when you step back and analyze what is being said, they do become apparent. One fairly easy example can be seen in the arguments made by the slave states at the time of the country's founding.

A major problem for the early government under the Articles of Confederation was money. One proposed solution was a bill that would levy a tax on the states based on population. As a general principle, this was seen as fair. The larger states would pay more, the smaller states less. But there was a sticking point: Should slaves be counted?

The slave states said no. In their view, slaves were property and should not be counted. Northern states objected that slaves in the South take the place of freemen in the North. The work of slaves, even if property, still "increase the profits of a state," in a fashion similar to the work of Freemen in the North. Thus, "the Southern colonies would have all the benefits of having slaves, while the

Northern ones would bear the burden."[116] Besides, they argued, "it is our duty to lay every discouragement on the importation of slaves." Excluding slaves would have the opposite result.[117] This dispute was the origin of the infamous three-fifths compromise. Eventually, a compromise was reached, but the bill still could not get the unanimous support required to pass under the Articles.

By itself, while despicable, the south's argument seems consistent. The problem entered in when the issue of proportional representation came up at the Constitutional Convention. The Virginia Plan, written by James Madison, proposed that,

> 2. Res^d therefore that the rights of suffrage in the National Legislature ought to be proportioned to the Quotas of contribution, or the number of free inhabitants, as the one or the other rule may seem best in different cases.

While there was a lot of discussion on this proposed resolution, the focus here is the proposal to base representation on "the number of free inhabitants." The slave states reversed their position and wanted to count slaves, the exact opposite of what they wanted when the issue was taxation. The Northern states reversed their position as well, arguing that if the slave could not vote, they should not be counted towards representation. Both sides reversed their position, but only one side was inconsistent.

To see this, consider the underlying rationales. When it came to taxes, the slave states did not want to count slaves because they claimed they were property. Slaves were not men to be taxed but property to be owned. Yet when it came to representation, the south wanted them counted as men. Now they were men to be represented. These arguments are at least inconsistent, if not contradictory. This was particularly true given the revolution had been fought

---

116 Taylor, H. (1911). *The origin and Growth of the American Consitution*. Retrieved 9 17, 2020, from https://archive.org/details/originandgrowth02taylgoog/page/n184/mode/2up

117 Taylor, H. (1911). *The origin and Growth of the American Consitution*. Retrieved 9 17, 2020, from https://archive.org/details/originandgrowth02taylgoog/page/n184/mode/2up

in part over the claim of no taxation without representation. The South did not want them considered for taxes but did for representation. There is a way that these can be reconciled, i.e., Count or don't count, whichever way works out best for the owners, but that is not one they would likely make.

Can the same charge be leveled against the north? Not really. The North wanted to count slaves when it came to taxation, but not for representation. Their reasons for counting slaves for taxation were twofold. First, they generated wealth similar to freemen in the North and so should be counted like freemen. Second, they did not want to encourage slavery.

Their reason for not wanting to count slaves for representation was also twofold. Slaves could not take part in the process of representation, i.e., they could not vote. Second, they did not want to encourage slavery. Allowing slaves to be counted for representation would magnify the representation of slaveholders. While the first reasons given for counting or not counting are different, they are not inconsistent. As for the second reason, they are effectively the same. So while their positions mirror each other, with analysis, it becomes clear that the South was inconsistent, the North was not.

Such inconsistent arguments still occur today. A politician can talk about how their new policy will only have positives and then seamlessly talk about how they plan to help all those adversely affected. There could be a way to reconcile such inconsistency. Still, the apparent inconsistency should at least cause pause as to whether the positives may be exaggerated and what are the adverse effects that need to be mitigated?

Avoiding Cons

This problem occurs when someone only wants to talk about the things that favor their position. For many claims, the amount of positive evidence is not as important as a single piece of contrary evidence. There was a massive amount of evidence that supported the wave theory of light. The evidence was so strong that the matter was considered conclusively demonstrated. Then came Einstein, who demonstrated that light was a particle. At that point, all the positive evidence for the wave theory became effectively irrelevant to the question of whether light was only a wave.

Suppose you are looking for the cause of a disease and think a particular virus is the source. In that case, the number of people with both the disease and that virus is important. But a single person who has the disease but not that virus is more important.

As a general rule, the evidence against a position is more important than evidence for that position. As such, a situation where someone only wants to discuss their position's positives while avoiding the negatives should raise a red flag.

Persuasion or Compulsion

A common thread that links all the issues above is an attempt to short circuit the discussion in some fashion to force the desired conclusion. As such, an important question to ask is: are they trying to persuade or compel? As used here, persuasion acknowledges people as individuals who can think for themselves and attempts to present a reasonable argument favoring the desired position by highlighting the pros, addressing the cons, and countering all objections. By doing this, they leave the ultimate decision to you. They do not need tricks or gimmicks as they trust in your ability to make the right decision.

While the tactics above attempt to short circuit this process, some go even further to interrupt the process. Rather than persuasion, they seek compulsion. To some extent, misplaced appeals to authority discussed above fall into this category. However, most still leave it to you to follow the authority. The focus here is on those tactics that fundamentally distrust your ability to listen to both sides and reach a conclusion. You cannot be trusted. You might be persuaded to reach the wrong conclusion. Therefore, various forms of compulsion are used to control, restrict, or even end your ability to decide.

This can happen in many ways, but the last area we will look at here is discouraging discussion. A constant theme in this book has been the importance of discussion in resolving issues and seeking truth. Any debate should seek to discuss the differences between the various positions, not shut them down. As such, one of the biggest red flags is the stifling of discussion. Unfortunately, it is on the rise. A sad commentary on our times is that polls show an increasing reluctance to discuss issues openly out of fear of reprisals.

Suppression of discussion can take many forms. It can be a refusal to discuss. After all, if there is no discussion, your side never gets heard. You can see this with candidates who refuse to debate their opponent. Another common form can be seen on many talk shows and political debates, which are the constant interruptions and talking over opponents. This can be very effective on television, where time is extremely limited. In a news program with three or four guests, each person will only get a couple of minutes to speak. As such, one only needs to interrupt and talk over someone for a limited amount of time to silence them effectively.

What makes this difficult is another common strategy on such programs, the filibuster. A guest may be asked a question they do not want to answer, so they begin a long discussion giving the "background" or "context," the main purpose of which is running out the clock. When someone interrupts, are they interrupting to keep someone from making an argument or stop a filibuster? It can, at times, be difficult to tell.

Of course, rather than interrupt, it is always easier not to invite them in the first place. A panel discussion that does not accurately represent the various views or where the views are mismatched is suspect. A mismatched panel is easy to mask. You just invite one member from each side and then have one or more "objective" guests. These "objective" guests can be drawn from think tanks or other organizations representing the desired view. Thus, you still have a panel stacked three or even four to one, but it has the illusion of being balanced.

More extreme versions of suppression are protests aimed at disrupting one side to keep them from speaking or simply to intimidate them. This is somewhat counter-productive, as it is an admission of failure. At this point, the protestors acknowledge that their arguments are so weak and unconvincing that their only option is to try and silence the opposition.

There are many such efforts in history, and as with the case of Galileo, these normally fail. The truth wins in the end. The only times they have succeeded are in very small groups or totalitarian states, groups with enough control to suppress the undesirable information effectively.

In the early decades of the internet, the tight control of information a totalitarian government needed to suppress non-official ideas was made much harder. China and other governments could maintain considerable control, but only by cutting off their country from the internet or vastly restricting access.

In the last few years, a new form of censorship has come to the forefront. This is Internet censorship made possible by two factors. One is the centralization of traffic through a few large corporations; these create chokepoints where censorship can occur.

Still, the vast amounts of information make monitoring difficult. This is where the second factor comes in—the advancements in AI that permit a level of control over information hitherto unimaginable. Now a major newspaper can print a story. If the gatekeepers of big tech do not like it, they can effectively suppress it from most people.

Even though this new tech censorship is still in its infancy, it is already pretty effective. As technology continues to develop, the effectiveness of censorship will only increase unless stopped. As usual, this is all done under the label of good intentions. It is done to protect people from misinformation or Fake News. But then censors always claim good intentions. There have already been several instances of stories that were censored later turning out to have been correct. Censorship protects lies; the truth needs no protection.

Derogatory labels

The final form of suppression that we will examine is the use of derogatory labels. Derogatory labels are effectively a combination of ad hominem attacks and argument by adjective. The goal is to make even the expression of disagreement so toxic that discussion is shut down. In the past, this could involve labeling some views as heresy, unpatriotic, or even treason. In more modern times, it could involve labeling something communist or racist.

As before, the mere use of these terms is not a problem. All these terms do have legitimate uses. There are communists and racists. It is the misuse of these terms, particularly to suppress discussion, that is the problem. For example, politicians can reject criticism of their policies, not by defending them but by labeling critics with a derogatory label. Often this will be combined with other forms of suppression.

While suppression does happen on all sides, normally, it does not happen equally. The reason is that shutting down discussion leaves the status quo. Therefore, this is an effective strategy only for those whose position is the status quo. As a general rule, the minority position always wants discussion so their alternative can be considered. It is the majority position that is resistant. One of the major advancements coming out of the enlightenment was that free speech was good and censorship bad, even for the majority. Sadly, that view is in decline, and there are growing calls for censorship.

A majority position does not necessarily mean a national majority. Censorship is very strongly tied to a group. The group may be the nation as a whole, but it can be any group regardless of size. Thus a minority position could still enforce strong censorship within their group. Censorship can even make sense in some cases, particularly when it is labeled or at least assumed.

We generally assume that any adult content will be censored from a G-rated film. What makes this acceptable and even good are two factors. First, it is clearly labeled. The second is freedom of choice. You know what you are getting, and you are free to choose something else if that is not what you want. This freedom to choose goes for the filmmaker as well. If they want adult content in their film, they can put it in and get a different rating. The only real problem occurs when a filmmaker tries to push the boundaries. But this is, in effect, trying to deceive people. People think they will see one type of movie; in reality, they get a different type.

Censorship becomes a problem when either of these two principles is violated. A political group that clearly labels where they are on the political spectrum can be expected to represent that part of the political spectrum. The Democratic and Republican Conventions can be expected to present their respective points of view. It would be unreasonable for the candidate of one party to demand speaking time at the convention of the other. On the other hand, a news program that claimed to be objective and yet represented a particular political view would be a problem.

The other problem is one of freedom and choice. This is what makes government and Internet censorship so problematic. If you do not want to see a G-rated film, you can watch something else. You do not have a choice to accept or reject views you never hear. You do not have a chance to factor in information you never see.

Any time there is the problematic suppression discussed here, you should reject the side doing the suppression. If someone has good arguments, they should use those rather than attempt to shut down the other side.

Reaching a Decision

Life would be a lot easier if you could just count the pros and cons in some mathematical fashion and total the result. Sadly, you can't. All the issues above are complex and will have exceptions. Rarely will the issues be clear cut, with all the problems and red flags on one side. While this certainly does happen, normally, it is with issues that are considered settled and where there is only a small minority that disagrees.

In short, when there are disagreements with significant numbers on both sides, there is no way around it; critical thinking requires thinking. Again, in a discussion where you have some expertise, you can evaluate the evidence and arguments themselves and reach a conclusion. In areas where you must rely on others, you will need to listen to the case being made by both sides. You will know you are ready to make a decision when you can answer the following questions.

> Why is there a disagreement?

> What are the core issues?

> Why do the sides take the positions they do?

When answering these questions, be sure to avoid self-serving answers that support your preferred position: no Ad hominem attacks or strawmen. You should answer these in such a fashion that both sides would say their positions have been well and fairly represented.

These questions will not always be straightforward. In this book, we have seen several inherently complex and difficult issues, such as tax policy. For such questions, there are no easy answers but a lot of competing and contradictory concerns. There are more fundamental differences, such as liberty vs. equality or what is fair. Then there are various concerns, such as one person's concern with immediate effects. At the same time, someone else is more concerned about the long-term consequences.

If you discover that you cannot answer these questions, more research will be required. A key point here is to realize it is the responsibility of a person making an argument to make it clear and convincing. Not all debates have to be of the caliber of the Lincoln-Douglas debates. Neither must they be the shouting matches all too common on TV. Still, with a little effort, you should be able to answer these questions, at least in a tentative fashion. At that, you are ready for the last question.

Seeking Truth

Who had the best arguments?

Again, as you seek to answer this question, rarely, if ever, will it be a clear-cut issue of all the errors on one side. You will need to make a number of assessments. Which side had the most errors? Which errors were the most significant? While clear-cut distinctions are rare, often, trends will emerge that point to a conclusion.

As a general rule, people can be counted upon to make the best argument they can. Suppose someone makes a bad case with little evidence, lots of emotional language, and personal attacks against their opponent. In that case, chances are their case is not very strong and should be rejected. If their position is the correct one, they can always improve their arguments and try again.

One final consideration is that confirmation bias still exists at this stage. As you look for problems with the side you reject, expect to find them more easily. The situation is similar to when you get a new car. As you drive it off the lot, it looks pretty unique. Until then, you had not seen very many on the road. Yet as soon as you drive it off the lot, you start seeing similar cars everywhere. In reality, they were there all along; what changed is that now you notice them.

As you find problems with the other side, a good rule of thumb is to switch labels. This simple check works wonders and eliminates a large percentage of the political controversies. Members of one party can be very critical of a particular practice yet justify it when it comes to their side.

In recent years, it has become common for the party controlling the Senate to be critical of the filibuster used by the minority party. Yet when the control of the Senate changes, the parties also switch sides on this issue. While some on both sides hold consistent positions, many who defended the filibuster when they were in the minority now attack it, while many who formally attacked it now defend it.

In any controversy, but particularly political controversies, changing the label can be very effective. Correspondingly, it is important to ask, are you consistent? Do you have one standard or two? One for those you agree with, and another for the other side. Is this something you would be concerned with if it was your side? Is this something you would attack if it were the other?

Once you have done all this, the only thing left is to make your decision. Does keeping track of all the various concerns highlighted in this book guarantee that you will have the truth? Sadly no. We are fallible. Then there will always be the issue of unknown unknowns. The things you cannot account for because you do not know they exist. Still, you will, on average, make better decisions.

Perhaps more importantly, the discussion will continue, and we get used to disagreement, the polarization will reduce. We will be able to disagree without demonizing. While some decisions are final, many are more like elections, settled for the moment but not long-term. There will be more elections and chances to change in the future. As the discussions go on, new information can be considered. Ideally, as people come to expect a better argument, those seeking to convince us will have to respond. They will have to make better arguments. Such methods can only improve the process of seeking and bringing us all closer to the truth.

www.ingramcontent.com/pod-product-compliance
Lightning Source LLC
Chambersburg PA
CBHW032036150426
43194CB00006B/303